Daughter of Adena

Margaret Worthington Mansfield, 1811-1863
from an 1852 portrait by Thomas Buchanan Read
Courtesy of Mrs. Edward Mansfield Swiggett

Daughter of Adena

Margaret Worthington's Personal Papers

1836 ~ 1839

Editing and Introduction
by Charlotte W. Wells

with Laura R. Prieto and Jennifer C. Davis

Freedom Press Associates

2005

Editing, Design, Typesetting by
Gail Holmgren Bickford and
Susan Hayes Clark

Cover design by Jarrod Clark and Shelley Stout
based on an original painting of Adena
by H.H. Bennett, 1908

Drawings of period dresses by Peg Scully

ISBN 0-945069-22-7

 Freedom Press Associates
PO Box 460
Freedom NH 03836

Dedication

For my children, granddaughters and great-grandsons
the only living descendants of
Margaret Worthington
and Edward Deering Mansfield

Richard Mansfield Dudley
Edith Dudley Sylla and
Alice Dudley Carmel

Anne Curran Sylla
Margaret Sylla Padua and
Genevieve Marie Carmel

Sunny Sompalli and
Leo Wheaton Padua

Contents

CONTENTS

List of Illustrations

Acknowledgements

The first person to support the creation of this book was my late husband, Winston M. Dudley (1912-1973), a great-grandson of Margaret Worthington Mansfield. He photocopied many of her papers, and those of her husband, Edward D. Mansfield. After his father's death, his mother, Lila Dudley, sorted and catalogued Edward's books, pamphlets and manuscripts. She gave us two diaries by Margaret W. Mansfield, several family Bibles, Swearingen and Mansfield genealogies, nine of the ten books Edward Mansfield wrote, most of his lectures, and many unpublished manuscripts. I thank Lila Dudley for these and for her comprehensive list of rare books.

I am also grateful to my husband's great aunt, Miss Edith Mansfield, for the portrait of Edward by Thomas Buchanan Read and the original oil painting of Adena by H. H. Bennett on the cover of this book. The late Mrs. Edward Mansfield Swiggett kindly gave me a picture of Margaret Worthington's portrait. I am thankful that his aunt, Miss Helen Dudley, left to the family her notes about her ancestors, Thomas Worthington and Edward Mansfield.

My children, Richard M. Dudley, Edith Dudley Sylla and Alice Dudley Carmel have supported me wonderfully. Dick, himself an author, advised me about hurdles in producing a finished work. Edith furnished me with helpful books about American women diarists. Alice, a genealogist by avocation, gave me books relative to the Ohio families and acquainted me with Rootsweb, which connected me with Worthington family genealogists, whom I thank for information about the origins of John G. Worthington of Cincinnati. Alice helped upgrade my computer hardware. My daughter-in-law, Elizabeth Martin, and son-in-law, Richard Sylla, helped with technical and historical resources. My granddaughter, Anne Sylla, reviewed some of the manuscript and advised me about the cover design. Genevieve Carmel, another granddaughter, helped with the title. I especially appreciate the interest of my nephew, James W. Wheaton, compiler of *Surgeon on Horseback* (1998), for proofreading and for the photograph of the painting of Adena on the cover.

I have enjoyed the help over many years of Mary Anne Brown, site manager at Adena. I have relied on her research into the birth, marriage and death dates of Margaret's siblings. Dard Hunter, Jr., Ms. Brown's predecessor at Adena, was also unfailingly helpful.

I am especially appreciative of Karel Whyte's carefully researched genealogy of the Swearingen family.

I greatly appreciate the expert help of staff members at the Ohio Historical Society's Archives/Library: Kenneth W. Duckett, Marjorie J. Myers, and Jeff Thomas. Pat Medert at the Ross County Historical Society has also kindly answered questions. I am grateful to personnel at the Warren County Historical Society in Lebanon, Ohio and at the Library of Cincinnati and Hamilton County for answering my inquiries.

I have been blessed with able assistants. Anne Imbornoni worked with me early on transcribing documents; Lois Kernan was especially helpful in computer technology and my early efforts to find a publisher. Laura Prieto, my research assistant, furnished important reference materials, making two trips to Ohio on my behalf. The authenticity of the notes rests largely on Laura's excellent work. I am deeply grateful for her contributions and her friendship. Dr. Carol Bleser, professor of history at Clemson University, kindly shared with us guidelines for editing manuscript materials. Beginning in 1997, Jennifer Crotty Davis helped organize my papers as an archive and to correspond with various historical societies to which I wished to donate Worthington and Mansfield documents. She has worked tirelessly on the present manuscript and is a whiz at the computer. I have delegated to her the work of obtaining permissions, preparing the bibliography and helping me with the index. Her warm friendship and complete dependability have made our work together a joy.

My deep gratitude goes to Gail Bickford, my publisher, and her able assistant, Susan Clark, who have put up with my reworking several parts of this book and have been patient with my slow pace.

The encouragement of my friends has been invaluable. Chief among them are Jean Allaway, Cliff and Joan Buehrens, Ruth Wells Caldwell, Ruth Charlton, Cate Culver, Mary Farr, Judy Flaherty, Pearl Frank, Constance Fry, Bee Grootweld, Mildred Haggerty, Caroline Hosmer, John and Josephine Lavely, Lynn McGee, Hester Rhodes, Alice Squires and Virginia Westervelt.

Finally, I would like to acknowledge the following historical societies, newspapers and individuals, who have kindly granted me permission to reproduce previously published or private materials: Thomas Barr, *Western Star*, (Lebanon, Ohio); Neal Hitch, Ohio Historical Society; Duryea Kemp, Ohio Historical Society; Pat Medert, Ross County (Ohio) Historical Society; Mark A. Neikirk, *Cincinnati Post;* Greg Ptacin, *Chillicothe Gazette;* Dr. George Parkinson, Ohio Historical Society; Elizabeth Plummer, Ohio Historical Society; Edith Sylla and Karel Whyte.
Charlotte W. Wells

Editorial Procedures

The procedures outlined below are designed to help the reader understand where and why Margaret's writings may have been altered in this edition.

Formatting: Date and place headings for diary entries appear flush left before each entry. Date and place headings for letters are flush right, and known postmark dates appear in square brackets. Margaret's signature is arbitrarily placed flush right at the end of her letters. The headings [Postscript (s)] indicate passages in the margins or outside of her letters after she folded and sealed them with sealing wax.

Editorial Intervention: Margaret's usual ampersand [α] is changed to "and," her "xc," for "etcetera" to "etc." Throughout the text, the convention of using an elongated "f" with a regular "s" to signify "ss" is changed to "ss." To break up some long passages, paragraph indents are introduced to indicate a change of subject, but not for her review of news items in one- or two-sentence bits. Her use of underlining is retained, appearing under individual words. The first word of each sentence is silently capitalized. When Margaret accidentally repeated words, duplicates are deleted. When she crossed out or corrected words, corrections appear without noting deletions.

Square brackets are used as follows:
- To replace an illegible word: [?].
- To supply a word surmised to be the [correct] one.
- To replace a word Margaret accidentally omitted.
- To use a surname to distinguish between two persons with the same first name.
- To supply the rest of a name for which Margaret used only initials. Explanations appear early in the diary and the letters, but are not necessarily repeated.
- To clarify the place from which Margaret was writing. For example, she wrote that she went "home" [to Eolia] while staying there with her sister Ellen, but while at Eolia also wrote that she went "home" [to Adena].
- To direct the reader, as in [See illustration on p. 00]. The abbreviation "cf." is used only in notes.

Spelling: Margaret's spelling of certain words: "Teusday," "to" (for too) "past" (for passed) is corrected, but her British-style spelling of "favour," "labour," "endeavour," "shew" (for show), "boquet" and "connexion," is preserved. Words like "gentles" or "gents" for "gentlemen," "enquiry" for "inquiry," and "furthest" for "farthest," her spelling of Scioto as "Sciota" and abbreviation for Cincinnati, "Cina," are retained. Other abbreviations, such as "Cha's relatives" are silently corrected to "Charles's relatives." Notes explain variations in the spelling of names: (Brown/Browne, Clark/Clarke, Douglas/Douglass and Irvin/Irwin), or the spelling in the 1840 U.S. Census for Chillicothe is used. Where Margaret used "tho" or "thro," the word "though" or "through" is substituted. Abbreviations for times of day ("mor'g," "eve'g") are left unchanged. Compound words like "anything" and "everything" are substituted for "any thing" and "every thing." She often hyphenated "to-night," "to-morrow," "good-night" and "good-bye." All such words are arbitrarily and silently hyphenated.

Capitalization: "Mother" for one's own parent and "mother" for another's parent replace both Margaret's and Edward's inconsistent capitalization of this word. Seasons of the year and compass directions are capitalized when Margaret personified them. Book titles are also silently capitalized.

Grammar: Expressions such as "tolerably looking," "many an one," and "why don't she write," and phrases in which Margaret seemed to be mimicking a southern or Scottish accent, as in "Ah little think" are retained.

Punctuation: Apostrophes are silently inserted to indicate the possessive of nouns, names, and contractions ("'tis", "'twas", "o'clock" and "can't"). The possessive of names ending in "s" is corrected.

Margaret frequently used dashes in place of periods; these are retained if they seem to express her rapidity of setting pen to paper. Occasionally dashes are silently replaced by periods or semicolons to make passages more readable. Dashes left at the end of sentences are sometimes replaced with periods. Ellipses (. . .) indicate omitted words.

Margaret's use of a series of "plus" signs in one or two places is preserved, although it is unclear what they mean. Her exclamation marks are retained.

Commas, periods, question marks and semicolons are silently inserted if lacking in the original but seem appropriate to the context. Periods have also been added after titles like "Dr.," "Gov." and "Mr." Parentheses are Margaret's.

Preface

My interest in Margaret Worthington (1811-1863) began in the late 1950s when my husband's mother, Lila McGaughan Dudley, read aloud to me excerpts from Margaret's 1836-37 diary, which she was transcribing on her portable typewriter. She laughed at the way Margaret used "Nemo" (Latin for "nobody") to disguise the name of Albert Galloway, to whom she was attached. Mother Dudley seemed to regard the diary as a quaint expression of Victorian sentiment, but I have come to regard it as more than a period piece because of its relevance to timeless issues of interpersonal communication, as well as to women's search for self-worth.

After Margaret's death in 1863, her journal was handed down to her oldest daughter, Elizabeth Phipps Mansfield Dudley (1843-1913), then to her son (my husband's father) Adolphus Mansfield Dudley (1877-1945). Soon after the birth of our son in 1938, Dad Dudley wrote to us ". . . through my mother's mother, born Margaret Worthington, Richard . . . through six generations goes back to Thomas Worthington, 5th [6th]Governor of Ohio and first U.S. Senator from Ohio." This was the first I heard about my husband's great-grandmother, Margaret Worthington, or her father, and realized that our children were linked genealogically to the people of Ohio's early history.[1]

After my father-in-law, Adolphus Mansfield Dudley, died in 1945, Margaret's papers passed into the hands of Lila Dudley, who completed her transcription of the 1836-37 diary before her death in 1960. The bound notebook, filled with Margaret's script within hard covers of marbleized design, then came to my husband, Winston Mansfield Dudley (1912-1973), and together we became its custodians. Winston also inherited many of Margaret's other papers, as well as those of her husband, Edward Deering Mansfield (1801-1880), Cincinnati newspaper editor and author, together with many papers of his parents, Jared Mansfield (1759-1830) and Elizabeth Phipps Mansfield (1776-1850).[2]

In 1963, when Win Dudley and I were preparing to move from Illinois to California, I re-transcribed Margaret Worthington's 1836-37 diary because I had found a few typographical errors in Mother Dudley's version. While re-transcribing the diary, I became more interested in Margaret as a person in her own right than in the fact that she was a daughter of Thomas Worthington (1773-1827), noted politician and entrepreneur. I decided in 1971 to prepare for publication a comprehensive edition of all her diaries and letters, under the title *Workings of the Heart.** But when I saw Win's chronic illness (Parkinson's) becoming worse, I decided to put personal plans aside.

After Win's death in 1973, I found myself the sole custodian of the Worthington and Mansfield papers he had inherited. I became so interested in the correspondence between Jared Mansfield and his wife after he was appointed a Surveyor General of the United States during Jefferson's administration that I wrote an article about his work that was published in a Special 1976 Bicentennial Issue of *Ohio History*.[3]

In recent years, I digressed again from my main objective to catalogue and distribute to appropriate historical societies most of the original nineteenth century manuscripts in my possession. Transcribing two of Margaret Worthington's later diaries, dating from 1847 to 1852 and from 1852 to 1855,[4] also took my attention. I read many of her letters, searching in all her writings for clues as to her development up to 1836. I came to understand her as a sensitive, often introspective young woman, sometimes peevish, but who appreciated the beauties of nature that she saw around her at Adena, the home to which she was intensely devoted. My major finding was that Margaret enjoyed a great many relationships of varying degrees of intimacy with her mother and nine siblings, and with many casual acquaintances, as well as a circle of eight close friends. Throughout all her writing she expressed her devotion to God.

In 1995, Laura Prieto, a gifted young woman, worked for me first as a research assistant, then became my co-editor, collaborating with me in an attempt to find a publisher for Margaret Worthington's first extant diary. I had already sent query letters outlining my project to several university presses and had been turned down by all. When this effort failed, we agreed that I would produce the diary by desktop publishing, while Laura may ultimately edit Margaret's later diaries and letters. I recently decided to include in the current work Margaret's letters during her engagement (1838-39) since they were also written at Adena, and fit well under the title, *Daughter of Adena.*

My work on the diary and letters, although often interrupted and subject to several false starts, has consisted of the usual procedures for a non-fiction work: library research, note-taking, filing, making genealogical and time-line charts and selecting possible illustrations. I have visited Adena on more than one occasion, conferring there with Mary Anne Brown, site manager, who has been most gracious in helping me.

I am greatly indebted to the scholarship of Alfred Byron Sears whose biography,

---

* See quotation from Charles Francis Adams p. *xvii.*

Thomas Worthington: Father of Ohio Statehood, furnished a wealth of details about the Worthington family.[5] The memoirs and biographies of Margaret's older sister, Sarah Worthington King Peter, have furthered my understanding of Worthington family life.[6] I have consulted many other books about Ohio, Chillicothe and Cincinnati, in order to piece together a better picture of Margaret Worthington's environment.[7]

Reading published women's diaries and biographies of women writers has helped me put Margaret's writings into perspective.[8] Martin Buber's *I and Thou* also influenced my thinking about Margaret's letters and diaries because of the distinction he makes between genuine person-to-person dialogue and those relationships that diminish one or the other party to a thing, an "It."[9] Her longing for I-Thou dialogue seems to me implicit in the disappointment she expressed over unrequited love and her impatience with unresponsive correspondents. Buber's descriptions in *Daniel* of orientation and realization as alternative responses to experience have helped me discern more clearly the processes I was using in working on Margaret's diary.[10]

Orientation, involving the usual procedures of research, gave me, as Buber says, a sense of security with regard to the myriad facts and persons Margaret alluded to, but by themselves did not necessarily help me "realize" the full non-verbal reality of a given piece of her experience. I briefly experimented with writing dialogues between Margaret and myself, in which I asked her questions and wrote down what I imagined her replies would be. This helped bridge more than a century of time between us and lifted her from being solely an object of my analysis into the role of a friend or sister.

Exercises in orientation nevertheless bore their own fruit. When I charted (on a large sheet of butcher paper) the major events that took place in the Worthington family — births, deaths, marriages (including those in the families of Margaret's siblings), and Thomas Worthington's political career— it became clear that her father had been absent in Washington D. C. or Columbus most of Margaret's early childhood. Perhaps she never felt close to him; at any rate, she never mentioned her father in this diary. The chart also showed what clusters of years may have been turbulent for the Worthingtons because of the frequent changes in the number of people meeting regularly around the dinner table. It also indicated those years that may have been relatively tranquil when Thomas was at Adena with his wife and children.

Quite early in my study of Margaret's diary I decided to suspend judgment about what psychological frames of reference (identity crisis, projection, transference, etc.) might explain her behavior. I would avoid if possible the temptation to read into her life what I thought I knew about my own! Even so, if I had not glimpsed what I took to be a developmental curve to her life's passage, I might not have thought it worthwhile to prepare her writings for publication. In a peculiar way, I have felt as if Margaret Worthington were editing and evaluating *my* life, motivating me to end my procrastination and to care for my health. One must be willing to pay a price to attain a state of consciousness clear enough to perceive another's.

Re-reading the diary after one of the lapses in my work, I realized that Margaret was the narrator of her own emotional drama, as well as the observer of external events such as contacts with relatives, friends and strangers. Sometimes she played the role of heroine in her life's drama, commenting, as a drama critic might, on how well or poorly she played her part on any given occasion. By trying out on paper the roles of friend, lover, nurturer and spiritual leader, she explored the dimensions of selfhood from the inside out. At times she looked to religious principles in familiar Bible verses to guide her self-evaluation, but journaling seems to have been most effective in helping her work on her own character.

She found that she need not be merely a passive recipient of hereditary or environmental influences. Something spoke to her from within about unlived life, unrealized potential. Otherwise, I cannot account for the willpower she summoned to become proactive when dealing with an entangling relationship she needed to end. The ten-month segment of her life represented in this early diary, together with the letters of her engagement period, can only hint at what she might become, but her writing brims with life lived in the moment—what Thomas Mallon has called "the flesh made word."[11]

I cannot claim to have plumbed to their depths the mysteries posed in Margaret Worthington's early writings, but they resonate sufficiently with my own experience to have earned my respect. I feel enriched for having vicariously experienced her unique way of making choices between fear and faith, withdrawal and engagement, selfish and unselfish love. At times she retreated into illness, withdrawing from society; but on the whole, her life demonstrated the triumph of courage over mistrust and fear. I am bonded to Margaret, as I believe other readers of her writing may become, because we all wrestle with uncertainties in our pursuit of meaningful lives. Amid relationships that are alternately joyous and vexatious, we are joined to women, like Margaret, whose claim to the respect of their peers is based on an honest and dearly won self-appraisal. In this effort, a journal may prove to be both a therapist and, as it was for her, a trustworthy confidante.

While the diary is intensely personal at times, it also contributes to our understanding of the cultural history of antebellum Ohio. Margaret wrote about her housekeeping duties, her sewing projects and her singing for family and friends. She also described many instances of calling on friends or neighbors, of attending or hostessing parties and of celebrating holidays like the Fourth of July or New Year's Day. She chronicled the social events she attended while on long visits among the politically and culturally elite residents of Cincinnati and Lancaster, as well as her one-on-one conversations with young men of her acquaintance in Chillicothe. She enjoyed a comfortable platonic friendship with Henry Massie and, on the other hand, found it difficult to allow James P. Campbell to propose to her because she was determined to marry only for love. Her long, confidential conversations with her best friend, Elizabeth McCoy, show the extent to which young women of her day shared intimate secrets with each other, and how much they helped each other make wedding plans. Her letters to Edward Mansfield during their engagement in 1838 and 1839 reveal the rather odd way in which they decided on a wedding date and how they chose their guest list. On the personal side, she expressed many misgivings about leaving her home and mother and becoming a stepmother to Edward's two young sons.

Private writings like Margaret's, having only oblique connections to political history, are sometimes dismissed as trivial. It is said that they do not report any great public achievements, any battles won, any laws passed. Ever since studying the novels of Virginia Woolf with their stream-of-consciousness style, I have been convinced that subjective feelings and intuitions are just as real, and reporting them is just as valid, as are objective experiences and the written records that describe them. A passage I found in the Introduction to *The Book of Abigail and John: Selected Letters of the Adams Family, 1762-1784* is particularly relevant. The editors cite Charles Francis Adams (from his 1876 edition of *Familiar Letters of John Adams and His Wife, During the Revolution*):[12]

> Students of human nature seek for examples of man under circumstances of difficulty and trial, man as he is, not as he would appear; but there are many reasons why they may be often baffled in the search. We look for the workings of the heart, when those of the head alone are presented to us . . . the solitary meditation, the confidential whisper to a friend, never meant to reach the ear of the multitude, the secret wisdom, not blazoned forth to catch applause, the fluctuations between fear and hope that most betray the springs of action,—these are the guides to character, which most frequently vanish with the moment that called them forth, and leave nothing to posterity but those coarser elements for judgment that are found in elaborated results).

This passage has become a personal manifesto because I believe what it affirms: that "workings of the heart" in either man or woman deserve to be valued along with the "coarser elements . . . of elaborated results." What Charles Adams highlights is the importance in both genders of those subjective elements that so often appear in Margaret's diary entries: "solitary meditation," "confidential whisper to a friend," "secret wisdom,"—amounting, as Adams suggests, to "the guides to character."

Margaret touched on "workings of the heart" in the paragraph appearing before her first diary entry, where she wrote about the contradiction she felt between free-flowing, spontaneous love and love as an exercise of the will. As her diary continues, we find her grappling with infatuation and how to manage her relations with suitors. Many passages reveal her emotional turmoil and self-doubt—"fluctuations between fear and hope." Other entries show her struggle for a sense of self-worth, for autonomy and agency with respect to her own character. She ultimately decided to act both on her own behalf and in service to others. Jill Ker Conway pointed out in *Written by Herself* that many women of Margaret's day did not realize the extent to which they exercised agency.[13]

In *A Private War: Letters and Diaries of Madge Preston 1862-1867,*[14] Virginia Walcott Beauchamp gives another rebuttal to the criticism that private writings are trivial:

> Such judgments are founded on an unexpressed assumption in the word trivial about what we mean by history. Somehow it encompasses great events—disruptions of large populations, conflicts within and between governments, structures of power. But when we read the personal papers of those who lived in such times, we discover that we stand history on its head.

Beauchamp goes on to quote Robert Fothergill, editor of *Private Chronicles: A Study of English Diaries* (1974): "Where we habitually thought of ordinary lives forming a vast background to historical events, now one's vision is of the great events dimly passing behind the immediate realities that comprise an individual's existence." She also forcibly states the case for publishing nineteenth-century women's diaries and letters:

> Reading [such diaries and letters] highlights how separate were the men's and women's cultures of that time and how sharply both men and women of our own century have been cut off from those earlier women's lives . . . . Conventional history speaks of the world of our male forebears—and then most usually of the elite group that wielded power. But for all people outside such groups, to discover their own history is to empower themselves. Through women's history, all of us can learn to respect the women who went before us—drawing strength from their examples of endurance and from the structures and models of relatedness in the female culture that supported them.

Margaret Worthington's writings between 1836 and 1839 provide insight into those very "structures and models of relatedness" that may be important to students of women's changing roles, who, at the turn of the twenty-first century, look back to see what they may learn from their sisters of the nineteenth. Her autobiographical writing is both historically valuable and personally relevant. It is candid and clear, sometimes impassioned, her descriptions often enhanced by apt metaphors, as when she likened the faded rose on her mantel to her shriveled expectations of returned affection.

My aim as editor of these early writings by Margaret Worthington has been to produce a readable narrative without doing violence to her original style. I hope the reader will appreciate this portion of her life story and not be distracted by either the eccentricities of Margaret's writing style or by my editorial intrusions. The book's subtitle, "Margaret Worthington's Personal Papers, 1836-1839" should not be taken to mean that I have included *all* her writings during that period. I have used those materials readily available but have not searched for the earlier or later diaries to which Margaret alluded in her 1836-37 diary. Nor have I tried to find other letters from Edward D. Mansfield to Margaret to add to the one included here.

With the aim of presenting Margaret's selected writings as part of her autobiography, I arbitrarily divided her diary into five parts, and her letters to Edward (and one from him) into three, consisting of about ten letters each. I have drawn a phrase from within each part to become its subtitle, each hinting at the progression of Margaret's feelings about her beloved home, from which marriage would ultimately take her.

I initially considered deleting passages from her letters in which she repeatedly complained to Edward about his not writing often enough, but ultimately decided to leave nothing out. The work presented here is thus "inclusive" to the extent that nothing in this particular diary or in this sequence of letters has been deleted.

I trust that my editorial emendations are clear and my annotations thorough and concise. Historians or other scholars who wish to study the materials in this book will find Margaret Worthington's original 1836-37 diary and the 1838-39 letters at the Ohio Historical Society in Columbus, Ohio. An accurate transcription of her 1836-37 diary (with no editorial changes save the rendering of her unique ampersand ["&"] as "&,") is deposited at Adena, the Ohio State Memorial near Chillicothe, Ohio.

For all the reasons stated earlier, I believe Margaret's diary and letters from 1836 to 1839 are worthwhile additions to the genre of American women's published autobiographic literature. While I have prepared *Daughter of Adena* with my children, grandchildren and great-grandchildren especially in mind, I hope that readers in the general public and the academic community will enjoy and benefit from reading the writings of this unusual young woman of antebellum Ohio.

I accept full responsibility for whatever omissions or inaccuracies may be found in the commentary and notes. It is understandably difficult to verify every detail, considering the large number of persons and events about which Margaret wrote. I hope this book—admittedly the work of an amateur historian and family archivist— will lay the groundwork for future editions of Margaret Worthington's writings.

❋   ❋   ❋   ❋   ❋

Lake Erie

Adena, near Chillicothe,
first occupied in 1807

OHIO

**Became a State
March 1, 1803**

Columbus •

Lancaster •

Xenia•

Scioto
River

Cincinnati

Chillicothe•

*Ohio map
adapted by CWW;
Adena picture detail
from 1908 painting by
H. H. Bennett*

Pomeroy •

Ohio
River

Portsmouth

Margaret Worthington's Ohio Environment in the 1830s

Introduction

A. Margaret Worthington's Formative Years 1811 to 1839

Margaret Worthington was born on July 25, 1811 at Adena, a stone mansion outside of Chillicothe, Ohio. Her parents, Thomas Worthington and Eleanor Swearingen Worthington, had moved to Ohio from what is now West Virginia in 1798. Their relative wealth and Thomas's political standing soon made them eligible to join Chillicothe's elite. Because Margaret was the seventh among the Worthingtons' ten children, and the fourth of their five daughters, she enjoyed a wealth of primary relationships which became more numerous as her siblings married and had children.[1]

At the time of Margaret's birth, the Worthington family had occupied Adena for only four years, so that in her earliest years she saw its elegant furnishings and French wallpaper when they were still fresh. Servants, former slaves who had been freed by Worthington when they left Virginia, waited on the family's needs in the mansion and worked the fields surrounding the estate. Margaret saw her parents entertain many distinguished visitors at Adena, particularly politicians and military men with whom her father was acquainted through his activities at both state and national levels. As a small child she took great delight in Adena's natural surroundings and in the life of her family.[2]

By 1836 when she began her diary, Margaret's home environment had changed markedly. Her father had died in 1827, leaving Margaret, together with her mother, two sisters and two brothers, still living at Adena. With fewer servants, the entertainment of distinguished guests had become a thing of the past.[3] But nothing changed Margaret's close attachment to her mother and her birthplace.

Incorporated in 1802, by the time of Margaret's birth Chillicothe had become a flourishing settlement of log houses and small businesses. It was the first capital of Ohio, later replaced by Columbus. Chillicothe was located on the Scioto River in the Virginia Military District, an area of Ohio set aside for veterans from Virginia who had fought in the Revolution. Trains of pack horses were driven over the trails leading into the Scioto Valley where boats were loaded with farm produce ready to be shipped down the Ohio River to Cincinnati or down the Mississippi to New Orleans.[4]

By 1836, Chillicothe had not changed much, although some liked to think it might become a great manufacturing town. In 1834, the Ohio Canal was completed linking Chillicothe to Cleveland on the north and Portsmouth on the south. From there steamboats carried passengers and freight down the Ohio. New houses were built on every street, many of elegant brick. But Chillicothe was no longer a center of political action and would be surpassed by Cincinnati in its prospects as a manufacturing center.[5]

Thomas Worthington helped establish the first legislature of the Northwest Territory, serving as its representative from Ross County. He also helped to create the political and judicial frameworks for the town and the state in their early stages. He is credited with successfully pleading the cause of statehood in Washington, D.C. while Thomas Jefferson was president.[6] Ohio entered the Union in 1803, eight years before Margaret's birth. The population in 1810 had increased to nearly 231,000, and the state continued to be settled by Easterners and European immigrants.[7] Between 1820 and 1840, the population more than tripled, with New Englanders joining Virginians as the state's most influential residents. Large numbers of German and Irish laborers also moved to the state during that period.[8]

When Margaret was born, only thirty-six years had passed since the Declaration of Independence was signed, and only twenty-two since George Washington took office under the Constitution. In 1811, Great Britain challenged the new nation's ability to defend itself on the high seas by blockading maritime trade and impressing American seamen into the British navy. These conditions led to the War of 1812, which resulted in conflicts between Ohio settlers and some Indian nations, who were allied with the British. In the fall of 1811, while serving a second term as Ohio senator during the administration of James Madison, Thomas drove his own carriage from Chillicothe to Washington, taking his wife and five of their children with him, including baby Margaret.[9]

Andrew Jackson's election as president in 1828 ushered in a time of political upheaval, but he was re-elected for a second term. Martin Van Buren succeeded him in 1836. By her own admission, Margaret did not care much about politics, but was aware of her brothers' interest in presidential candidates. She was also interested in the report about the passage through Chillicothe of the Mexican President, General Santa Anna, who had been defeated and taken prisoner at the Battle of San Jacinto in Texas.

Her own marriage prospects were the main focus of Margaret's attention in her twenty-fifth year. She enjoyed relationships with a large number of young men and women of her age group, not only among those of her inner circle in Chillicothe (who are listed later), but also among others in town and those she met during lengthy visits to Cincinnati and Lancaster. Since the telephone, e-mail or even the telegraph were not available in the 1830s, she could only cultivate relationships by face-to-face meetings or by exchanging letters. Her highly emotional reactions when one or another of her friends failed to answer her letters in a timely fashion indicate just how important to Margaret was a free give-and-take of thoughts and feelings.

Margaret's education in a series of private schools was quite different from that offered later by public schools, and in some ways seems more advanced. As a small child she learned the rudiments of reading, writing and arithmetic in a log cabin schoolhouse on the property line between Adena and Fruit Hill, the estate of the McArthur family.[10] When she was about ten, Margaret and her sister Ellen attended the Young Ladies' Boarding School in Chillicothe run by Mr. and Mrs. Daniel Steinhauer. She made friends there with Julia Galloway, Elizabeth McCoy and Elizabeth Waddle, all of whom appear in her diary entries fifteen years later. The girls had classes in reading, writing, arithmetic, bookkeeping, English grammar, geography, the use of globes, elements of astronomy and history. Ellen wrote to their brother Albert that she and Margaret had also begun music and drawing lessons.[11]

By 1824, Margaret and Ellen were attending a school in Chillicothe run by Miss Mary Baskerville, who was noted for her devotion to teaching "the King's English."[12] Perhaps there Margaret began to develop her expressive writing style. Their father took the two girls to Troy, New York, in August of 1825 to enroll them at Emma Willard's Female Seminary. In her one year of attendance there, Margaret gained the reputation of being a gifted student.[13]

Mrs. Willard, a pioneer advocate of higher education for American women, had opened her seminary in 1821, offering women and girls advanced courses in history, mathematics and science.[14] She also offered religious and moral instruction and classes in literary, domestic and so-called "ornamental" subjects.[15] Mrs. Willard succeeded in training a great many young women for the teaching profession, but colleges for women equivalent to those attended by young men did not open until later. Oberlin, the first coeducational college in the United States, opened in 1833 in Oberlin, Ohio, but by then Margaret was needed at Adena and there is no evidence that she wished to go there. In later life, however, she expressed regret that her education had been cut short at about the time of her father's death in 1827.[16]

Significant relationships opened up for Margaret in December of 1828 when she attended the marriage of her brother, James T. Worthington, to Julia Ann Galloway in Xenia, Ohio. Friendships developed between Margaret and Julia's sisters, Sally, Amanda and Rebecca (who became Mrs. George Myers and moved to Lancaster).[17] Margaret had some tensions in her relationship to Julia's brother, Albert, whom she occasionally called "Nemo" in her diary. He had given her a piece of sheet music, a love ballad, inscribed "Feb. 9, 1835 from A. G.," and in June of that year she visited the Galloways in Xenia.[18] Unfortunately, we do not have her first diary which might have shed light on an earlier stage of her relationship to Albert.

Chillicothe. Dec. 21, 1821

Dear Parents

As you wish Ellen or me to write to you every week while you are in Columbus, and it is now my turn, I will with pleasure attempt to write a few lines to you for the first time in my life. Ellen and I are very well in health. We feel very lonesome when we go home and hope that you will soon return. We went home last Saturday and read the history and adventures of Robinson Crusoe. I wish I had been with him on his island to help him to milk his goats; he must have been very lonesome before he got his man Friday. Thomas and James are well. I hope you will soon write to us and tell us how you and the children are. Sister Mary and sister Sarah and the children are all well. Mr. and Mrs. Steinhauer send their compliments to you. I remain

Your affectionate and dutiful daughter

Margaret's first letter to her parents, written at age ten

[A copy of the original is shown on page 5]

Chillicothe. Dec 21. 1821

Dear Parents

As you wish Ellen or me to write to you every week while you are in Columbus, and it is now my turn, I will with pleasure attempt to write a few lines to you for the first time in my life. Ellen and I are very well in health. We felt very lonesome when we go home and hope that you will soon return. We went home last saturday and read the history and adventures of Robinson Crusoe. I wish I had been with him on his island to help him to milk his goats; he must have been very lonesome before he got his man Friday. Thomas and James are well. I hope you will soon write to us and tell us how you and the children are. Sister Mary and sister Sarah and the children are all well. Mr and Mrs Steinhauer send their compliments to you. I remain

Your affectionate and dutiful daughter

Margaret's first letter to her parents at age ten
Courtesy of Ohio Historical Society

Adena in the Late Nineteenth Century
From the estate of Winston Mansfield Dudley

B. Adena from 1807 to 1839

At the time of Margaret's birth in 1811, Adena must have appeared much the same as in 1807 when Fortescue Cuming viewed the mansion shortly before its completion. Cuming, a European, was visiting Duncan McArthur's home, Fruit Hill, when he recorded these impressions:

> I walked before breakfast half a mile through the woods to . . . an elegant seat belonging to Col. Worthington. It will be furnished in a few weeks and will be one of the best . . . houses not only of this state but to the westward of the Allegheny Mountains. It is about sixty feet square with a square roof and large receding wings. It has two lofty stories, with six rooms on each floor, and cellars and vaults beneath. The wings contain kitchen, scullery, apartments for servants, etc.
>
> Like Col. M'Arthur's it is built with freestone, but the stone of the front is all hewn and squared like the generality of the houses in the new part of Glasgow, Scotland, the stone being very similar both in colour and quality. The situation is like Col. M'Arthur's, being on the brow of the same ridge of hills, and affording the same prospects.[1]

When the Worthingtons' new house was first occupied, it was called Mt. Prospect Hall, but was renamed Adena in the fall of 1811, after Worthington had come upon the term in a work on ancient history which said it applied to "places remarkable for delightfulness of their situations."[2]

There is a tradition that the view from the Adena property was the source of the design of the Ohio State Seal. After an all-night meeting, Thomas, Edward Tiffin, the first governor, and William Creighton, first secretary of state, stepped out of Worthington's house, Belle View, in the early morning. Their view of the rising sun above Mt. Logan is believed to have suggested the motif for the state seal.[3]

In *Personal Memories* (1879) Edward D. Mansfield recorded his impressions of Adena as he knew it in 1838 and early 1839:

> It was so remarkable [a] house at the time that great numbers of people came to see it when finished . . . It is situated on the brow of the ridge or upland which separates the North Fork of Paint creek from the Valley of the Scioto and overlooks the valley, the town and hills beyond . . . The state of the country was such that almost all manufactured articles were

brought from the East at more than double the expense that would now be required. The workmen came from Washington City, the glass was made at the glass works of Albert Gallatin, Geneva, Pennsylvania. The marble fireplace fronts came from Philadelphia and hardware was also from the East. At the time it was built it was the most elegant mansion in Ohio . . . [Adena] stood in the midst of a garden and orchard where the finest shrubbery and the richest variety of fruit furnished delight to the lover of natural pleasures.[4]

The design of Adena and its extensive grounds was in the eighteenth century tradition of colonial Virginia. While in Washington in 1805, Worthington commissioned Benjamin Latrobe, noted architect and surveyor of public buildings during the administrations of Presidents Jefferson and Madison, to draw the plans.[5] Talbot Hamlin, Latrobe's biographer, writes that the details of Adena's architectural plan are very simple:

. . .the emphasis is on geometrical power and the distinction that comes from restraint . . . The orientation, with the entrance to the north between sheltering wings and with the chief rooms to the south, follows the scheme of the Dickinson College building [in Carlisle, Pennsylvania]. Heavy stone cross walls, containing fireplaces, divide the main block into equal thirds.

The master bedroom was part of a private suite on the ground floor of the eastern third of the building, with an exterior door leading to the garden. The western third of the house where the dining-rooms and other areas for the entertainment of guests were located, was also arranged for ease of service and privacy. Rotating servers leading to the state dining room and the drawing room made it possible to serve food and drink without the servants being present, and Latrobe arranged it all so that on special occasions the family dining room became a convenient serving space.[6]

The Worthingtons' furniture was largely in the Hepplewhite and Sheraton styles popular at the time. They brought family heirlooms from Virginia, including a spice chest Eleanor Worthington later gave to Margaret. Many chairs, tables, beds and the like were made on the estate by the carpenters who built the house.[7]

Margaret's mother planted the semi-formal gardens extending eastward from the house. She planted more than forty varieties of roses, many on the upper terrace, along with other plants and shrubs, some of which came from the eastern states. She discovered one rose in the woods near Adena and domesticated it as the Worthington Rose.[8] Vegetables and fruit bushes grew in the next two terraces, beyond which a large grove of ornamental trees and flowers was laid out in geometrical patterns. West of the house Worthington developed a fine orchard, from which grafts and seedlings were sold to Ohio farmers. Outbuildings were also arranged on this side in a layout common to

Virginia plantations.[9] Historians generally agree that the area surrounding Adena consisted of 1,500 acres throughout Margaret's lifetime.[10] Immediately around the house some native trees had been left to shade the lawns, and Lombardy poplars lined the drive leading to the entrance gate. In front of the house a circular driveway curved out across the lawn, affording panoramic views of the surrounding countryside.[11]

A visitor approaching Adena from the north would have found an open terraced court and a flagged porch by the front door. The *Scioto Gazette* published an extensive article about the house during the 1903 celebration of Ohio's first one hundred years, comparing it to an Italian villa, with its terraced garden at one side. Entering the house, according to the *Gazette* article,

> . . .one finds the low, wide doorway is still the same, and through it one enters the reception hall, with its old wood fire, its walnut mantel, and the ivory-white chair rail and woodwork. Here the dominant note is red [in wallpaper with conventionalized scrolls, etc.] with the ceiling a soft buff. Here the floor, as that in all the main parts of the house, is of oak . . .dark and shining.[12]

These particulars help us imagine the scene at the front door when Margaret received visitors. One can see from floor plans (see pages 11 and 12) how they would be ushered from the hall to the reception room. From there they could enter the state dining room or the formal drawing room on the western side of the mansion. The breakfast room, north of the state dining room, could also be entered from the hall. Margaret sometimes went to the kitchen, located in the west wing, to help make biscuits or preserves and pickles.[13]

After Adena's first restoration in 1953, a Columbus newspaper reported it was to be "the most complete and authentic restored property in the Middle West." Many original documents, drawings and legal records were examined in order to reproduce as accurately as possible Adena's original interior decoration.[14] A handsome book, *Great Houses of America* (1969), includes a ten-page chapter about Adena. Illustrating the text are many pictures, some in color, showing the beautiful features of the mansion's design and furnishings.[15]

From the time they first occupied Adena, the Worthingtons entertained many notables. Mr. and Mrs. Henry Clay, for example, made annual visits. Mrs. Clay had befriended Mary and Sarah Anne when they were in school in Lexington, Kentucky. The great Shawnee chiefs, Tecumseh and Blue Jacket, were guests in 1807.[16] President James Monroe was a visitor in 1817.[17] Even Aaron Burr visited the Worthingtons in the vain hope of enlisting support for his dreamed-of empire in the southwest, later sending Mrs. Worthington gifts of a moss rose, honeysuckle and yellow jasmine.[18] DeWitt

Clinton, governor of New York, and John Jacob Astor, financier, came to Adena by special invitation at the time Worthington was nearing completion of his Ohio canal project.[19] Among well-known women who visited Adena were Mrs. John Pope, sister of Mrs. John Quincy Adams, and Dolley Madison's sister, Mrs. Todd.[20] The opening of Adena's doors to so many people of local and national importance undoubtedly set the standard for "generous hospitality," which Edward Mansfield described in his memoirs.[21]

Margaret may be said to be a "daughter of Adena" more than any of her sisters because she actually lived in the mansion for the greatest length of time. Her older sister, Ellen, lived there for twenty-three years, and her younger sister, Elizabeth, for twenty-one. Adena was Margaret's home, however, for almost twenty-eight years, between her birth in July, 1811 and her marriage to Edward Mansfield in 1839.[22] Sarah also had a special fondness for her childhood home, habitually returning each spring to renew old times at Adena. She remembered the olden days when, as her biographer writes, "[t]he halls rang with [the children's] shouts and laughter. In more quiet hours they loved to gather downstairs in their mother's sitting-room. There, circled around the table, they read the plays of Shakespeare and Plutarch's *Lives* (abridged), or stole into the adjoining nursery to watch the newest baby. When tasks were done, there was always a troop of neighbor children to greet."[23]

Margaret's love for her home is a further reason for considering her a special "daughter of Adena." Among the features that held great appeal for her were the garden flowers, especially roses, from whose blossoms and thorns she derived powerful metaphors for her emotional ups and downs. She also believed Adena to be a wholesome environment. In September, 1838, she wrote to Edward, "All [Mother's] grandchildren are sent to Adena when they are sick and we have strong faith in the efficacy of the air and treatment which invariably cures them." This was particularly true during epidemics such as the cholera outbreak of 1832.[24]

Adena has undergone many changes since Margaret's time, but was freshly restored to its nineteenth century appearance in time for Ohio's bicentennial in 2003. It is a State Memorial, with a Visitor Center on the grounds.[25] Inside the mansion, one may go upstairs to Margaret's bedroom, view the furnishings and see the mantel that held her little vase of roses, and the fireplace where she sat to record the events of her daily life and her sometimes turbulent feelings.

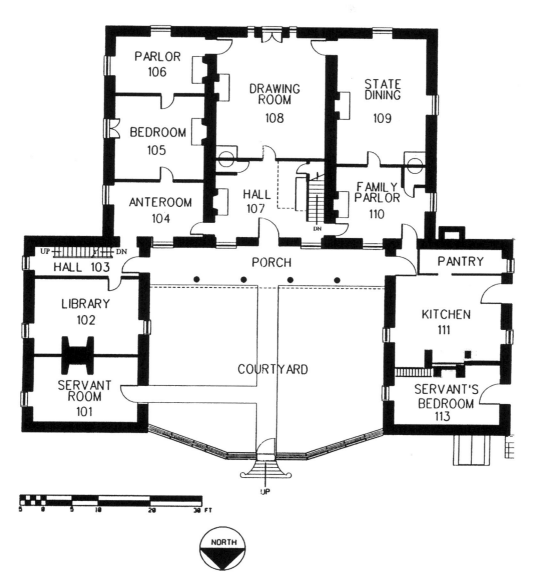

Plan of First Floor of the Adena Mansion
Courtesy of Facilities Management, Ohio Historical Society

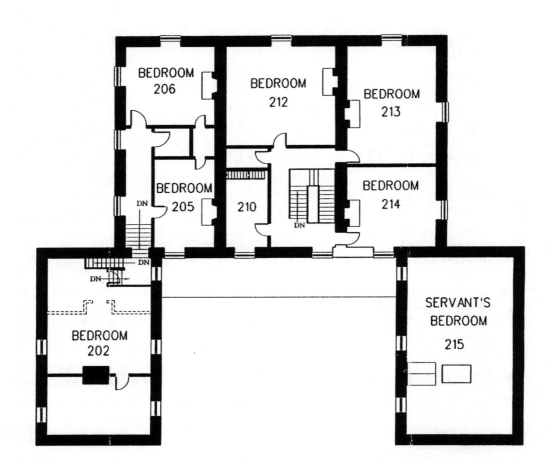

Second Floor of Adena Mansion
Courtesy of Facilities Management, Ohio Historical Society

C. Chronology of Margaret's Parents from 1773 to 1827

1773   On July 16, MW's father, Thomas Worthington (TW), was born near the present Charles Town, West Virginia, youngest of the six children of Robert Worthington II (1734-1779) and Margaret Matthews (d. 1780). His grandfather, Robert Worthington, "the Quaker," after moving from Cheshire, England to Ireland, emigrated in 1714 with his wife, Alice Taylor, and their family to Salem, New Jersey, then relocated near Philadelphia. Upon Alice's death, he moved in 1730 with Mary Burtis, his second wife, to the Shenandoah Valley in Virginia where he obtained a Crown Grant of 3,000 acres and built a stone house, Quarry Bank. When his son, Robert II, (first of three children by Mary Burtis) came of age in 1748, he obtained 600 acres of his patrimony and took up farming, surveying and land-dealing. TW thus became heir to a family tradition of land speculation and large-scale farming.[1]

1775   TW's father and General William Darke volunteered their services to George Washington at the beginning of the War for Independence.[2]

1777   On September 22, MW's mother, Eleanor Swearingen (ESW), was born at Shepherdstown, Virginia (now West Virginia), the oldest of the four children of Josiah Swearingen (1744-1795) and Phoebe Strode (1757-1786), who was the daughter of James Strode (d. Apr. 1795) and Anna Hamilton Forman, of Berkeley County, Virginia. Eleanor's great-grandfather, Thomas Swearingen (b. 1688 in Maryland) settled with his wife Lydia Riley (1691-1764) near Shepherdstown, Virginia. The earliest emigrant ancestor to this country was Gerrett Vansweringen [sic] (b. 1636 in Holland, d. 1698) who m. (1) Barbarah de Barrette (b. in France; d. 1670); m. (2) Mary Smith of St. Mary's, Maryland.[3]

1779   TW's father, Robert Worthington Jr., died, leaving an estate worth $200,000.[4]

1780   TW's mother, Margaret Matthews Worthington, died, leaving him heir to about 1,400 acres. Due to his parents' early deaths, Thomas was deprived of parental guidance in his formative years. Although initially educated by private tutors, he received little instruction while cared for by his older brothers.[5]

1786   ESW's mother, Phoebe Strode Swearingen, died at age 28.[6]

1789   TW chose General William Darke as his guardian and resumed his education.[7]

1792   TW went away to sea, buying passage on a British ship; swindled out of his money, he shipped home as a sailor.[8]

1793   TW ultimately inherited a modest home, Prospect Hill, and a few slaves, some of whom emigrated with him to Ohio.[9]

1795   ESW's father, Josiah Swearingen, died; she inherited one-fourth of his estate as well as one-fourth of the estate of her maternal grandfather, James Strode, landed proprietor of Berkeley County, Virginia, who died the same year.[10]

1796   After purchasing warrants for land in the Virginia Military District, including some from Gen. Darke, TW joined a party going to the Ohio Country where he employed men to survey a choice piece of land northwest of Chillicothe.[11] On December 13, TW married ESW at the home of her maternal aunt, Mrs. Abraham Shepherd, in Berkeley County, Virginia.[12]

TW was almost six feet tall, robustly built, with ruddy complexion and sandy hair. In later years, MW remembered her father's energy and deep-set blue eyes.[13] A contemporary of ESW described her as a "rather slight woman with a finely shaped head. Her black hair became silver-white as she aged. Her face was oval, her eyes a bright blue-grey, and her mouth well-shaped. At home she wore a white scarf of fine material around her shoulders, and her tasteful dress was always plain black."[14]

1797   TW returned to Chillicothe to build a house in readiness for his family. On November 19, Eleanor gave birth to Mary Tiffin Worthington in Berkeley County, Virginia.[15]

1798   On April 17, after an arduous journey of thirty-four days, TW and ESW arrived in Chillicothe with their infant daughter, several Swearingen and Worthington relatives and a number of freed slaves. They also brought with them trees, shrubs and farm animals, as well as fine china, silverware and other furnishings. TW was soon elected to the First Territorial Legislature, which met in Cincinnati, and at age 25 joined a group of young men who opposed the policies of Arthur St. Clair, governor of the Northwest Territory.[16]

1800   On May 10, ESW gave birth to Sarah Anne Worthington in Ross County, Ohio. TW built the first mills of any importance on Paint Creek in Chillicothe.[17]

1801   Over an eight-month period, TW presented Ohio's petition for statehood to Congress at Philadelphia, then at Washington, D. C. The citizens of Chillicothe celebrated TW's successful lobbying efforts which reached fruition in April, 1802.[18]

1802   On May 11, when TW again returned home from the East, he found ESW, Mary and Sarah Anne had already moved from Chillicothe into Belle View, the new log house he had built northwest of town, close to the site where Adena would be erected. On May 31, Eleanor gave birth to their first son, James Taylor Worthington. TW helped to frame Ohio's new state constitution, which he delivered to President Jefferson and Congress later that fall.[19]

1803   On March 1, Ohio became a state; TW was elected one of its first two senators.[20]

1804   On August 18, ESW gave birth to Albert Gallatin Worthington at Belle View.[21]

1805   Construction began on Adena.[22]

1807   On March 18, ESW gave birth to Thomas Worthington "Jr." The family moved into Adena. ESW took major responsibility for designing the flower gardens. Back in Ohio, when his term as senator ended, TW was again elected to the Ohio State Legislature.[23]

1809   On February 27, ESW gave birth to Eleanor (Ellen) Strode Worthington at Adena.[24] During the winter of 1809-10, TW brought members of the Ohio Legislature home for the night as often as two or three times a week. Although no longer a legislator himself, he liked to attend the sessions in Chillicothe to keep abreast of state politics.[25]

1810 TW was again elected U.S. senator from Ohio.[26]

1811 On July 25, ESW gave birth at Adena to her seventh child, Margaret Worthington, possibly named for Thomas's mother, Margaret Matthews. ESW and the youngest children spent the winter with TW in Washington, but returned to Adena in April.[27]

1812 During the War of 1812, when Margaret was still an infant, TW entertained at Adena several military leaders, including Generals William Henry Harrison and Return J. Meigs, as well as Regimental Commanders Lewis Cass, Duncan McArthur and James Findlay.[28]

1813 ESW was among the leading ladies of Chillicothe who presented a sword to Col. George Croghan in honor of his brilliant defense of Fort Stephenson. When TW returned to Washington for the next session of Congress, he took ESW and Sarah Anne with him.[29]

1814 On May 28, ESW gave birth to Elizabeth Rachel Worthington while visiting relatives in Berkeley County, Virginia. In December, upon being elected governor of Ohio, TW resigned his seat in Congress and returned to Adena. He imported Merino sheep and hired German redemptioners to help begin the culture of grapes. Bishop Francis Asbury, Methodist circuit-rider, on a visit to Adena, found ESW's religious instruction of the Worthington children and the family's servants admirable.[30]

1816 On March 13, MW's sister Mary married David Betton Macomb at Adena and on May 15, her sister Sarah Anne married Edward King who had been at Adena since the fall of 1815, studying law. On June 15, ESW gave birth to William Darke Astor Worthington. TW visited son James at West Point and while there addressed the cadets. TW was re-elected governor of Ohio; Ohio's seat of government was moved to Columbus.[31]

1819 On July 16, ESW gave birth at Adena to Francis Asbury Worthington, last of her ten children. During this time, TW suffered financial reverses.[32]

1821   TW represented Ross County in Ohio's 20th and 21st General Assemblies.[33]

1823   TW and ESW went on a business trip to New Orleans, where they were met by son Albert who had begun to accompany loads of TW's produce to New Orleans, and had become his father's business agent there. TW and ESW became ill with fever, a condition that persisted even after their return home.[34]

1825   In August, TW took MW and Ellen to New York to enter them in Mrs. Emma Willard's Troy Female Seminary. He continued on to Saratoga Springs, hoping to find a remedy there for his poor health.[35]

1826   Sarah accompanied TW to New Orleans where the latter had been invited by the city to participate in a reception prepared for General Lafayette. TW recommended routes for the general's tour of the West.[36]

1827   TW served as an Ohio Canal Commissioner. By late spring his health was failing; repeated summer trips to Saratoga Springs had brought him no benefit. In June, following his long sea voyage from New Orleans, TW was met in New York City by Edward King's brother John, who notified both ESW at Adena and young Tom at West Point that TW was seriously ill. Tom hastened to his father's bedside. On the 20th of June, TW died in New York City. ESW, accompanied by Edward King, went to New York to bring TW's body back to Adena where they were met by a crowd of mourners.[37]

    The worth of TW's estate at the time of his death was estimated to h a v e been $146,000, including 15,000 acres of land and many town lots. ESW and her oldest son, James, were named co-executors of the will; it would take them twelve years to settle TW's complicated business and personal affairs. Adena and its 1,500 acres were left to ESW and the unmarried children.[38]

D. Eleanor Worthington's Life from 1827 to 1839

After Thomas's death in 1827, Eleanor Worthingon's role as mistress of Adena was of necessity redefined. She no longer had occasion to entertain notable politicians in her graciously appointed mansion, nor was there enough income to support a large number of servants. At home or in Chillicothe, Eleanor guided her children

Thomas Worthington
(1773-1827)
Courtesy of Ohio Historical Society

Eleanor Swearingen Worthington
(1777-1848)
*From the estate
of Winston Mansfield Dudley*

in accordance with their various states of development. As co-executor of her husband's estate, she continued her efforts to sell tracts of land and town lots, while also supervising the farming operation at Adena.[1]

By 1827, Eleanor's two oldest daughters were married and her three oldest sons well on their way to independence. Mary and Sarah had moved away from Adena with their husbands; James at 25 and Tom at 20 were continuing to maintain their father's manufacturing and business interests. Presumably, Albert was taking care of shipments from the Worthington interests at New Orleans, until his death in 1834 at age 30.[2]

Between 1827 and 1839, Eleanor's immediate concern was the education and welfare of her five youngest offspring. Frank, who in 1827 was eight, attended schools in Chillicothe before entering college. Willy was eleven when his father died, but by 1834, he too, had left home for college.[3] Lizzy, age thirteen, was at Adena with her mother until about 1831 when she went to live at Sarah's home in order to attend a school in Cincinnati. Margaret and Ellen, sixteen and eighteen respectively, were obliged after their father's death to leave Emma Willard's school, and after that possibly received more schooling in Chillicothe, but were at Adena most of the time. Thus in the first twelve years of widowhood Eleanor was guiding her youngest children in ways she would formerly have shared with Thomas. Eleanor also fulfilled her role as a loving, nurturing grandmother. By 1836 she had twelve grandchildren and by 1839, fifteen, whom she loved to have visit her at Adena.

Having inherited wealth when she was orphaned at an early age, Eleanor may have developed more wisdom in finance and land management than was usual for women of early nineteenth-century America.[4] Advertisements for the sale or auction of parcels of land or of town lots appeared repeatedly from 1834 to 1836 in editions of the *Scioto Gazette* over her name and that of James.[5] One parcel of Thomas's estate was a farm in Madison County where cattle were raised on land usually leased to tenant farmers.[6] According to Margaret's letter to Edward, September 14, 1838, Eleanor was willing to visit the Madison place to tend to whatever business arose in regard to that farm, which came into Margaret's possession when her father's will was finally probated in 1839.[7]

Eleanor also took her husband's place as supervisor of farm operations at Adena. This was not an entirely new task because from the beginning of their residence outside Chillicothe she had designed and supervised the gardens about the mansion. During the War of 1812, when Thomas was in Washington, D.C. for many months at a stretch, and women servants replaced men as field workers, Eleanor's brother, James Swearingen, moved into the mansion to supervise the farm work.[8] Eleanor, although undoubtedly preoccupied just then with the care of seven children under the age of fifteen, probably shared with her brother whatever she knew about her husband's methods of farming. In later generations, family lore held that Eleanor was "the best farmer in Ohio."[9]

How did this demure-looking little lady find the strength and stamina to carry all the new responsibilities of widowhood? Her faith in God's providential care was undoubtedly a major bulwark against adversity, a faith nourished by a thorough knowledge of Scripture, and a habit of daily prayer. The experiences of earlier years such as moving an entire household from Virginia to Ohio in 1798, plus having had to manage Adena during her husband's frequent absences, also armed her for the new challenges. She merited and won the devotion of her children; her daughters all professed their admiration and deepest love for their mother, none more than Margaret. In spite of Eleanor's load of cares, Margaret's writings never hinted that her mother ever remonstrated with her three youngest daughters about their getting married and leaving her at Adena.

Later historians praised her for her management skills:

> Eleanor, wife of Thomas Worthington, was a woman of fine mind and remarkable business capacity. Delicately brought up, she faced the dangers and hardships of the new settlement in the Northwest Territory with a brave spirit. Her husband being mostly in public life, she managed his property in his absence with great skill and success. She was left a widow in 1827, with ten children and a large estate deeply incumbered with debt. She contributed greatly, by her economy, frugality, and self-denial, to the education of the younger children, and, by her wise counsel, secured to them all a large part of their inheritance.[10]

E. Margaret's Siblings from 1836 to 1839
Bold print indicates the names of persons Margaret mentioned in her writings.

Only two of Margaret's siblings still lived at Adena in the spring of 1836, their number greatly reduced from the ten children shown in the Worthington Family Table on page 21. Her favorite brother, **Albert**, had died in 1834, and by 1836, five other siblings had married and moved away from Adena.

Margaret's eldest sister, **Mary Macomb**, and her husband, **David B. Macomb**, had moved to Florida in 1826 and later moved on to Texas. **James** and **Ellen** had

WORTHINGTON

FAMILY TABLE [1]

Compiled by Charlotte W. Wells

Eleanor Swearingen
1777-1848

m. Thomas Worthington
1796
10 children

Thomas (Tom)
1807-(1884)

unmarried

Albert Gallatin
1804-1834

unmarried

James Taylor
1802-(1881)

m. Julia Galloway
1828
8 children
m. Martha Piatt Reed
(1856)

Sarah Ann
(Sally Anne)
1800-(1877)

m. Edward King
1816
5 children
m. William Peter
(1844)

Mary Tiffin
1797-1836

m. David Macomb
1816
7 children

m. Eleanor Swearingen
1796
10 children

Thomas Worthinton
1773-1827

Birth and death dates
on chair-backs.
Marriage partners & dates,
no. of children on tabletop

m. Arthur Watts
1832
8 children

Eleanor Strode
(Ellen)
1809-(1863)

m. Edward D. Mansfield
1839
4 children

Margaret (Maggie)
1811-(1863)

m. Charles R. Pomeroy
1835
11 children

Elizabeth Rachel
(Lizzie)
1814-(1852)

unmarried

William Darke Astor
(Willy)
1816-(1850)

m. Jane Tayloe Lomax
(1843)
2 children

Francis Asbury
(Frank)
1819-(1849)

Note: Dates in parentheses mean they occurred after 1839

— 21 —

established homes in nearby Chillicothe. As Margaret's diary opened in April, 1836, her sisters **Sarah** and **Lizzy** were both at Adena, attending the family meeting on April 7. But later that month both of them returned to their homes in Cincinnati, accompanying Margaret as she made her first trip to the city by steamboat down the Ohio River. Her brother **Tom** was unmarried and living at Logan, Ohio, where he operated flour mills on property he had inherited from his father.[2] Logan had been founded by the older Worthington in 1816.[3] Thus, in 1836 Margaret and her two younger brothers, **Willy** and **Frank**, were the only children still calling Adena their home.

Recapping the status of Margaret's siblings, **Mary Tiffin Worthington**, born in 1798, married **David Betton Macomb** at Adena in 1816; they had seven children, two of whom died in infancy. As noted above, by 1836 the Macomb family was in Texas. Margaret's diary entry of December 3, 1836 reported that Mary had died there on the 19th of October. The surviving children were:

> **Eleanor**, b. 1816; m. Joseph Harrell, May 15, 1839
> **Thomas**, b. 1820
> **Louis**, b. 1821
> **Mary**, b. 1824
> **David B.**, b. 1827

In February of 1837, Mary's husband committed suicide, causing consternation among the orphans' Ohio relatives. The three youngest children, Louis, Mary and David, were sent to Adena to be under the care of their grandmother, Eleanor Worthington and their aunt Margaret.[4] (Further details are given in the Interlude, between Parts Five and Six.)

Sarah Anne Worthington, born in 1800, married **Edward King** (b. 1795) at Adena in 1816, and had five children. Only two of them survived to adulthood, **Rufus King** (1817-1891) and Thomas (**Tom**) **W. King** (1820-1851).[5] As youngsters, Rufus and Tom were often at Adena where they played like brothers with their uncles Willy and Frank Worthington, who were almost their age.[6]

From 1816 to 1831, Edward and Sarah King had lived in a Chillicothe home supplied to them by Sarah's father.[7] Margaret would have had opportunities to visit their home many years before either James or Ellen had houses in town. In the summer of 1835 Sarah accompanied their son Rufus when he entered Harvard College. Edward, meanwhile, stayed at Adena while he recovered from malaria. Catharine Beecher made a brief visit to Adena in that interval. She disagreed with Eleanor who called adherents of abolitionism, "peace destroyers in the church."[8]

Several months after the death of her husband in February, 1836, **Sarah** decided to take her son Tom to join his older brother, Rufus, at Harvard. She also invited two King nephews and her own youngest brother, **Frank**, to join her sons at college. She maintained a home in Cambridge for all five boys until they completed their courses in 1840.[9] **Tom King** was still in Cincinnati in the spring of 1836, appearing occasionally in Margaret's diary accounts of her social activities in the city. **Sarah** lived to become one of Cincinnati's great philanthropists and a patron of the arts.

Margaret's brother, **James** T. Worthington, born in 1802, married her school-mate, **Julia Ann Galloway**, in Xenia, Ohio, in December, 1828. The couple subsequently established a home in Chillicothe. Of their eight children, Mary (1832-1883), Thomas (1835-1891) and James (d. 1863) appear in Margaret's papers; Elizabeth and Martha died young; Eleanor, Julia and Richard were born in the 1840s (Chillicothe cemetery records and Drummond 1971, 33-36). Several of Julia's siblings, listed below, figure prominently in Margaret's 1836-37 diary.

> Richard Galloway, b. 1806
> **Julia** A. Galloway, 1808-1856, m. **James** T. Worthington
> **Henry** P. Galloway, b. 1810
> **Albert ("Nemo")** Galloway, b. 1811
> **Rebecca (Beck)** Galloway, b. 1814; m. George Myers in 1835
> **Sarah Ann (Sally)** Galloway, b. 1816; m. **Robert Patterson**
>   **Browne**, October 31, 1837
> **Amanda** Galloway, b. 1818; m. George Trotter, June 12, 1839
> Frances (**Mary**) Galloway, b. 1820
> Robert A. Galloway, b. 1822
> James E. Galloway, b. 1825[10]

Eleanor (Ellen) Worthington, born in 1809, married **Arthur Watts** at Adena in June, 1832. Occasional diary entries that Margaret headed "Eolia" were written at the Watts farmstead in the Scioto Valley which was within walking distance of Chillicothe. Three children were born to Ellen and Arthur Watts between 1832 and 1839: Eleanor (**Ellen**), in 1834, **John**, in 1835, and **Lily**, in 1837.

Elizabeth (Lizzy) Worthington, born in 1814, married **Charles R. Pomeroy** at Adena in November, 1835. In the spring of 1836 they were living at Mrs. Lodge's

Cincinnati boarding house. Charles was associated with his father, **Samuel W. Pomeroy**, in the coal business in the city.[11]

As early as 1831, Lizzy had become acquainted with the advantages of city life, and had grown familiar with many of Cincinnati's prominent citizens. At Sarah's invitation, she had gone to live with the Kings who had recently moved to the city from Chillicothe. Sarah enrolled Lizzy in a fine private school for girls, an arrangement that lasted for two years.[12] Lizzy's letters from Cincinnati to her mother and Margaret in the 1836-39 period show that she willingly executed shopping errands for them and their friends in city clothing stores.[13]

Lizzy and Charles Pomeroy eventually had a family of eleven children, two of whom were born during the 1836 to 1839 period: **Eleanor W.**, whose birth at Adena on August 6, 1836 Margaret recorded in her diary; and **John Alsop**, born September 28, 1838.

Willy attended Ohio University at Athens, Ohio, in 1834, but by 1836 seemed, according to Margaret's diary, to be at Adena most of the time.[14] He never married. **Frank** returned home from Kenyon College at Gambier, Ohio, in April, 1836, where he had been since 1834. In the late summer of 1836, he left for Cambridge, Massachusetts, where he entered Harvard College, graduating from that institution in 1840, later obtaining a degree in medicine.[15] Frank was married in 1845 to Jane Tayloe Lomax and had one surviving daughter, Alice.

F. What Was Margaret Worthington Really Like?

After all our catalog of persons to whom Margaret was related in one way or another, what can be said about her relation to herself, her self-image? Other than the critical self-characterizations in her diary, we have only Henry Howe's description of her. Howe, an itinerant chronicler of early Ohio communities and personalities, visited Margaret and her husband after they established a home outside of Morrow, Ohio, in the 1850s. He wrote that Margaret was "large and commanding, a blonde with a sweet smile and ways and sensibilities, a Christian woman of the finest type," mentioning also that she had executive ability.[1] Margaret's portrait by Thomas Buchanan Read, reproduced in the frontispiece, and again on p. 126, was painted when she was forty-one,[2] at about the same time as Howe's visit.

Readers may judge Margaret's character for themselves after reading her diary and letters. Motivated by her strong religious convictions, she often expressed a desire to be more faithful to God. One reason she kept a diary at all may have been her wish to evaluate her day-to-day experiences in the light of her Christian faith. Given the strength of her religious convictions, as well as the passionate nature of some of her attachments, it seems apparent that writing in her diary gave Margaret the benefit of putting subjective feelings into an objective form. Her diary was like a soul-mate to whom she could confide almost, if not quite everything, that was uppermost in her mind and heart, so that she could better determine her priorities. The epigram on the flyleaf of her diary expressed her idealistic view of life:

Earth will forsake. Oh happy to have given
the soul's unbroken fragrance unto Heaven.[3]

APRIL,	3	4	5	6	7	8	9
	10	11	12	13	14	15	16
	17	18	19	20	21	22	23
	24	25	26	27	28	29	30
MAY,	1	2	3	4	5	6	7
	8	9	10	11	12	13	14
	15	16	17	18	19	20	21
	22	23	24	25	26	27	28
	29	30	31				
JUNE,	..	..	..	.1	2	3	4
	5	6	7	8	9	10	11
	12	13	14	15	16	17	18
	19	20	21	22	23	24	25
	26	27	28	29	30		
JULY,	..	..	..	..	..	1	2
	3	4	5	6	7	8	9
	10	11	12	13	14	15	16
	17	18	19	20	21	22	23
	24	25	26	27	28	29	30
	31	..	..	..	..	..	..
AUGUST,	..	1	2	3	4	5	6
	7	8	9	10	11	12	13
	14	15	16	17	18	19	20
	21	22	23	24	25	26	27
	28	29	30	31	..	..	..
SEPTEMBER,	..	..	..	..	1	2	3
	4	5	6	7	8	9	10
	11	12	13	14	15	16	17
	18	19	20	21	22	23	24
	25	26	27	28	29	30	..
OCTOBER,	..	..	..	..	..	..	1
	2	3	4	5	6	7	8
	9	10	11	12	13	14	15
	16	17	18	19	20	21	22
	23	24	25	26	27	28	29
	30	31	..	..	..	..	..
NOVEMBER,	..	..	1	2	3	4	5
	6	7	8	9	10	11	12
	13	14	15	16	17	18	19
	20	21	22	23	24	25	26
	27	28	29	30	..	..	..
DECEMBER,	..	..	..	..	1	2	3
	4	5	6	7	8	9	10
	11	12	13	14	15	16	17
	18	19	20	21	22	23	24
	25	26	27	28	29	30	31

This is a copy of Margaret's calendar for the nine months of 1836 covered in her diary. It was attached to the inside cover. The relevant calendar weeks for January and February of 1837 were fastened to the flyleaf, opposite.

Courtesy of the Ohio Historical Society

Daughter of Adena

Margaret Worthington's Diary of 1836 - 1837

It is a hard thing to love from a sense of duty to wring from the heart those feelings which will not flow spontaneously—who would prize such love, who receive it—who be content with such worthless . . ., not those truly whose warm hearts have throbbed with the delightful consciousness of returned affection from those most dear. Yet there are some whom I feel it my duty to love—well I do love them but with a love so forced I cannot be happy in it—

Part One
"Oh, how reluctantly I leave home . . ."
April 1 - May 21, 1836

Adena, April 1, 1836

Lizzy and I walked to town yesterday to meet with the circle of industry at James's[1]—passed a pleasant evening—gave Mr. Taylor a needlebook he had bespoken. The honorable Judge did me the honor to make himself agreeable to me—so he intended it at least and so I took his intentions.[2] Passed the night at Uncle James [Swearingen's] and walked home this morning.[3]

Gathered in the woods the first spring flowers whose delicate beauty always delights me. I do not know why it is that I love them best—it must be that I have cherished the feeling that they are Nature's free will offering to her admirers. They are always more welcome to me than exotics or garden flowers. These last delight me by their coming, but towards the blossoms of the wildwood there is a wild undefinable emotion of delight, of rapturous pleasure; from my childhood I have felt it and I well remember when my apparently crazy joy on discovering the first wild flowers called forth the merriment of my playmates.

A few mild days have quite changed the aspect of things, though not a leaf is yet expanded, the buds are swelling to burst their folds and the flowers are springing as if by magic. Sweet are the smiles and delightful the voice of Spring; flowers are her smiles and the carolling of birds her voice—who does not love them? Stern Winter would fain have caught a peep at the charms of Spring, and bright Summer too, and perseveringly thwarted and checked sweet Spring in her progress. At last he has been obliged to yield, to resign his dominion to gentler sway.

I am aweary to-day—no sooner did I arrive at home than I began to reset my exotics and was busied till night. Put up some flowers for Rebecca Myers.[4] Frank returned last week from Gambier.[5]

Adena, April 2, 1836

Sat. Came to a full determination to visit Cincinnati with Lizzy. Charles can't come for us so we, that is, Sister S[arah], Lizzy and I and perhaps Misses Delano[6] and Irvin[7] are to escort each other and next Tuesday[8] week is the day appointed for leaving home. I am foolish maybe, but oh, how reluctantly I leave home even for so short a time as three weeks. A few warm days have wrought wonders in vegetation. The buds are swelling almost into leaves, and obedient to the voice of Spring her first-born flowers are timidly looking out to the sun's light. Does it not seem as if flowers came at the call of birds?

Cousin Henry Massie spent the evening with us. He improves surprisingly on intimate acquaintance. I esteem him highly; it would be strange if I did not, knowing his good qualities, his intelligence and amiability.[9]

Adena, April 4, 1836

Monday. As I was sitting in my room this morning making the first arrangements for my visit to C[incinnati], I was much surprised to receive a summons below to see Mr. Cranch.[10] He came principally to escort us home he says, and his company would add greatly to our pleasure but he must go to-morrow and we cannot, as I have just begun to think on the necessary arrangements. Walked through the garden and gathered a boquet [sic] for him. In the afternoon Mr. Randolph called, an odd genius he, too.[11] After tea Sally S[wearington], the boys and I went to Fruit Hill.[12]

Adena, April 5, 1836

Tuesday. Anne James and Mr. Taylor and Mr. R. [called].[13] The latter stayed to dinner and I gave him letters to Xenia to Sarah and Mary [Galloway]. A letter this evening from Sally.[14] Fear she will not be able to meet me in C[incinnati].

Can't write! and why? What said I that might not readily be replied to? <u>Can't write</u>—I'll think of that—I have thought of it—and it strangely affects me, too—oh, that I could school my feelings better. Those two words may mean nothing, and yet I have suffered them to make me unhappy. My head aches, and 'tis well it does, for it oft as now has served to conceal a heartache. <u>Can't write</u>, well then, be silent, and though I die in the effort, so will I. Sally says her parents have decided to take Mary to Steubenville.[15] I regret it but—have no right to say aught.

Adena, April 7, 1836

Thursday. To-day we had a family meeting, all of us but Tom and Sister Mary, the first meeting since Mr. K's death.[16] How hard, oh, how painful for me to realize in truth that he is gone forever from us. Death has taken one, and another and another—my heart aches to think of the now vacant places once filled with those so loved—when they were only absent we could speak of them and in imagination have them with us—but now—though we must all think of the departed we hesitate, we fear to speak of them. To-day we were present, sister Sarah, James and Julia, Ellen and Arthur, myself, Lizzy, Willy and Frank.[17] God grant we may oft meet in happiness again. Arthur's mother was here too—poor lady, what an affliction is hers to be perfectly sensible of what she wishes to say, yet unable to express herself intelligibly.[18]

As for myself, this day I am not well, in consequence of agitation of mind, or it may be the latter is caused by the former, my enemy of lang syne having assailed me without the slightest provocation.[19] There is an arbour being put up in the garden which I claim—it will serve in future to recall this day.

Adena, April 8, 1836

Friday. I walked to town to Miss Luckett's, remained three hours and then walked home again, which as I was not very well I consider worth boasting of.[20]

Adena, April 9, 1836

Sat. night. This time next week I shall probably be in Cincinnati, and this will be the last time I shall write at home a journal of my—what?— for some weeks. It has been a day of unceasing rain, hard showers in succession through the day. 'Tis a pleasant sight to look on the green earth again, to see the naked shrubbery assuming its first and beautifully delicate-colored leaves. I have been <u>sick</u>, <u>sick</u> all this week and preparing to leave home. Was somewhat surprised and gratified to receive a letter from Miss Irvin in answer to our invitation to accompany us to C. Cannot go with us—I was in hopes she would, as I wished to become well acquainted with her and discover if it were possible for me to love her.

Adena, April 11, 1836

Monday. 'Tis well to be prepared for disappointments. The rain of Sat. has caused several breaches in the canal and the streams are too high for fording, so we must defer our journey for several days. A breach in the canal Sat. night caused by the giving way of the bank caused much alarm and considerable destruction of property. Most Providentially, no lives were lost and this is somewhat remarkable as the accident occurred between midnight and the break of day when mortals are least prepared for such exigencies.[21] Mrs. Coons spent part of the aft with us.[22] I—am—foolish—simple—I'm ashamed of myself—but ah me, that cannot prevent . . .

Chilly weather, frost for several mornings past. Poor little flowers, I feel as though they all needed clothing. I breathe on them to melt the frost which benumbs them—do they know me? It seems as if they should, and love me too, for I daily visit them and hold converse with them. They seem to me possessed of feeling and sometimes I reproach myself for plucking them. Were I a flower, I'm sure I should wish my birthplace my grave. If it were possible, as my fancy often suggests, that flowers should be possessed of feeling, sensibility, how must they suffer from the wanton waste inflicted on them! With what indifference do we pluck a beauteous flower from the parent stem, mindful only of the gratification caused us by the possession of it—utterly unheeding of what pain the separation may be producing. I love flowers, I dearly love flowers—they awaken within me the deepest, the most delightsome emotions. How many wild fancies I have about them too. I laugh at them in my sober hours but they yield me innocent pleasure, these same wild fancies.

Adena, April 12, 1836

Tues. Lizzy and I passed the evening at Gen. M[c]A[rthur]'s. Weather still gloomy and unseasonably cold, and I have incessant <u>head</u> <u>aches</u>.

Adena, April 15, 1836

Friday. I walked to town to breakfast and then, in company with E[leanor] S[wearingen], went to Eolia.[23] Sister S. and Julia were added to our party shortly and we had a very pleasant day, only a little interrupted by the presence of Mr. Randolph.

Went to the river with him, then to town to church and Saturday morning walked home, calling on my way at Mr. Walke's[24] and Gen. M^cA's. The canal is not yet repaired and the streams too high for fording so we must remain yet several days.

Adena, April 18, 1836

Monday. I came home last night supposing our journey would be delayed indefinitely. Lizzy stayed in town to make enquiries about the possibilities of getting off. I was industriously making pickles when she came home this morning and warned me to prepare for departure in the evening. All was bustle—hurried my pickles, had clothes washed, and left home about five o'clock aft., with a feeling of sadness not to be shaken off. Walked in the garden and gathered some lovely flowers which I intend to take to Cincinnati. They will bear with them thoughts of Adena's bowers—friends among strangers, and their fragrance will refresh me and say sweet home.

Adena, April 19, 1836

Tues. We left James's home this morning about ten, later than we wished, but as Mrs. Woodbridge was travelling the same route we waited for her party, consisting of herself, [her children] Lucy and Charles W., Mr. Buchanan and child and nurse; our party, Lizzy, Susan Delano and myself.[25] Several friends called to bid us goodbye, Annie J[ames], Louisa A[twater], Mr. Randolph, etc.

Nothing particularly interesting occurred to-day; crossed the creek safely and found the roads better than we had expected. At Piketon[26] we crossed the Sciota [sic] —'twas just before sunset. The river was much fuller than usual and makes here a very pretty bend. The reflection of the trees on the water, the bright tints of the setting sun formed a pleasing scene, one of beauty such as the world is full of, did we but notice them.

Was miserably accommodated at Piketon—bad beds, dirty house and ill fare. It quite sickened me. I felt worse for it all day. Arrived at Portsmouth about three in aft. I will leave a page to fill up when Portsmouth fulfills the destiny marked out for it. Now it does not promise much though it is prettily situated I think, from the hasty view I could give it.[27] Mr. Buchanan, Mrs. Woodbridge's brother, resides here. He was polite and seemed anxious to shew us the beauties of the town which as yet are but few. About 9 in the eve . . .

En route to Cincinnati, April 20, 1836

A boat arrived about 9, and we got on board.[28] Susan and I sat on deck till the moon was down, endeavouring to form some ideas of the scenery as 'twas the first trip for us, and we rose by daylight next morning, but alas for our curiosity! A rain came on and we sought shelter most reluctantly in a cabin. I should think the scenery must be beautiful, very beautiful in summer. The river rolls between wood-crowned hills, sometimes sloping gently and at times descending abruptly to the water's edge. I had not a fair view however, and must see again before I can form a just conception of the scenery of the Ohio. As we descended the river, vegetation was more advanced than at home where the trees scarce presented a shade of green. We reached the far-famed proud City of Cincinnati about ten o'clock Thursday morning, April 21.

Cincinnati, April 21, 1836

My heart almost failed me when I looked from the steamboat on the bustling scene at the wharf, compared with our own little quiet town. As we neared the city the rain ceased and we hoped to be able to go on deck, but the weather had changed several degrees colder and the wind was high. I observed some very pretty country houses and the towns of Newport and Covington opposite Cin'a [sic] on each side of the Licking River. The approach to the city is beautiful. It is surrounded by hills now covered with the tender green of early spring, ever so delightful. Many boats were lying at the wharf. Lizzy and sister [Sarah] went on shore, leaving Susan and me to wait for an escort. By and by, Mr. W[orthington][29] came and soon we were all in Mrs. Lodge's parlour.[30] In a few minutes E[lizabeth] W[orthington], having heard of my arrival, came in and wished me to go immediately to her house, but I could not till to-morrow as mine and Lizzy's things are so packed together that 'twill take some time to <u>right</u> them.

April 22 to May 19, 1836

May 19. I can scarce believe it that I have made a three weeks visit to C[incinnati] and am safely at my beloved home again. I never can write with pleasure when I am abroad for several reasons. One very important one is that implements of writing are not always at hand when I am in the mood, and another, anywhere but in my own room I am liable to interruption. I wish to remember my visit to the Queen of the West and will endeavour to narrate a few circumstances and events which were productive of most interest and pleasure to me.[31]

Cincinnati

The first two days [April 22 and 23] after my arrival I was under the operation of a dentist.[32] I remember the time when I thought I could not bear to have artificial teeth in my mouth. Now I have two and thankful for them. The pain of extracting several teeth and the filing irritated my system, and for two days I was kept in my room, nervous and feverish.

I took up my abode with dear E[lizabeth] W[orthington] the day after my arrival and remained with her ten days. Many ladies called to see me. I was not well the whole time and felt anxious on Elizabeth's account as she is in a very feeble state of health and was in perpetual trouble about servants. She had one most diabolical creature who, in revenge for being sent away, threw some caps and collars in the gutter and trampled them beneath her feet.

Mrs. S. Pomeroy was engaged packing up furniture preparing to leave town. I like her more than any of Charles's relatives. Willis P. [Samuel W. Pomeroy] was polite and is a pleasing man. His wife is a very agreeable woman, in bad health unfortunately. Except [for] Charles's mother, all his kin treated me as they would have done any other stranger, Yankee fashion I suppose, and I was not at all pleased as I had expected different treatment. I am truly fearful my Yankee kin and I will never level the mountain of formality lying between us. I am anxious, but they don't seem to care or to expect anything else.[33]

E. W. has one child, a beautiful boy of five years, too great a pet with both his parents to be under very good government. Mr. W. is a <u>gentleman</u> well bred, polite and was very attentive and kind to me, but I am afraid my friend is not happy. Mr. W. is of but little importance in society, wants energy, decision and I hope he may not want morality in one point. My heart ached for E. for she was a noble girl, spoiled 'tis true by admiration, but with a husband of a different character she might have been a blessing to society. She used to be energetic, gay [but] now she seems listless unless when under excitement. She is as she ever was, heaven bless her, warmhearted and affectionate. Oh, that she may find in religion a balm to her crushed and disappointed hopes; I think she is seriously concerned about religion.

I found a letter from Sally [Galloway] awaiting me at C. saying she could not join me, but, *nil desperandum*, I wrote to her again urging her to come even for a few days. The second week after my arrival [May 2 to 11] I stayed at Mrs. Lodge's with Lizzy. [We were] badly enough off here, too, for servants—only one old woman, Mrs. Lodge lame, and her poor daughter deprived of the use of her lower limbs so that she cannot even stand. Sister Sarah left for New York with Mr. and Mrs. Pendleton[34] a week after we came down. I had several pleasant rides, one especially a few miles down the river, to Mr. Oliver's. There are many beautiful country seats on the river bank.

On Monday [May] 9, Sally, Mary and Albert G[alloway] arrived, much to my joy.[35] I never in my life felt so oppressed, restrained, bound by the feeling of being a stranger, as since I have been here. It must be an art of Cin'ians. I spent one evening at Edw[ard] Mansfield's and felt as if I had been bound in boards and cold pressed.[36] Both gentlemen and ladies seemed to think it unnecessary to trouble themselves about either Susan or me. Another eve'g I spent at Dr. Drake's and must thank Judge Hall for all the evening's enjoyment, as I was quite unacquainted with almost everyone present, etc.[37] The Judge loves the Universal Nation as little as I do, but oh, I've kindred (bah) of that same nation.[38] Mr. Ben Drake is certainly agreeable sometimes.

When Sally arrived, I was dressing in unwilling mood to go to E. W.'s to meet some company. Sally and A[lbert] did not send word who they were and Charles told S. we were engaged!—but the dear child waited 10 or 15 minutes and then, out of patience, came up to my room. I was heartily glad to see her and wished to remain at home, but it would not do, and Sally could not go with me. Albert and [my nephew] Tom King accomp'd me to Mr. W[orthington]'s ladies; two I had never seen before but all of the gents I knew. The Misses Carneal are pretty girls and called accomplished, the younger especially so; she is seventeen, has confidence enough for a woman of 40, sings like an actress, very fine voice if she would only sing naturally.[39] None of the ladies gave themselves any concern about me. However, I did very well among my friends: Mr. Whiteman, Judge H., Dr. Ridgely, Mr. Graham, Mr. Hodges and Mr. [Ben] Drake, all of whom are old acquaintances.[40] I sang and was frightened almost out of my wits, foolishly enough, but I could not help it—and was glad when the time came to go home to Sally.

Tues. [May 10], we visited the school formerly under Miss Beecher's care and A[lbert] made arrangements to enter Mary as a pupil.[41] They all know best, but I fear Mary will do no good here as respects the formation of her character. After we returned, Miss Groesbeck called and then Miss Shoenberger, the lady to whom Mr. Cranch is devoting himself.[42] I must, by the way, mention that Mr. C. called twice for 15 or 20 minutes to see me during my stay in his city. I had expected him to be very kind even, but he lacked common courtesy. Charles and Lizzy gave an after tea party, a room full of merry people, Sally as gay as any. I tried too hard to join the merriment and the cord snapped and I had to take myself off and—oh, that long evening, and Lizzy reproaching me for my dullness, when I could but just refrain from tears—and wherefore was it so? Alas, my old enemy! Will it never give me up myself?

[May 11] Albert and Mr. Whiteman promised to call and walk with us before breakfast. A. disappointed me. Mr. W. came and we walked to the reservoir on the hill. Unfortunately, the smoke and fog obscured the view of the city, river and country. We had a pleasant walk but I could not but think that Albert might have kept his promise. After breakfast, Sally and I went shopping, then came back and packed up our things to be sent to E. Worthington. Called with A. to see my highly valued friend Mrs. [Elizabeth P.] Mansfield.[43] How very much I enjoy her society; found William Crane at our house; poor fellow, his misfortune deserves our warmest sympathies.

A sailing party was arranged for today and Sally and I held ourselves in readiness at the time appointed, but much to our surprise, and somewhat to my disappointment, all of the ladies, and there were ten of them, sent excuses for not joining us. Two gentlemen, Mr. Graham and Mr. Eells, came and after waiting two hours we determined not to be thus cheated of our pleasure and the gents proposed, instead of the sailing party, a ride.[44] We assented, and with the addition of Tom King, we set out for the Hygean Well about 4 miles distant from the city on the Kentucky side.[45] We had fine horses, the gents were entertaining and we in a mood for enjoying the ride. On arriving at the well, we found the house deserted. It is a large frame building with a porch extending all around it—looked dreary enough too, all silent, the grass overgrown and the trees untrimmed. The only inhabitant we could descry was a peafowl who greeted us incessantly with his discordant voice. The water is pleasant with a slightly medicinal taste. We had some difficulty, too, in getting even a taste of it, having nothing to drink from but the well bucket. Each one had a different device, one from his hands (Mr. E.), Sally and I from leaves made of <u>cups</u>, [sic] and Mr. G. and Tom from the bucket itself.[46] Returning, the ride was delightful —a glorious sunset—balmy air and our way lay through a beautiful beech wood. I enjoyed it exceedingly and so did dear Sally. <u>If only I were not so simple</u>, how much enjoyment might I have had for two weeks past. "But 'tis done, all words are idle." We reached home just at dusk and took tea in our riding dresses. Let me not omit to mention that this day I first touched the soil of old Kentuck.

Albert and Mr. Rankin called, then Charles and Lizzy with Susan D. and Mary G. and we all sallied out to see Miss Afong Moy, the Chinese girl who was exhibited at the Bazaar.[47] The <u>exhibition</u> for the eve'g was over, it being late when we arrived and her ladyship, of small understanding, had retired. However as our party was large she consented to reappear. She seems about 16 or 18 and below the middle height, a large Dutch-looking [broad] face [and] oblong eyes. It seemed to me her head was disproportionately large. She was dressed in her native costume with a little additional finery. I had not conceived it possible for a person of her size to walk at all on such small feet, no larger than a child's of a year-and-a-half old, and most shockingly deformed. How are the blind creatures of the earth to be pitied—amongst us who boast our refinement there are customs ridiculous.[48]

Thursday May 12.[49] My last day in Cincinnati and though there be some here that I love, yet oh, my heart longs for home, my peaceful home. I had a letter from Julia on Monday, telling me how sweetly flowers were blooming there and since then I have been doubly anxious to leave this noisy, worldly city.[50] My tastes are all for country life; I scarce think even a sense of duty could make me happy in a city— it seems to me emphatically the world; cold hearts, and insincere smiles, warm words and chilling tones and an affectation of deep interest where none exists. These I cannot bear and I fancy I have met some of this character here—they are in, and must be of the world. In a village like ours I could live, and with pleasure, too. I'm learning every day, "There's no place like home" for me.[51] For true happiness and enjoyment, give me a country life. It has so much more of interest and innocence, too, than town. God has wisely given to his creatures different tastes and sources of pleasure in things directly opposed. His wisdom is infinite and how great is his goodness; let my heart rise in grateful thanksgivings for the blessings vouchsafed me and for none earthly more than friends and dear home.

Called with S[usan] D[elano], Mary and Albert G. at Mr. Longworth's. Eliza was not at home to my regret,[52] then at Mrs. Mansfield's to tell her goodbye, and then to Mr. W.'s again, where I found W. Crane who stayed till afternoon. Sally made ready and we went out and made a number of calls. The day was warm and had it not been for a confectioner's by the way, we should have been quite exhausted.

Today is Charly [Worthington]'s birthday, and in honor of it his mama gave him a party of boys and girls of his own age. About 30 or 40 children came and I never in my life enjoyed a scene more than they presented—so free from restraint, so joyous. Compared with grown up people, they seem as wild flowers beside exotics; and yet there were two or three that seemed to have caught the affectation of their elders—I pitied them so soon to lose what is rightly their due. Mr. Drake came in and romped with the little people and seemed to enjoy it as much as I. Judge Hall, too, and Misses Booth and Carneal.[53]

Went to bid Mrs. Pomeroy goodbye, then according to promise, to Mrs.

Lodge's to take tea with Charles and Lizzy. On my way I was overtaken by a shower and fortunately met Mr. Drake with an umbrella. We called at Mr. Groesbeck's where Sally was and waited till the rain was past. Miss Wallace was there. She and Miss G. and the Misses Drake are the most interesting ladies I have met here, unmarried ladies I mean. I think I should like them all extremely.[54] Charles and Lizzie, with Susan, Mary and Tom returned from a sail on the Ohio. I wished I could have joined them.[55] After tea, A. and Dr. Ridgely came in, then M— —P. and Annie. I said my goodbye at nine and called—stayed an hour and then made my obeisa[nce]. Sally and I had a laugh extraordin[aire]. [The page containing the next paragraph was torn].

I felt a little fainthearted at the thought of travelling alone with only Susan, and was more delighted than I ever expected to be at the sight of Mr. Carlisle.[56] Our friends soon left us and just as the boat was pushing off, Albert came to bid us goodbye. They all . . . stood watching us from the shore till our boat swung . . . back [and we could] see each other no longer . . . [The remainder of this page was torn. On part of it, MW wrote that she felt "more miserable than (for) many years."]

The Ohio is well named "beautiful river."[57] There is nothing of grandeur in the scenery of its shores but much of beauty generally—hills on one side, and lowlands on the other. Occasionally a town adds variety but there is much of sameness in the scenery, though 'tis all beautiful—lovely. I marvel that I have never seen any views of the river—there are some I should think well worth the sketching. By night I had quite recovered from my fit of despondency (the remembrance of which even now is grievous) and sat out on the guards and sang with some ladies, our fellow passengers. Mr. C. did not trouble us much, but it was a comfort to know we had a friend on board who would, in time of need, be at hand.

Reach'd Portsmouth at 5 next morning [May 14] and, as no canal boat was going till eve'g, we took seats in the stage which was at the door when we arrived. Mrs. A. and Sarah were in it. Whilst our baggage was being put on I sent up and had a few minutes talk with Mary Irvin[58] who looked rather sleepy and no wonder. In half an hour after we left the Steamboat, we were on our way home in the stage coach. Bad road. [I was] sick, very sick most all day, only kept up by the beautiful wild flowers which covered the woods. Made a terrible mistake about flowers. Reached James's a little before sunset, but so sickened that I could scarce feel as happy as I wished.

[May 15] Went to church and was pleased to meet again my Sunday scholars and many friends. Sunday evening, I returned home. Everything seemed to welcome me.

Adena, May 16, 1836

      Monday morning. I took my accustomed walk before breakfast in the garden. Home, dear home, how I rejoice to feel at home—almost I can say, would I had not left it this last absence. The snowdrops are gone and but a few withered stocks of the lily-of-the-valley remain. Cruel ones, why did ye not await my coming? You that I love so dearly, whose appearance I hail with such exulting delight, why not stay for me—will you, too, pain me by neglect? My precious flowers, I blame not you. 'Tis your destiny and ye must fulfill it. A few short days and your transient existence is begun and ended—ye will bloom again, but it may be I shall not see you. Yet forget me not, sweet flowers, for the love I bear and have ever borne you, forget me not. What have I gained by my visit? My sweet favorite flowers have bloomed whilst I was away. I have missed the season which ever fills me with rapture, the first budding of vegetation. +++ I fear I have not even the gratification of knowing that I have pleased my friends in C., for whilst there I was sick, sad and terribly out of humour with myself, and it's hard to please others when one is in such a case. One thing I know, my heart is far sadder than when I left home, and why? Because—that is a woman's reason, they say, and it must serve me now. They all at home say I don't look well—thinner and paler—can't help it, and regret it sincerely, more than anyone else can do. Don't, and fear I cannot soon say with sincerity that I like Cincinnati in the usual acceptation of the phrase. It's too much world for me—a log hut in the far west would, I think, be my choice the rather. I may change. Mrs. James, Annie and Charlotte Bush called this even'g.[59]

Adena, May 17, 1836

      Tuesday. I went to town to bid Uncle James's family goodbye. Miss Luckett accompanied them. They went off in good spirits. [I] rode with Ellen, Willy and several other friends a mile or two. Came home fully determined to go to Lancaster on horseback—wrote to Beck [Rebecca Galloway Myers] to that effect and was busy all the week renovating my riding dress. Several of my friends called to see me, among whom was Miss Baskerville—an honor I can't forget.[60]

Adena, May 21, 1836

      Sat. eve'g. I rec'd a letter from Mr. Myers, saying Rebecca had gone to Xenia to make a visit, so my visit was . . . Well, I'll go when she returns—a single suspiration.

The First Page of Margaret Worthington's 1836-37 Diary
Courtesy of Ohio Historical Society

Adena in 1971

Courtesy of Edith Dudley Sylla

Part Two
"I would not be a belle"
June 1 - August 31, 1836

Adena, June 1, 1836

Summer again—I remember with what joyous feelings I greeted this day last year. To-day I merely write the fact without feeling much interest about it; is my heart freezing—or maybe it's undergoing the process of ossification—or maybe it "has bled, and is healing itself callous." For the last ten days it has rained incessantly; not a day without a cold rain and we've not had a peep at the blessed sun in all that time.

Judge and Mary Irvin[1] were here last week on their way to Lancaster, spent a day with us, and went to town through a hard rain to spend the eve'g at Mr. Douglass's.[2] Mary didn't go. Quite a pleasant party, but I was and am tired of hearing my name in connexion with . . . a very clever fellow and I like him very much more than I thought I ever should, but that's all.

Tuesday, May 31st was James's birthday. Julia gave a party in honor of the occasion and for Mrs. Bush but she left in the morning to our disappointment. Rain, rain, a pitiless eve'g and only a few ladies came and plenty of gents—tired myself talking to half a dozen at a time. I carried down a great variety of roses and other flowers this morning and arranged them to look beautifully. The roses during the past week have been in perfection; nothing could be more beautiful had they only a gleam of sunshine. The whole garden is perfumed by them—the air is indeed laden with sweets. 'Tis beautiful and conveys to my mind sensations of delight and enjoyment which I cannot express; my mind is full of beautiful thoughts and images, yet when I would convey them thence by words they fade, they vanish, they are despoiled of their loveliness by the attempt. My arbour is yet bare, an unsightly object with its skeleton frame, but it will be beautiful in time. When, though, shall my thoughts be clothed in the graceful drapery of language? I have dwelt too much in Utopia; <u>now</u> I feel its tendency. But I am foolish again—go back, ye thoughts that "strive to win your way," that I <u>can</u> but will not now write. Heard a day or two since of Mary Wallace's marriage to Mr. Shillito[3]—it was unexpected when I saw her in C[incinnati], maybe not to her, but to her friends.

My first thought on opening my eyes this morning (June 1st) was how many foolish things I said last night—and yet how the . . . seemed interested and edified thereby. I would not be a belle if I could. I have in truth too much conscience if nothing else—one hour's reign wearies me.[4] Went shopping, purchased a muslin dress,[5] received a present of some new music "from my friend J.," rode home to dinner—tried my songs, some beautiful, one especially so—simple, pathetic, touching—'tis called "The Angel's Whisper."[6] Jamie likes it—I'll learn it for him.[7]

Adena, June 3, 1836

Friday. Received a visit from Mr. B'n[8] of five hours—I hope he was pleased. He tried to say what I was determined he should not, for I was most obstinately dull of comprehension. He must, if he have any discrimination, perceive my determination. I am to spend next week with E. McCoy, a visit I have been promising for a long time. Truly I hope the weather will prove more favorable; for two weeks past there has been rain daily and not half a day's sunshine during all that time. "The heart knoweth its own bitterness;"[9] how true that saying of the wise man—how forcible the expression; who has not felt it?

McCoy's, Chillicothe, June 5, 1836

Took up my abode to-day at Mr. McCoy's, and passed a week very pleasantly. On Tues. eve'g we paid a long promised visit to Mrs. Hoffman. E. McCoy, Anne J., Fanny K. and Mrs. Alexander [went with us]; Cousin Henry M. and W'm M^C. came after tea. I think we were all possessed for I never witnessed such merriment, and as for myself I laughed till I had no strength. We went to McKee's and took ice cream[10] and then returned to Mr. McCoy's where we found Mr. and Miss Madeira[11] and Mr. J. P. C[ampbell]. Received from him a beautiful boquet [sic]. Made arrangements for passing the next day at Arthur's. E. M^cC., Mr. C. and I went down [to Eolia] to breakfast—a pleasant day.

In the evening Mr. C. came to accompany us home, supposing we would walk to town. As E. and I had two of Arthur's horses and he had not returned, Mr. C. was furnished with an old horse, Fox by name, with a blind bridle and whose every step was accompanied by a noise very similar to the puffing of a steam boat. We laughed at Mr. C.'s equipment and E. suggested that her horse was better able to carry two than Mr. C.'s one, and inveighed against his cruelty. The gentleman took the hint and in a moment was mounted (with a little of my assistance) behind

Elizabeth on the redoubtable Peter Pancake and, somewhat to the surprise of E., I rode off at a canter, Mr. C. and E. calling after me in vain and endeavouring to overtake me, but poor old Fox, with all his puffing, could not accomplish it. I kept before [them] all the way to town and was so convulsed with mirth that I could scarcely keep my seat at the rate my horse was going. It is as well the night was dark or we should have had a boy mob about us.

A letter yesterday from Sally [Galloway]. Poor girl, she is not well and the death of two persons in whom she was much interested has deeply affected her: Eliza Anderson and Henrietta Carr. What sad havoc death makes among our loved ones.

Chillicothe, June 8, 1836

Wednesday. Judge and Mary Irvin with Misses Clarke and Irvin arrived last night, and this morning E. and I called to see them.[12] Miss I. as usual, Miss Clarke an amiable benevolent looking girl. Elizabeth invited them to take tea with us to meet some other company. Went shopping with Mary, then home where I found Mr. B'n who stayed till I was called to dinner—ahem. A good deal of company, everyone seemed in a pleasant mood and I should have been much happier but that I had to play till I am sure half the company was weary. They will make me play, 'tis unkind. This day last year I was in Xenia. Called to see the ladies this mor'g. In the afternoon some gents, Mr. B. and Mr. Massie, came. I went out home with William M^{c}C. to get flowers, and in the eve'g we went to a party at Mr. James's which was also characterized by the prevalence of merriment; every one seemed in good spirits, and J. certainly? Disappointed in not meeting with Mary Irvin. She has treated me like a Yankee—never gave me a hint that she was to leave town in the morning. Sat. The Lancaster ladies left town, I hope pleased with the attentions shewn them by our townsfolk. We, that means E. M^{c}C., A[nne] J[ames], Miss Haughton and Ellen, Arthur and Messrs. W. M^{c}C. and Taylor spent the eve'g at James's. "The cheek may be tinged with a warm sunny flush."

Adena, July 9, 1836

June, sweet June that I love so well has passed. Why was it that I this year thought less of its beauties, cared less, I might say? The moonlight that has ever seemed to possess a charm unclaimed by any month beside—now, why was it that I must force myself to observe it? 'Twas beautiful—two nights I cannot but remember. The roses are all (except the monthly) gone. I have plucked the last moss bud and oh, how beautiful it was. But the lot of beauty is upon it and it must perish, but not as soon as its mates. I have pressed it and will keep it to greet the roses of next year. What tales may it not have to tell of days yet to come? If I love them I surely must take it to its parent stem.

The last two or three weeks have not been passed to my satisfaction as regards my conscience and my happiness. I have been sick, sad, sour, cross, sleepy, lazy, oh, what a catalogue! Julia has been to Xenia, made a week's visit and home again, bringing Amanda[13] with her and a letter from Sally to me. Sister Sarah arrived two weeks ago. Tom K. is here—a bad boy too, I fear. Our town has been very sociable indeed, a number of little parties and [a] great deal of visiting. I have attended most of them and have been thought very happy, and merry; "never was so animated," I hear—aha—"While the cold heart runs," etc. Lizzy and Charles arrived this morning whilst I was busied putting down the dining room mat. "Sister, what is the matter?"

Adena, July 11, 1836

Monday. Went to town shopping with Elizabeth and remained all night—attended prayer meeting for [Sunday School] teachers[14]—oh, how I wish [we] were more zealous in our Master's cause. Much need of an efficient Superintendent. Ours is a willing, but not a capable man. Went with E. MᶜC., Ellen Waddle, Mr. Lee,[15] Mr. C., and Lizzy to MᶜKee's to eat ice cream. There is a large party tonight at Mr. Douglass's in honor of Gen. Harrison[16] but I had no spirits to attend it and was happier at prayer meeting. Gen. H. with a party of ladies and gentlemen called this morning at our house. Heard to-day from Mr. C. that John [Walke] and Fanny K[ercheval] were soon to be married, and was rude enough to say I did not believe him though I knew he spoke truth.[17] John has not used me well and I'll tell him so.

How could I forget to mention the celebration of the 4th in our town? I remained all night at James's with Amanda and was awakened before daylight by the drum and fife which I mistook for a serenade, but the cannon corrected my error. Immediately after breakfast we went out shopping, then to the Sunday School Anniversary. Our children marched in procession to the Methodist church where several addresses were delivered. It was a pleasing sight and one full of interest to a Christian, this gathering together of our little ones to teach them how to celebrate this day, to lift up their hearts to Him who has given us all that we enjoy. After the meeting of the S. S., we went to witness the presentation of a flag by a young lady to the Scioto Guards.[18] Can't say the ceremony was very imposing or that I was quite as much interested as I was some five years ago in a matter of a like nature. Then came the oration, Mr. Murphy, the Orator,[19] cousin Henry, reader of the Declaration. After dinner a <u>pleasure</u> <u>party</u>, a boat party on the canal which detained us till night. There was an abundance of mirth and merriment and the votaries of Terpsichore,[20] though few, lacked not enthusiasm. After tea, we all adjourned to the ice cream house and so ended the day. Now where I left off.

Adena, July 13, 1836

Wed'day. Amanda and I with Mr. Campbell rode home to breakfast. A. stayed all day. Mr. C. left and returned in the eve'g. I am not well today in consequence of—I don't know what, just the same feeling that has weighed on me for months past.

Last evening I attended a party at Mrs. Waddle's where I met many of my friends and might have been happy but a fit of unfitness came over me and I was dull and disagreeable. I have been perpending the cause. A., Mr. C., Charles and I rode to Gen McA.'s where I made all necessary enquiries relative to the anticipated wedding. A most lovely evening.

Adena, July 15, 1836

Friday. Rode to town with Charles to bid Amanda good-bye but she has determined to wait for the wedding. After breakfast, James and Julia and A. made us a visit, talked about preparations for the event. In the evening I was surprised to see A. and Wm. McC. Amanda has again changed her mind and will go to-morrow. John Walke and his Cousin from Va. were at Adena yesterday and we talked over the matter of his want of confidence in me, and he quite cleared himself too; talked of the <u>future</u> and the past, themes ever full of interest. We have ever been friends. I have loved John like a relative. But why is it that young gents never, or very rarely can have the same feelings towards ladies? They always seem to think more is meant than really is, and an unguarded expression, a warm word or affectionate look may do wonders of mischief. 'Tis a check which I have felt with all my young <u>gentle</u> friends and too often with John, <u>who</u> <u>once</u> <u>nearly</u> <u>lost</u> <u>my</u> <u>friendship</u> by . . .

Adena, July 16, 1836

Sat. John W. came up for me in his gig and we rode to Ellen's and made a visit of an hour or so, then to town to James's where I remained all night.

Adena, July 18, 1836

Monday. Rode to town to breakfast intending to make calls. Called on the Misses Belt, and after some few others on Mrs. and Miss Carson with both of whom I was much pleased.[21] Mrs. Nelson <u>tolably</u> [tolerably]. Dined with E. MᶜCoy, then to the mantua maker,[22] then to James's where Sister [Sarah] was making ready to leave. Mother had not, as she promised, sent for me—forgot it and I was beginning to <u>fret</u> about going home, when who but J. P. C. should come for me in his gig. With many thanks, I accepted his offer to take me home. We stopped at Mr. Jacob's where I found Mrs. and Miss Carson and Miss Wallace, Mr. Thacher, and Mr. F. Campbell.[23] Stayed to tea and passed the time very pleasantly. The evening was beautiful, a bright and delicately tinted sky and young moon, balmy air and very agreeable companion, so how could the ride be other than pleasant? I enjoyed it. We walked in the garden a long time, and I discovered as I have often done before, that "some things may be done as well as others."

Fruit Hill — the Home of McArthur
From *The Weekly Scioto Gazette,* May 23, 1908.
Courtesy of The Chillicothe Gazette[24]

Adena, July 19, 1836

Tuesday. I rode to Gen. McA.'s and breakfasted there, making offer of assistance, etc. Then I went to Mr. Walke's where they had not breakfasted and stayed an hour or two. John rode home with me—to-morrow is his wedding day.

Adena, July 20, 1836

Wednesday. Lizzy and I went over before dark to Fruit Hill and had some difficulty in dressing. The rooms were crowded to suffocation—nothing visible but moving heads. The bridal party stood in pairs and could not, on account of the crowd, appear to great advantage. John and Fanny, how much I am interested for them both—may God's blessings, spiritual and temporal, rest on them. Gen. McA. was not present; poor man he neither knows or cares much about it.[25]

Adena, July 22, 1836

Thursday morning I went to assist Mrs. Walke in preparations for a party. Found the evening much more agreeable than the preceding—rooms full but not crowded. I like J. P. C.'s relations very much; the niece especially. She sings pretty well, wants a little life in music which she does not lack in conversation or manner. I sang and played an hour or more, I truly believe, but I was so urged that I could not but comply. Spent Friday at Arthur's—they leave to-morrow for the Springs.[26]

Adena, July 25, 1836

Monday. My birthday!!!! I cannot fill this page now, but yet should I live another year, I may wish to recall the actions of this day—the thoughts I need not record; they are the same, painfully impressed, of this day last year. Then hope was bright—what has dimmed it? My folly; I am a very child. On this day last year I gathered a boquet [sic] of new born flowers moistened and beautified with the soft morning dew—they are now before me; though withered, they are with me still. To-day I have not touched a flower—I will let them fade in their birthplace, 'tis fittest so.

After attending to domestic matters, I wrote a long letter to Sarah G., then took my work and sat awhile with Lizzy, then to my own room again and to meditation on subjects more puzzling than profitable, maybe. And thus has passed my 25th birthday. O Lord, so teach me to number my days that I may apply my heart unto wisdom.[27] I have done that this day which my heart prompted, against my pride, sorely 'tis true—I hope I may never have cause to regret the act. The advice I gave S. I have little hope will have any effect. I <u>felt</u> the impossibility (should I call it so) even whilst I was writing, "We are not made of wood and stone, and the things which connect themselves with our feelings and affections cannot like bark or lichen be torn away without our feeling their loss." As for the hint I gave, I thought that my duty, too, and my selfishness assented. If 'tis taken, <u>well</u>, if not—?—why . . .

Adena, July 26, 1836

Tuesday. Mother, Lizzy and I rode to town to make some purchases and the carriage was well stowed with them. Mother and I called on Mrs. Nelson and Mrs. and Miss Carson. Heard of a riding party and returned to Adena to prepare for it. At half past two Mr. C. and Daniel Webster appeared[28] and we set off to meet the other members of the party at Gen. M^{c}A.'s. Bade John and Fanny good-bye. They leave home to-morrow for a visit to the eastern cities and Virginia—happiness attend them!

Our road lay along the bank of the creek at the foot of a steep hill or cliff and continued so for several miles, so it appeared to me. We dismounted in a delightful shady spot where the pale monotrope reared its drooping, spirit-like form— 'tis well called, "the ghost flower."[29] The party scattered over the woods in groups in search of enjoyment, each mayhap finding it in a different manner. A leaning tree, beautifully and softly carpeted with moss, tempted some among its branches. 'Twas a linden tree and we had, "Oh Linden when the sun was low," from Miss Waddle. We returned home about dark, witnessed a lovely sunset and a glorious <u>moon rise</u>.

Words fail me when I would speak of the exquisite feelings caused by the contemplation of such a night as this—words seem powerless. Why cannot our ideas burst forth in their beauty and not come forth remoulded and lost, as it were, in the slender vocabulary of words which express loveliness. O, why can hearts not speak? Mr. C. spent the evening—

Adena, July 27, 1836

Wednesday. Rode to town before breakfast to make arrangements for company and spent the day in preparation. Was somewhat disappointed that so many apologies were sent—however, the few that were gathered together seemed [to], and I hope did in reality enjoy themselves. Mrs. and Miss Carson leave early in the mor'g. I like them more on better acquaintance. If possible the night was more beautiful than the preceding—the sky cloudless—the fair moon hung "alone in her glory." A ramble in the garden. The company left early as Mrs. and Miss C. had packing to do—put out the lights and put myself to bed.

Adena, July 30, 1836

Thursday, Friday, Saturday very stupid and far from well. Thursday mor'g Sister S. returned.

Adena, August 1, 1836

Monday. I brought little Mary[30] home with me yesterday—she is to remain with me during the absence of her Parents. Poor little child, with what different feelings I take charge of her from those which were mine when my darling [Elizabeth, age 6] was left in my keeping. She is not an interesting child to me. The contrast with her sister is painfully unfavourable to Mary.

Wrote to dear Sally—my precious friend, how I feel for her. I fear her health is forever undermined—oh, what an undermining, wearing out of life is this hope deferred [Prov. 13:12]. Truly it makes the body as well as the heart sick, poor Sally. 'Tis a hard conflict and I fear she will think me unkind in saying what I did to her; but I could not bear the thought of her dying, as it were, before my eyes without one effort, however painful, to relieve her. A hard task to cease to love when we believe the object of that affection to be worthy, when we have been gladdened by the deep proving of their fond love. Poor Sally. James and Julia came to say adieu. They leave early to-morrow.

Adena, August 2, 1836

Tues. Charles arrived before breakfast this morning—<u>he</u> <u>is</u> <u>Lizzy's</u> <u>husband</u>—

Adena, August 4, 1836

Thursday eve'g. I rode to town to see my old schoolmate Araminta Rice, lately married, now Mrs. Walton and residing in New Orleans.[31] She looks much as she used to and her husband is quite prepossessing in his appearance. Rode with Charles to Arthur's, took tea and then home again. Was waked about midnight and at 7 next morning had a new niece, Lizzy's daughter, an unexpected guest, and we were rather unprepared for her, wardrobe very incomplete. Lizzy and the child very well.[32]

Adena, August 9, 1836

Tuesday. Aunt Collins[33] spent the day with us. Sister S. was preparing to leave us and the kitchen was a complete scene of bustle and confusion—made me dizzy. In the ev'g Sister and Tom left us—it may be a long parting but I cannot realize it.[34]

Nothing yet—and I am striving against my rebellious heart—how childish I seem to myself when I think on it.

Adena, August 31, 1836

  'Tis the last day of summer and oh, how many vain regrets are striving to slip from my pen's point. This past summer, 'tis gone now, why speak ill of it? It might have been [as] full of happiness as it has been of mercies to sinful me. But it has rather worn away than passed with me. Many domestic cares (such as a large family and no, or very poor, servants) have contributed their share. My health has been only tolerable, Mother's the same, and though 'tis a sin, I must acknowledge that never in my life have I suffered as much from dejection and why, I shame to acknowledge, I hardly can tell, but [of] this I am fully sensible, that I have been incapacitated from performing my duties as I should have done. I have had but little enjoyment in society, reading, writing, or any thing once delightful. I have been perpending the matter and have, I hope, by God's assistance come to a determination that it shall be so with me no longer. I have duties which I must not dare neglect. I owe my friends a cheerful countenance and my God a grateful heart. How selfishly have I given way to my own sorrows, real or imagined! How have they taken possession of every faculty. It must not be—rouse thee, my soul—strengthen thee, my heart. There are in the world more objects than one deserving of regard. Eternity, eternity, eternity, oh, how have I neglected eternity in my thoughts for months past. The freshness of summer has passed—my early youth, too, is gone—the bright tints of Autumn will soon again be here—ah, they remind me of daydreams too bright, too beautiful to remain.

  For a month past I have remained closely at home and have been much engaged attending on Lizzy and her babe and my charge, Mary. I have had a severe cold and cough and though I do not rejoice in <u>it</u>, yet I am glad that it has been in my power to remain entirely at home.

  I know not in what words to express my horror of a late transaction in our town. Words seem a covering of the sin, a palliation of the enormity—so weak, so powerless are they to express this unheard-of crime. I cannot detail it—oh, that I had never heard, or could forget it. Two strangers, brother and sister, Vanderm by name, with the highest recommendations, professing themselves to be followers of Jesus, have proved the vilest hypocrites the sun ever shone upon.[35] Oh, let me be humble, let me mourn for the depravity that is in man, in my own heart, and pray, Lead me not into temptation.

Margaret's Jam & Jelly Record from inside the back cover of her 1836-37 diary

June 20 4 $\frac{1}{2}$ lbs raspberry jam   4 $\frac{1}{2}$ lbs
"   22 Currant jelly   8
"   23 do--[ditto] for Julia   8 $\frac{1}{2}$
"   25 Jam for Lizzy   4 $\frac{1}{2}$
"   do-- Mother   3
"   28 do-- Sister Sarah   4 $\frac{1}{2}$
"   31 Jelly   3 $\frac{1}{2}$
"   Blackberry   4
"   Pears   6
"   Peaches   13
"   Marmalade   30
"   Grapes   7
"   Quinces   5
"   Marmalade   12

Courtesy of Ohio Historical Society

Part Three
"Fairly caught in a net of . . . my own"
September 15 - December 1, 1836

Adena, September 15, 1836

Two weeks have passed since I last wrote; in that time Charles has left us, James and Julia returned (12th) and I, of course, have delivered up my charge Mary. My health is better and with my heart I thank God my mind is more at ease and my resolution has not failed me—<u>yet</u>! Lizzy is learning to nurse the baby which relieves me from duty. Poor little Moll, I must say I parted with her without regret. Maybe I am more selfish than formerly but I certainly think she is the least interesting child I ever had the care of; she is selfish, more than ordinarily so, and has not an affectionate or generous disposition. What she may be, I can't pretend to predict. I hope more than she now promises, but this I can say, that there is a fearful responsibility resting on those who have the rearing of her—so fearful I would not for anything incur it.

Vegetation has not yet lost its verdant hue. The trees wear—'tis true, a tarnished aspect, and here and there a shade of brown is seen but other than this there is no indication of Autumn. The weather is warmer than in July, and oh, how I enjoy it, more perhaps that it so soon will be gone, and I hope, too, because my mind is more at rest. I cannot bid good-bye to summer while its roses and all its beauties remain. Yet I love the fall, and the only reason I so cling to summer is because winter so soon follows Autumn.

I rode with Charles to Mr. Rowe's to bespeak peaches some ten days ago. On Monday I went in the dandy to get them, taking Mary with me. The old folks seemed pleased to see me and were very kind. How forcibly was I reminded of my ride on the same errand with Miss Kelly[1]—a year! A short time, and yet a long period when I revolve [?] its events and my feelings and their effects on my conduct. I've been preserving,[2] as usual—a tedious business truly, and one that requires patience, which virtue does not <u>obtain</u> with me in such quantity as formerly.

On Sat. 3 Sept., Charles, Mrs. Jacob, Mr. C. and I rode to the hill on the opposite side of the river. The afternoon was pleasant and I enjoyed the ride bravely.

By way of variety we had a scramble down a steep hillside which rather annoyed Martha and Charles but afforded much amusement to Mr. C. and myself. The view is very beautiful—a lovely valley surrounded by gently rounded and beautifully grouped hills, some nearer, others peeping above in the blue distance, here and there the river showing its calm surface through its woodsy banks. I well remember a steamboat story with which Mr. C., a second time, gulled me.

A letter from John Marye[3]—oh, how it pained me for he says he is no longer a Christian, that he is so fascinated by worldly pleasures he cannot attend to religion. Oh, can it be so—my heart has been in sorrow for him ever since I received his letter. I answered it immediately and with impatience await his reply. May God in mercy save him from the misery, the guilt of turning away from his Creator.

By Julia I received a letter from J. B. Hearne,[4] accompanied with a large present of music, some very good and valuable. I do not know what to think of him. He has been, and is yet, one in whom I am much interested and, not having full confidence in his principles, fear lest his mind may be led astray by his passions, which, if I know him, are very violent. He speaks of me as having been of service to him and as being his true friend. How I have evinced it I don't know, but am happy if I have been useful to any of my fellow beings. How often are the best gifts of God thrown away—worse than that, perverted to the worst purposes. Poor John, I feel for him.

Sally has not written to me. Can it be that she is offended? What I said was dictated by the best motives, the sincerest friendship and a severe sense of duty. It pained me and I fear wounded her. Yet I feel I did right. Could I act as I have advised Sally? Alas, my heart indignantly, sinfully throbs, no; a higher power must aid in such an effort. Julia says Sally's health is improved—I am thankful for it. Oh, that her heart reposed on her Saviour, that she could fully resign herself to his will. I fear she never again will enjoy health; the spring's life will be sapped by the sickness of the heart. Who can cure it? Ah, weak and languid and sad—sad, too [two words crossed out].

Adena, September 17, 1836

Sat. Went to town and stayed all night at James's, singing at Mr. Carlisle's. Oh dear, how Mr. Hill does bellow—and is a singing master, too.

Adena, September 21, 1836

Tues. and Wednesday I was busied making Mother a dress. To-morrow is her birthday (many happy ones to her) and it must be finished Thursday. Lizzy and I appointed to spend today with Aunt Collins. Willy returned and gave us an account of the capital Young Men's Whig or Harrison Convention. Several thousand from every part of the state met at Columbus. "Old Boys" sent two hundred. They left town in high style, banners flying—music—cheering and a speech or two.[5] Poor Willy sounded quite tired and worn out.

Julia came up and dined with us and gave us some particulars of her journey. The carriage did not come till late so we "tea'd" with Aunt and rode home by moonlight. A lovely night—when the last moon shone, I felt sad that ere her beauteous light should again visit the earth, summer with all her glory should have passed away. To my happiness I was mistaken, and but that the month is called September, who would know it from July? (I love more than ever the music of insects.) The weather has been very warm—the thermometer as high, I believe, as it has been during the summer. The nights, too, are much warmer than is usual in August. No indications of Autumn save the ripening of fruit and here and there a changing sugar tree. Moonlight, sweet moonlight—I walked about the garden and sat me down presently in Frank's arbour and meditated on the chances and changes of this life and finally came to the conclusion that I had best study amiability, as cross old maids are disagreeable creatures. Bless thee, sweet moonlight, bless thee for the sweet, the profitable thoughts caused by thy influence, and for thy soothing effect on the sad heart.

Ellen and the children spent the day with Mother—Lizzy and I were sorry to leave her. I have risen later this past summer than ever before. I've been languid all summer; now that I am much better, my nights are so restless that I can't rise early. I miss my morning walks through the garden.

Adena, September 26, 1836

Sat. eve'g [Sept. 24], I had a pleasant canter to town. The Choir met to practice at James's. Mr. C. and Dr. H. stayed quite late—never saw Jamie look handsomer. Another letter from John Marge, he is evidently unhappy; how, alas, can he be otherwise? Monday, Mrs. Luckett [6] and Mr. G., Sr.[7] for several hours. On Sat. night the weather became much cooler and has continued so for some days. Oh winter, must you come?

Adena, September 29, 1836

Thursday. Went to town and aired Uncle James's house. They will soon, I hope, be here. Remained in town all night and went to a concert where I heard some delightful music, the first time I have ever seen a harp or heard a good performer on the violin. Mr. C. [was] my escort. Ellen and Arthur went with us, that is, Lizzet and me. Stayed with Lizzy and came home early next morning. Mother went to Methodist meeting; the conference is now in session. Sat. eve'g, as I was going down to town, I met Misses James, Belt and Bond[8] on their way to Adena. I returned and we took tea at home, and then walked to town where we did not arrive until long after dark— quite a <u>wonderful</u> <u>feat</u>, <u>Col.</u> <u>Taylor</u> <u>said</u>, <u>for</u> <u>ladies</u>. Stayed an hour or so at Col. Bond's and they <u>made</u>, yes, made me sing several songs, and among them (oh cruel) "The Messenger Bird."[9] Cousin Henry went home and spent an hour with me, very agreeably to me, and I hope to him also—I do like him. Poor little Mary is sick and looks shockingly.

Adena, October 3, 1836

'Tis the first of Oct., my favorite month—the weather is again moderate and pleasant. Monday. Mr. Hamlin, of the Methodist church, preached yesterday in our house to an overflowing congregation. I remained in town all night—saw Mr. Grover of X[enia].[10] Came home this morning. Called on my way to see Sarah McArthur[11] and her sister, Mrs. Rheinhard, who are on a visit to Fruit Hill. Mrs. R. is a very interesting looking woman, but in very poor health.

Adena, October 4, 1836

Tuesday. Mr. and Mrs. Gooding[12] spent the day with us. "Snowed all day!"

Adena, October 5, 1836

Wednesday. Early this morning I received a note from Effie telling me that Mrs. R. was at the point of death and requesting me to come over and assist in nursing her. As speedily as possible, I obeyed the summons and found Mrs. R. very ill, and poor dear Sarah in great sorrow. Mrs. R. has had consumption for several years and was in a very weak state when she left home. Sarah thought she would be benefitted by a journey and advised her coming here. For some days she was better, but Tuesday mor'g she was attacked with palpitation and difficulty of breathing; her extremities became cold, pulsation almost gone, and in this state she has been suffering agonizingly, but in great resignation, confiding herself to her Saviour.[13]

Adena, October 12, 1836

Wednesday. To-day, Elizabeth and baby left us—I shall feel her loss more than I ever have done. Yet, 'tis best she should go. Never within the space of a few months did I see any one so changed in feeling as is Elizabeth. She seems to have few thoughts beyond Charles and the baby. Her other relatives seem to have sunk alarmingly in her mental thermometer. The dear little babe I shall miss and regret (to speak honestly) more than her mother. I have been hurt at Lizzy's indifference—'tis selfish in her. Oh, we are too, too selfish in our love. And so she is gone; I have not before felt it so sensibly. Now that she is a mother, the tie seems loosed which bound her to her childhood home.

Mother accompanied Elizabeth to Portsmouth—there they will meet Charles. William has been quite sick and needs a good deal of attention. He is, and it grieves me, very unamiable, and so very obstinate about taking medicine. I passed the day in arranging the house to my liking.

Adena, October 14, 1836

A week[?]—Mother returned on Sat. eve'g. I remained closely at home during her absence and accomplished a good deal of sewing. As soon as she returned I went to town to be in readiness to attend Sunday School in the mor'g. The trees were beautiful. 'Twas twilight and their shadowy, misty-looking foliage made them appear like spiritual things. Ah, the seal of mortality is on them as on all of earth "passing away!" How mournfully does the rustling of the Autumn leaves proclaim this sad truth.

Found Rebecca Myers at James's and her little boy whom I saw for the first time.[14] He is a gentle little creature, such an one on whom we involuntarily place our love. Remained in town till Monday. Spent the morning with Rebecca, then to see Miss Clarke, then shopping with Beck all over town. In the afternoon, selected Sunday School books with E. Carlisle[15] and Lizzet McC.[16] We have had too many story books in our library. Though good for children at ordinary times, I cannot but think them decidedly injurious in a S. S. Library. The children read them on the Sabbath, usually omitting [and] overlooking the moral, and catching eagerly the story. I fear we shall have a generation of novel readers if S. S. teachers are not more cautious. Synod is to meet in Chillicothe during this week and the miserable looking old church is undergoing a cleaning—chandeliers <u>painted</u> a most beautiful gold color.[17]

When we had finished the books, E. McCoy and I called at Mr. James's to see the Misses Belt, then again to see Miss C'ke. Then [we] parted, I to James's, she home. Met Tom in the street. He is just recovering from a severe fall. My poor brother, he is involving himself, I fear irretrievably, and will take no caution or word of advice. Rode home after tea by moonlight with Matthias only for my escort. No letter yet from Sally; what does it mean? Why don't she write and oh, why don't . . .

Adena, October 18, 1836

[MW wrote the following paragraph across the script of her diary entry for October 18]

Sunday was a day of trial to me. Thoughts would intrude, vain, sinful thoughts+++++++ yea, even in this sanctuary. I have never wished for foreknowledge, knowing and believing in the wisdom of God, but oh, this irritating, vexatious matter. I am a dolt, a fool, a sinner. I cannot think of marrying—heavens no—strange, oh incomprehensible one am I!

Tuesday. "Busy as a nailer" all day, sweeping and setting the house to rights. Put down the drawing room carpet—no light job either.[18] In the eve'g Rebecca came up. She is a very kind amiable woman—she should have been married at fifteen and saved herself and others a world of vexation. Mother returned from Gen. M^cA.'s and seems in much anxiety respecting Mrs. M^cA.[19] who has been sick a long time and is now much worse.

Adena, October 19, 1836

Wednesday. We spent the day very quietly and were much <u>vexed</u> (ungrateful) that we were obliged to spend the evening out—anywhere but to Mr. James's, I would have refused pos[itively]. A comfortable room full—did not feel well or happy. Don't like Miss Deane's singing.[20] The latter part of the eve'g it rained fast—Jamie as usual—ehem! Uncle George Townsley arrived.[21]

Adena, October 20, 1836

Thursday. This month, usually so delightful, has this year been uniformly unpleasant. A week since, we had very severe frost which has sadly marred the beauty of the country. Snow fell last night, not in any quantity, but yet enough to give everything a dreary aspect. Mother sent a new boy for me, who, finding me at breakfast, left my horse and went home without my knowledge. After waiting a long time I set off alone, not without a misgiving either, for I never ride alone. Just as I came to the crossing of 2nd and Walnut riding at a canter, Fanny took it into her head to turn up Second St., contrary to my usual custom. Of course, as it was unexpected, I would be thrown upon the right horn of the saddle; and unfortunately, the saddle being half a yard too loose, it turned backwards and I lost my balance and turned a most beautiful somerset [somersault] into the mud—alack and welladay! Gratitude to God for my preservation was my first impulse and then the ridiculous appearance I must present. I was entirely unhurt, not even bruised, which seems almost a miracle as I turned completely over and fell on my left side. I never scream when alarmed for which I am thankful, as if I had, I should have had a mob about me in a moment. I was conscious I was falling and remember holding up my head for fear it would be injured. The instant I touched the ground, I started up and called to a little boy, who was the only witness of my feat, to assist me mount again. A man came out of the shop, Mr. Robeson, and tightened my saddle girth and assisted me to remount. All the injury sustained was by my shawl and riding dress which were sadly defaced. I was clad truly in a muddy vesture; nevertheless, I cantered home and related my catastrophe to Mother, urging her to keep the secret—and thus much for my second tumble. I must do Fanny justice; she stood perfectly still as if she knew she had done her share of the mischief. One would suppose that which takes place in the s[tree]t was no secret.

   Mother went to church though the weather was unpleasant. Friday is the opening of the Synod. In the eve'g Mother returned by way of Fruit Hill and found Mrs. McA. worse—no hope that her life, so invaluable to her family, can be prolonged more than a few days.

Adena, October 21, 1836
   Friday. Supposing of course there would be church, I went to town to remain till Sunday—no service till night, however. Ellen, Julia, Rebecca and I rode out to Gen. McA.'s—alas, we could do nothing.

Adena, October 22, 1836
   Saturday. R. and I walked to Arthur's, taking Jimmy in his coach. Poor Arthur heard whilst we were there of the death of his mother, not to us an unexpected event. After we returned, we, that is, Rebecca and I, made some calls at Mr. James's, and

admired Mrs. J.'s beautiful plants and well-arranged green house, and at Col. Bond's to see Miss Clarke—absent however.

Adena, October 24, 1836

Monday. We heard yesterday with the deepest sorrow of the death of Mrs. McArthur. God does all things well—his wisdom is infinite—but oh how mysterious, how inscrutable is this heavy dispensation of his will. Who, by searching, can find out God?[22] Gen. McA. has been for a long time a charge and burden to his family, from the derangement of his mental powers and bodily infirmity.[23] All, yes all the management of his business and the farm and house has devolved on Mrs. McA. It has been too much for her and hastened, I fear, her to the grave—while he, the imbecile, is left. Oh, what distress, what anguish will the death of this dear one inflict on her family, first, and also a large circle of friends. God comfort them. He can do it, for she died in the full hope of a happy eternity. Poor Mary, the youngest daughter and her mother's darling, is absent at school. She has been sent for, but too late to arrive before her mother's death. This morning I was sent for to go and comfort the bereaved and assist in the necessary preparations with Miss Cook and Miss Welsh.[24] Found them all in great affliction—words are idle, vain, at such a time—'tis well for us to ponder on these things—to lay them to heart and pray and profit by them. "For us they languish and for us they die." Of all the sorrows of earth, none are so bitter, so heart rending, as the death of beloved ones, even though we may have the blessed assurance of their eternal felicity. Yet, oh, how agonizing the knowledge that we must on earth see, hear and be with them no more. We may love them—yes, love cannot die—and may we not justly hope they too love us in the bright world to which God hath received them? Do they love us? Oh yes, I know it, and sometimes in the dark silence and solitude of night I almost fancy the spirits of beloved departed ones hovering about me. "Friend after friend departs"[25]—tie after tie is loosening from the Earth as dear friends leave us—and are not they, should not they, be as treasures laid up in heaven that our hearts may follow and dwell with them there?

I remained at Fruit Hill till Wednesday Mor'g, except a few hours on Tues. aft. I am, or have been, making some preparation to accompany Rebecca to Lancaster. On Wednesday, Misses Clarke and Bond and Cousin Henry called. Miss B. is just coming out and needs no "pushing." She affects a dislike to her native place which I fear made me rather rude to her.

Adena, October 27, 1836

Thursday. Uncle James's family returned last Saturday after an absence of five months. They left Sarah in Virginia, or I believe she is to go to Philadelphia to school. Hope she may not be spoiled or learn any affected city airs—danger of it. I was right glad to see them, and glad to see their house inhabited.

Mr. Buchanan is in town wife-hunting again—sounded a <u>little</u> on Sunday. Thought I had satisfied him last summer. They say he is courting Miss E. Belt. Surely she will not marry such a man. I'd as leave have a sensible fish for a help <u>meet</u>. To-day all the family were to spend with Rebecca [Myers] at Arthur's. I could not go as I was busy in that momentous and tiresome employment, "doing up" muslins. Mother went.

Adena, October 28, 1836

Friday. Made a cape this afternoon which I think pretty, and think too, I was smart about it. Rebecca sent for shubbery [sic] etc. and says her boy is sick. I am writing after a week's intermission and my events are not chronologically arranged. I received letters on Sunday, very gratifying and interesting. One from dear Lucy[26] in which she tells me how proud she is of her husband! They are going to Mississippi and I hope to see her yet.

And one letter from Sally, and what reason does she give for not having written sooner? None worth a care or thought, much less the pain her neglect has caused me—I wrote to her by Uncle George Townsley.

Adena, October 29, 1836

Sat. Busy in my room getting things ready for Lancaster.[27] James and Dr. Goodale[28] called; [I] promised to visit Columbus if possible during my stay in L. Friday, I went with Mother to town and found little Jamie Myers very ill indeed—stayed with him all day, and Sunday night sat with E. Carlisle and nursed him all night. I discovered some excellent things in E. C. which I ought to have done before, but this circumstance afforded the first key to the hidden worth of this excellent girl. She is possessed of a more intelligent, cultivated and refined mind than her sister (<u>I</u> think), whose society I have usually preferred, merely because I was unacquainted with E.

Adena, October 31, 1836

Monday Mor'g. Made calls with E. McCoy. In the afternoon went to Mr. James's to see Annie and the Misses B.; found Misses Clarke and Bond there. Mr.

[George] Myers[29] arrived yesterday in a hack to take us home but the child is too sick to travel, and when we do go we must take a canal boat. He is some better but still very sick. Mr. M. took me home in the coach.

Adena, November 1, 1836

Tuesday. Packed my trunk in the expectation of leaving in a few days and was surprised at Willy's summons to be ready immediately, as Jamie was so much better. Mr. and Mrs. Myers would leave the same evening on a boat. Felt a little sad at leaving home. Last Saturday, Mr. J. P. C. sent me a valuable charge! [or] so I choose to consider it, in a white moss rose, [also] some pens for which I am grateful, and a song he has often spoken of to me, "The Raindrops Minstrel," the words of which are very beautiful, and from the hasty trial I gave it, I think the music appropriate.[30] I am very, very much obliged—but—can't I manage as I have often done before? I really am fearful 'tis a harder case than I have yet had to manage—well, I'll do my best—++++

Rode to town and found Mr. M[yers] and R[ebecca] making preparations for departure. E. M^cC. was at James's. Oh, how I wish she was going with me. Mother, too, was there on her return from Arthur's. Mr. and Mrs. Watts have arrived, and I am much disappointed that I shall not see them. We took tea at Mr. McCoy's and then hurried to the boat which we found tolerably looking, not many passengers. Said good-bye to our kind friends, E. M^cC., E. Waddle, and Mr. Lee. I like this youth.

Lancaster, November 16, 1836

I have been in Lancaster two weeks and not an incident noted in my journal. I have been much engaged by company. Rebecca, too, is kind enough to like my society, and all the time I have for writing must be, or has been, devoted to my absent friends. I will endeavour to think of those occurrences which may in future be pleasant to recall. They would have been better sketched at the time of their occurrence. However, the two past weeks have not been so very full of interest as this preface would seem to imply.

Well, we arrived in L. on Thursday mor'g [Nov. 3] before day—very early. Mr. Myers left the boat and went up to the house to have fires made and whilst we in the meantime made ready to depart. Jimmy was much improved in health. Mr. M. with his brother, Henry,[31] soon made their appearance and by 7 we were snugly seated by the Ingle side.

I passed the first day unpacking and arranging my things to my liking, in which I succeeded admirably. I could almost fancy myself in my own room at home. Gen. Harrison passed through Lancaster on his return home from the Eastern states. He was cordially, almost enthusiastically, received by the citizens. Made a speech at a dinner and was exhibited in the evening at Mr. Ewing's to a great multitude. We looked in an hour or so, found some among the crowd of strangers whom I recognized: Mrs. Reese, Miss Irvin, Miss Clarke and one or two others.[32] Came home and slept soundly.

Friday [Nov. 4], Mrs. Fall and Miss Irvin called, Mr. Belding too, and I was glad to see him.[33] Poor fellow, how pale and languid he seems. He and Miss I. took tea and my muslins suffered. Henry Myers is a clever fellow, a wee bit vain but experience will cure him. He is in a delicate state of health.

Monday [Nov. 7], I do not remember what happened, but I remember feeling hurt that no letter was forthcoming from Sally. The town of L. is prettily situated in a valley on the side of a slight hill. The noble little run, the Hockhocking, flows along the south border.[34] During the greater part of this week Mr. [George] M[yers] was absent and Rebecca passed it very quietly. A good many ladies called and one or two gents. We spent one evening at Judge Irvin's. Ellen quite agreeable. Sat eve'g. [Nov. 12] We were out walking and Mr.[Myers] returned. On Sunday I attended the Presbyterian Church, a neat but small edifice—Mr. Cox, the minister. He does not suit my ideas of a clergyman. He is not gentle or persuasive in his manner, [saying] I will, and you shall, instead of, let us endeavour.

Monday [Nov. 14]. My kind friend, Mr. Belding, in company with Ellen I[rvin], accompanied me to a hill near L. called Mt. Pleasant.[35] Mr. B. proposed a ride on horseback but as he could not join it, I begged he would accompany us in a carriage as I much wished him to be with me. Accordingly, he came and we set out in a barouche. The day was lovely for the season, the air soft and bland as October and we in good spirits. When we reached the foot of the hill, E. and I parted from Mr. B. whose weak state of health would not admit of the exertion of climbing the hill. We reached the summit and never have I been more pleased, even though I had heard the view so much extolled. The hill of itself is a curiosity—it rises perpendicularly, shewing a bold front of jagged and projecting rocks which seem artificially piled together. Occasional pine trees springing, as it were, from the rocks themselves, seem like fastening pins to a large structure. The top or brow is covered with the shrub laurel, a beautiful evergreen.

Whilst we (E. and I) were admiring the view, I heard a rustling of leaves and exclaimed, "There is some quadruped!" Nor was I at fault, for on our hastily going to the spot whence the sounds proceeded, we discovered a quadruped mounted by a biped—in short, our friend, Mr. B., seated on the carriage horse in harness with the cushions for a saddle. Joyfully and mirthfully we greeted him, as our pleasure would have been naturally lessened had we known he was waiting below.

We remained for two hours on the hill gathering laurels (ah me, how much more easily than ancient heroes) and clambering about the rocks. I planted a laurel in a cleft of the rock, and Ellen I. promised to watch it for me. Mr. B. had one without a root in his hand—Ellen planted it. Ah! I fear me it is too much like him, bright but fading. A pleasant ride home—the azure demon flapped the tip feather of his wing across my spirits, but I frightened him off. Of late some feelings of months past have been flitting past me. Oh, if they do come again, I cannot, I cannot, indeed I cannot bear them. I brought some laurels from the hill and we each planted one—Mr. B., Ellen and myself. We gathered some beautiful bright sumach berries and I wish long to preserve them, and long, long will I remember the visit to Mt. Pleasant.

Tuesday afternoon [Nov. 15] we spent at Mr. Myers's. In the evening we went to a small party at Mr. Ewing's—very pleasant. Had to sing too much—bad piano for the voice, and I was miserably out of tune—however, that was not my fault. The evening had been very rainy and boisterous. We returned home about eleven and 'twas beautiful moonlight. Mr. B. accompanied us home, that is, as far as we would permit him. I must say I think our gentles shew off advantageously by these. I do not mean Mr. Belding—I like him, poor fellow. Wednesday, 16th. Made calls in the morning—afternoon, assisted Rebecca in making preparations for a wine party. Beautiful moonlight—and I was wild.

Lancaster, November 17, 1836

Thursday. We were washing glasses, etc. Miss Irvin came and passed an hour or two sans ceremony—wonderful.

Lancaster, November 18, 1836

Friday. Wrote letters in the morning. Mr. Belding spent part of the morning and dined. He is to leave for the south next week; my best wishes go with him, but I fear all in vain. Oh, if he only were a true believer. I am much interested for him, more every time I see him. He is very amiable and has a great depth of feeling, only discoverable in private conversation. From his diffidence I should never have surmised it. A few evenings after my arrival we were alone together for a long time and I learned more of his character than ever before. I have forgotten exactly the day, though I should remember it on account of a violent storm, almost a hurricane, which whisked leaves and sticks in the air, laid the grass flat, and I believe did a little more material damage down [the] street.

Friday afternoon Henry Myers and I set out for a ride. The weather was fine and we [were] enjoying the ride when Henry's horse gave symptoms that we judged it best to return. Though we had scarce been out of a walk, the horse was sweating violently. I stopped at Judge Irvin's—found Ellen suffering from cold and headache. Her sister's horses were standing at the door and her father and I prescribed a ride, so she equipped and we set out and rode half a mile or so. So I did eke out my ride—came home and spent the evening quietly with Rebecca.

Lancaster, November 19, 1836

Sat. Returning calls, though the day was unpleasant—the business is somewhat the same and I wished to get over it.

Lancaster, November 20, 1836

Sunday. Rained all day and I did not go out. Mr. Belding came in, suffering from toothache. He gave me a new edition of a work, *Language of Flowers*, a very pretty thing, and as a gift from him I shall value it, though I do not like the emblems as well as Mrs. W.'s *Flora's Dictionary*.[36]

Lancaster, November 21, 1836

Monday. Rained and tried to snow through the whole day. Mr. Tennant and Mr. Belding took tea with us. Mr. B. wrote my name in the book he gave me and presented me with a seal, the motto of which brought painfully to my mind his own apparent destiny. The device, a bunch of roses, and motto, "We bloom to-day, to-morrow we die"—alas, it is true of all that earth possesses—"There's nothing true but Heaven."[37] We were all sad. I tried to sing, but could not. After tea Mr. B. and I went to see Ellen Irvin.

Lancaster, November 22, 1836

Tuesday. Went out this mor'g, cold and snowy, freezing and muddy though it was, to find some things for Mr. Belding. [Found] nothing to my fancy but a seal which I thought very pretty and appropriate. Soon after we returned home Mr. Belding came to say adieu—we were sad. I tried to be cheerful but my heart reproached me. I had some old music, [was] looking over it, and so concealed the emotions which I did not wish observed. I never felt so much interest for one, almost a stranger. His situation called for it. In ill health, with scarce a hope of recovery, he was going amongst strangers as it seemed, to die—no female relative and only one friend to minister to his wants. When we parted, Rebecca kissed him—she has been indeed a kind friend to him. He took, he wrung my hand, as if he too thought we might never meet again. Tears would come, why should I stay them? God comfort him. We wrote letters to send by Mr. B. E. Myers came to spend the day. In the eve'g, we went to Mr. Myers's to a candy making. My thoughts were too much on poor Mr. Belding for me to enjoy it, and I was glad to get home to my own room. A letter from Anne James.

Lancaster, November 23, 1836

Wednesday. We spent the eve'g at Mr. Reese's. Mr. and Mrs. R. very <u>genteel</u> and <u>interesting</u>, ahem. Ellen I. spent the mor'g and dined though she was not dressed, whereat Bec[k] said, "marvellous!" We had some very interesting conversations this morning.

Lancaster, November 24, 1836

Thursday. We had company this evening. Alack for me, my face ached all morning—made me useless to R. After dinner—better, [in the] evening—well, almost, and in pretty good spirits. Ladies agreeable, Mr. Ewing is very much so, too; pity his manners are not more polished. Mr. Willock, a bonny Scotsman, Mr. <u>Heart</u>, a youth who greatly admires himself.[38] It is a source of mortification to me that my voice, owing to a cold and in a measure to the cool days, has been sadly out of order ever since I came. The good people here have learned <u>somehow</u> that I sing tolerably, and they must be <u>somewhat</u> disappointed. However, I shew my willingness to do as well as I can. The evening passed off very pleasantly. Sorry my friend, Henry Myers, was not with us; health would not permit. A letter from my friend Harry,—can't come now—sorry.[39]

Lancaster, November 26, 1836

Sat. R. and I made calls—bright day but cold. In the eve'g, Henry M. took tea, then Ellen I. came and Mr. Willock to practice the "Pilgrim Fathers."[40] We are progressing. Mr. Heart, our "audience," was charmed surely. Ellen I. is improving in my esteem. Certainly she can be very agreeable and has been exceedingly so to me.

Lancaster, November 28, 1836

Monday morning. I walked out soon after breakfast to the canal reservoir about a mile from town—a pretty walk too, and from the hills which are near it, a fine view of the country and Mt. Pleasant which looks like a castle of *romaunt* [romance]. The reservoir frozen over and some boys skating added life and interest to the scene. I mused on—and came to a conclusion—which for the moment satisfies me, but gave not rest to my feelings—sad, but exhilarated by my walk. When I returned, Rebecca called out, "A letter from Albert!" I soon possessed myself of it and found 'twas from Sally with postscript from Albert. "I'm na ashamed to own," etc. Sarah is, I trust, recovering from the mental malady which has caused her so much suffering. As for me, it is useless for me to attempt denial to myself that I have most completely mistaken my feelings. Had I been in doubt before, the experience of a few months past would prove most forcibly the strength, but it is not as he would. Yes, it is even so, and though no better understanding should be effected, I will here make some acknowledgements—all I dare not—fairly caught in a net of—my own. And I not the least aware of it! Never thought of such a matter other than in jest, and thought esteem and regard and (I shame to write the word) friendship were my only emotions. Now I begin to understand why I was always so careless and indifferent to other gents, but in sooth it is a mystery to me that I did not sooner discover the true state of the case. We have both been wrong, but I am inclined to think I have suffered most—I do hope so. How did I bear the depressing feelings of the last summer? I do not think I could do it, or rather—suffer it, again. Oh marvellous—I am wonderstruck. I have often wondered if I could be so very different from "a'body" else. But as to marrying! No, never. So I did wrong—how or when, I can't say—oh, I am so proud—it is dreadful to be so.

Lancaster, November 29, 1836

Tuesday. Finished Mother's frock and am ready to go home. Began to feel a little uneasy as to my mode of doing so, when, who should arrive but my dear Elizabeth [McCoy] and my esteemed friend, Mr Lee. They had both promised to come for me, but I was incredulous. Mr. M. had invited company to tea and I was dressing when I heard of their arrival. Mr. Lee and Mr. Graham tea'd with us. Mrs. McCracken would not let Lizzy come. After tea Mr. L. and I, with Miss Irvin, went to visit Mrs. Ewing. To my regret, she was absent, and as Miss C[larke] was not as interesting as usual, I soon wished myself at home, and prevailed on Misses I. and C. to accompany me. Mr. Graham and H. Myers, and presently Mr. Willock, [arrived and] at nine, Elizabeth came over and we had a very pleasant evening. E. stayed all night with me. Ellen Irvin has treated me very kindly. I like her. Her greatest fault is formality, precision—and rid of this she would be "charming" ac'd'g [to] Col. T[aylor].

Lancaster, November 30, 1836

Wednesday. The last day for me in L. and the last one of Autumn. The weather during this month has not been severe but a good deal cloudy.

This morning Mr. Lee called early and we agreed to take the Columbus route.[41] Lizzy then went to her Uncle's, and Mr. L. and I had two hours confabulation. Then I went to dress to make calls and before I had finished, Ellen I. called and surprised me somewhat by the information that she was engaged and might be in a certain case married soon. We are alike in <u>some</u> <u>things</u>. Made calls and returned to dinner.

Mr. and Mrs. Reese have pleased me more than any acquaintances I have made in the place. Mrs. Ewing, too, is an agreeable woman. After dinner Mr. L. came but soon vanished when I said I must pack up. So I packed up and was ready by tea time to see company. Mrs. McCracken behaved in, what I deem, a very shabby manner towards Elizabeth and myself, and I was woefully out of temper about it. Mr. H. M., Messrs Heart, Willock and Graham came and after awhile, Ellen I. I had a cold and sore throat and was peculiarly stupid, sang like a peacock, and was highly complimented by Mr. G. Ellen spoke again to me of Dr. Wolfley[42] and wished I could see him. She can love for she loves him. I believe she is a noble girl—yet, not exactly the one that I should love best of any.

Departing Lancaster, December 1, 1836

Thursday. Early this morning we bade adieu to our kind friends and set off in the coach for Columbus—roads fine, Mr. Lee very agreeable, weather delightfully cold—little cloudy, full coach, etc. We reached Columbus at two o'clock—sent my cards to some acquaintances. Dr. Goodale came immediately to see me. We did ample justice to a good dinner. Found Miss Kelly in the parlour who seemed pleased to see me; Lizzy did not know her. Dr. G. returned, bringing with him his nieces, Mrs. S. and Miss C., and we all walked out to see the town, etc. The bridge is one of the most beautiful, it is said, in the Union. It is to me very beautiful, uniting in its appearance the ideas of strength, lightness and grace—it seems at a little distance to hover, as it were, over the water. I wished to see the buildings of the State Prison, and no more; but my friends (they are used to the sight) insisted on my visiting the shops where the convicts were at work. The discipline necessarily is very severe and I felt humiliated to see the poor creatures who dare not so much as look up, much less speak, for fear of punishment. My heart wept for them and I <u>begged</u> to go from the scene.

Mr. Lee, Lizzy and I took tea at Mr. Kelly's where we met Miss Espy[43] and some gentlemen. Miss E. is an interesting girl [and] sings with feeling. I never was so urged to remain in my life and wished it had been in my power, but was forced to refuse the most pressing invitations and promised if I could to come again. Dr. G. and Mr. M^{c}C. stayed till very late, then we went to our rooms and packed and at half past one or two fell asleep. At four we were awakened and prepared to start. At six we were off—weather and roads fine. Lizzy napped a good deal and Mr. L. and I chatted on divers subjects. Reached home just at sunset, thankful and happy. Arthur came in just after me. Stayed all night [at James's]. Went to Mr. M^{c}C's—saw for the first time Dr. Foulke.[44] He made a silly speech which struck me as very ridiculous, and I in reply made a very rude and unladylike answer. So we rest.

The Zanies[45] have gained the Presidential election, and to-night they disgraced our town by a jollification. Our Flag waving on high—that's well—below it the emblem of their party, a full grown hog!! Oh Chillicothe, oh! what a fall was there. I do not meddle in politics but I am much interested in my country and fear her downfall, should the present party remain in power.

Dresses of Margaret's Period

Courtesy of Gail H. Bickford

Part Four
"Why . . . lingers the thorn?"
December 3 - 31, 1836

Adena, December 3, 1836

Sat. To-day is the anniversary of James and Julia's wedding and we hoped to spend a delightful day. Mother was to come down and I returned. How glad I was to be at home once more. "My spirits flew in feathers then that are so heavy now," and I walked to Uncle James's and breakfasted and then made a good many calls for the pleasure of meeting my friends—not formally, truly. As I returned to my brother's a thought came over me—what shall I hear to-day to make me sad [after] I have been so excited and gay this morning? Alas, it came too soon. A letter from Mr. M[acomb][1] announcing the death of my beloved, though long-parted, sister Mary. How are we reminded by the frequent removal of our dearest friends not to love them with a supreme affection. "It is indeed a fearful thing to love what death not only <u>may</u> touch," (as the poet says) but what we are certain he will take. Death is making painful vacancies in our family circle—do the living lay it to heart? Alas, it seems all in vain that we have these painful warnings so often exhibited in the change or removal of the objects of our earthly affection. It is the voice of God proclaiming to his children, "Thou shalt love the Lord thy God with all thy soul and with all thy might and all thy strength,"[2] but ah me, from our actions it might be supposed that this voice said rather, "Make to thyself a dearer idol," than "Thou shalt have none other gods before me."[3]

This dear sister has been absent for a long time indeed. I was but a child when she left us, but oh, how well I remember her affectionate and endearing disposition—how happy it made us as children to hear that sister Mary was coming—or we gained permission to visit her. What a loving heart was hers—if I had favorites in our circle (and I know I had) my loved Albert and Mary were those to whom my heart clung closest in childhood. Oh, my brother, God alone knows the depth of my love for him. Both now are gone.

I have heard and read of instances of the devotedness of women but never did I hear or read of a more complete devotion than in the instance of my sister—my sacrificed, my suffering sister. Married young to one whom her heart approved, though against the wishes of her parents, her trials seemed to begin with her married life. Her husband was a schemer, a dreamer and a follower of every idol [sic] fancy that crossed his imagination, and, as is usual with such men, was ever most sanguine of success as his phantoms were eluding his grasp—the death of one hope was the bright birthplace of a brighter one. The hand of God laid on him heavy pecuniary losses—but, to-morrow all would be well. And she, my uncomplaining sister, saw nothing in him but what was right. Alas, how like a woman—devoted, disinterested, caring only for the happiness of her husband; he loved her—but oh, in comparison, how selfish was his love. And now she is dead—God only knows, but I fear her heart was broken. In that lawless land with none but her husband and children, not even a friend to wipe the death drops, she yielded her Spirit to Him who gave it. What rending of heart must it cost her husband that he dragged her, a willing victim, but a victim, there to die. I cannot forgive him for all the anguish he has caused her—may he have God's, and the forgiveness of his own spirit.

Oh, what a different aspect has this day from what we had hoped. Poor Mother went immediately to Ellen's. I remained in town till Sunday evening—walked out with V[irginia] S[wearingen] and Mr. C. On Monday, I set about putting my room in order, but company came and I was interrupted.

Adena, December 6, 1836

Tuesday. Company again and I was so sinful as to be vexed almost to anger, for they were people who have no share in my affection—selfish mortal that I am. Put up my curtains, and arranged my room in winter style. My dear little room, how much of pleasure and of pain have I felt within its small compass. Looked over my drawer of precious nothings — faded flowers — ribbons, small keepsakes and what is more precious, the hair of many loved ones. A lock of dear sister Mary's, taken from her head at least twelve years ago and preserved with much care, called forth gushes of feeling.[4] Oh, in the days when she gave me that hair! Am I the same being now? I could not but smile to see how carefully I had preserved every trifle ever given me by my friend. I wonder I never noticed it before. Made a visit to Gen. McA.'s—all well—called to see a new arrival in the way of baby—a nice little what? Not negro—Maria's child.[5]

Adena, December 7, 1836

Wednesday. Willy went to the Barrens[6] yesterday, tempted by the uncommonly fine roads and weather. I went to Arthur's and spent the day, that means from 12 till 3. Promised Ellen to come and stay a week when . . . what dear children she has.

Adena, December 9, 1836

Friday. How speaking are the merest trifles at times. Amanda gave me a little vase last summer to keep on my mantel with flowers and I always, whilst roses lasted, kept it supplied. I was this morning dusting and took up my little gift to give it a renovating touch, with a sad feeling that I had <u>no</u> <u>roses</u> wherewith to fill it, Ah! "Summer's gone" indeed—and so have summer's roses but <u>why</u> <u>in</u> <u>their</u> <u>stead</u> <u>lingers</u> <u>the</u> <u>thorn?</u> I was so forcibly reminded of too many of the joys of earth that I set down the vase and preserved the thorns in it; aye, like thousands of roses of life, the thorns have outlived the <u>roses</u>. Let them live—there are some few in my heart perhaps that will bear them company—new roses will come to my vase and my heart—the sweetness must repay me in both for the thorns.

I wrote to dear Lucy to-night—ten years since we parted and yet has "Absence conquered love?" No, no, and though I doubt whether we should recognize each other's faces, we could never be mistaken in the language of the heart. My own Lucy—I shall be so anxious to hear from her. I wrote a long letter too, to . . . . Pride cried, "Shame" with a fearful energy—but feeling and affection approved with a stronger, yet more unobtrusive power and so I, womanlike, followed feeling— judgement and reason merely gave a negative assent—not full approbation—-or maybe pride's thundering tumult stifled the sound. Said feeling, "There is surely a misunderstanding." Said pride, "Whose place is it to seek an explanation?" Said judgement, "You should have been more clearsighted and foreseen the state of your heart." "But," again urged feeling, "write, and give an opportunity; your last may have been a damper." "Well," quoth pride, "if you choose, but if you suffer for it, don't blame me." Nay, my pride of iron strength, you are clear of aught in <u>this</u> matter and so the letter was sent, and when the answer comes, then we'll see.

Adena, December 12, 1836

Monday, midnight. I have just finished reading a horrible Irish tale of murder and am afraid to go to bed lest "thrice ere the morn" I should dream it again and with very different emotions from the poor soldier's dreams of home. I've been engaged in stopping airholes, listing [weatherproofing] windows, etc. against severe weather. As yet, the winter has been charming—mild sunbright weather almost like Indian summer at noon—fine roads, too. How much it reminds me of the winter eight years ago when I made my first visit to Xenia and returned home on horseback the day before Christmas—since then we have had, every winter, very cold weather. There goes [my] watch ticking away with might and main as if 'twould burst its case to remind me of my resolution to keep earlier hours—it is not imagination—it does repeat its strokes much more energetically after 11 o'clock—little monitor. I obey, though with reluctance, for I hate to go to bed, and to-night I am afraid of dreams.

It is really too ludicrous and too good a joke on myself to pass by. I missed one of my garters this mor'g and was obliged to get another and just now found both on the same leg—worthy of record truly, but the laugh it caused me was wonderful.

Adena, December 13, 1836

Tuesday. My mother's wedding day and its <u>fortieth</u> anniversary! I have had many sage thoughts to-day on the subject of matrimony and, were it not too late, I should like to record some of them but Julia kept me up till past my hour for bed and I must remember my resolution. Health is sweet; now I am beginning to feel it so more than ever and wish to preserve it. To-morrow, if my humour fail not, I'll write again.

Adena, December 14, 1836

Wednesday. The humour's off and "what if it be so?" To-day mayhap <u>it</u> has reached its destination and I have been surmising the effects—I think I am prepared for the event in either of two cases. Pa-ti-ence, Mistress Margaret of "spinster's joy." Yesterday was a most unpleasant day—rain, unceasing rain, but for all that, Ellen and Arthur and the children, Aunt Swearingen,[7] hopeful Harry and Aunt Collins came and we spent a pleasant day, though regretting Julia's absence. James is away. Oh, <u>Aunt Ina</u>, you do gossip unmercifully and are so perfectly ignorant of it, too—heard more news than has reached my . . . for a length of time. [It] tired mother and can't say I was particularly interested except it might be by a repetition of that undoubted fact, my speedily approaching marriage to J. P. C. [I] laughed! and thinks I to myself, <u>maybe</u>. Won't say. Do I know? Just at dark Julia came bringing Mary. Tom has been here for two days, "being weaned."[8] To-day we have passed quietly and agreeably. 'Tis past midnight. I have just written a very foolish letter to Bessie McC., so trifling and ridiculous that I am ashamed to look over it and shall send it without. It was written in a most rapid manner and doubt if it is readable. I do believe the girl has some matrimonial ideas in her head which she wishes to tell me but thinks I have deceived her with regard to Mr. C. I wish I could be believed, but nobody is in these troublesome affairs.

Adena, December 16, 1836

Sat. We have had a variety of weather in this week: rain, beautiful bright weather, snow and quite cold. Snow fell yesterday 4 or 5 inches—rain in the eve'g. Julia left us this morning—children with me. I have been thinking much this week of the probable issue of a certain matter and find I do not repose as I would do. A little foresight! might set me at rest.

The year is hastily drawing to a close; in two short weeks and it will be numbered with the past—Oh, who can number the hopes, fears, loves, tears, all that have been blighted or fulfilled, banished or realized in the space of 12 months? This time last year I was yet grieving for Lizzy's loss[9] and my own folly—'tis well we can sometimes in a measure forget past feelings. Would that I could blot yet more than I have done from my too faithful memory. Received a paper with Oscar's[10] name on it and a request that he might write to me—he surely knows it would please me—I love to be remembered and loved. There be some on the earth who love me or I could not live—without the love. [With] esteem alone, but without the warm affection of some hearts, life to me would be a burden. I am expecting a letter to-morrow, or by the next mail—shall I be disappointed?

Adena, December 20, 1836

Tuesday. Yes, of a truth, I am—to-day a bare acknowledgment (without even thank you) on the margin of a paper. Well—the course of true love, etc.

Adena, December 21, 1836

Wednesday. Last night when I went to bed the thermometer must have been above temperate—a warm rain was rapidly dissolving the snow. About midnight high winds came, and this morning the thermometer stands but a few degrees above zero—four or five, I believe. These sudden changes in weather act painfully on our physical nature, as reverses in fortune do upon our moral nature. I have no cause but for gratitude; thus far my health has been excellent—oh, how I enjoy the blessing!

My heart aches are less frequent and less severe—I have prayed against my sinful heart and I do believe God has helped to conquer its rebellion. Oh, this cold, dreary weather. How many things in the natural world seem but figures of those in the moral! How full of instruction is every thing around us, [would] we but give our minds to the contemplation? But we are so filled with the world, aye, the artificial world, that we give our souls no time for far more delightful musings. I love solitude—not always, but I love to be much alone. I am unfitted by it maybe for the society of the generality of people, but not for that of my friends.

My poor little birds, how I pity them this cheerless morning—they can't find the crumbs I daily give them, for the snow. I love the little creatures—my poor flowers—spring is coming.

Mr. Gus. P't brought a youth here a day or two since, a young John Bull who says I sing <u>very</u> <u>nicely</u> and in expressing his doubts as to his singing correctly said, "I don't know whether I did it right or not." He has a very fine, musical voice—it is really a treat to me to sing with a good bass voice. None of our gents can sing tolerably—maybe they might, but they don't.

Adena, December 23, 1836

<u>Friday</u>. Cold—very cold weather. Yesterday, Mr. Campbell and Dr. Foulke paid me a visit—[I] made my apology to the Dr., sang a song or two very badly and talked a good deal of nonsense—in a glee, wherefore, I don't know. I must become acquainted with Dr. F. If he is to [be] Lizzet's, he should be a clever fellow—I cannot form my opinion of him yet. I wish Jamie would not take such especial pains—if I am not called coquette, I shall be mistaken, yet heaven knows I do not deserve it. No letter yet from my crony—I am really surprised to feel myself in such a state of comparative quiescence—hope it will last. I must learn to keep my thoughts under better control and feelings, too—they lead me hither and yonder, gathering a wreath of wishes bound together with <u>hopes</u>—ah, if <u>they</u> break, away goes my beautiful wreath, as many an one of less import to my happiness has done. Oh, what a deceived mortal I have been and yet indeed, indeed, the fault was not mine. The week is almost gone—this evening, I go to town, as I promised, to spend to-morrow with Julia, [the] next day being Sunday and—what—Christmas again?—aye, Christmas again.[11] I must look into my last volume and see what were my musings this time last year.

DIARY

Adena, December 26, 1836

Tues. I returned to-day from town. We have had a communion season in our church and I attended the services and enjoyed and I hope profited by them. Mr. C. united with the church—this has given me and all his friends much pleasure. He is very kind to me. Called with E. M^cC. and E. W. at Mr. Walke's. I spent yesterday with E. McCoy. As usual, we spent most of the day in the streets. At night, Lizzy revealed to me what I have been suspecting: that she was engaged to Dr. F. Oh, what a long talk we had—at two o'clock I rose and lighted a candle and read some of his letters, and we talked till nearly daylight. How many confessions on either side that ought to have been made long, long ago. I withheld from her one that I will soon communicate, be the issue what it may. 'Twill maybe ease me to have her sympathy. She spoke of J. and wished that . . . and I found it in my heart to join her—but alas, it cannot be without a complete revolution within me. And so this staid friend of mine has been carrying on a sedate kind of flirtation for nearly two years past. Heaven help her and the object of her choice. He is pious—ah, what a blessing; my dear, dear Lizzet—she does love unworthy me, as well as I could wish and oh, how will I pray for and desire her happiness. Will she love me less when married? I will believe not. She says if she is married I must be also—we will see. Oh, that it could have been otherwise with me—that I could undo even now the riveted links of affection from one heart that may be values them not. I am incessantly reproaching myself and this makes me unhappy—for the last two days especially—no letter—no message. Can such neglect, such pointed neglect—such coldness betoken warm affection? I said last night to Elizabeth that in comparing her and my chances for happiness I found them exceedingly in her favour. God alone knows—but 'tis the most rational conclusion. One who has acted so blindly as I should be very cautious in erecting "castles." Years, if they come to us, will prove. Oh, sometimes I dare to wish I could lift, as it were, a corner of the veil of futurity—that I might know some things. All I would not, for the universe, behold; and I fear I have sinned in wishing to know anything. Let me but conscientiously continue my path, "looking unto Jesus" for help in time of need, and all will yet be well. I have had some misgivings that I was to be consumption's victim—yes, and they have come over me since my health seems quite restored. Oh, that I could live in a state of preparation for death. This time last year I find I was in much such a state as at present—my journal says so.

Adena, December 28, 1836

Wed. What a creature of hope am I—a fancy has taken possession of me to-day which has made me quite another being—surely I am not right in giving way to these feelings. Dr. Foulque [sic] and Mr. Campbell have just left here and 'tis nearly 11 o'clock and a cold night too. J. promised to teach me chess and this afternoon offered but I refused so it is my fault. I think I shall like L. W. F. I <u>will</u> like him. The gents came up to the foot of the hill on the ice and I supposed of course they w'd remain all night but Dr. F. would not—poor gents, they will have a dreary walk. The moon is up but not as brightly as for their sakes I could wish. Now I must write to Annie J. Mr. C. says he will cut my name on the ice of the "Lake" and I have promised to go in the morning to look at it—hope they may reach town with uncracked pates.

Adena, December 29, 1836

Thursday. According to promise, I went this morning to the pond and, according also to promise, found my name engraven in several places upon the ice. I put on Willy's skates and was surprised to find that I could stand on them. I really hope I shall be able to acquire this much desired art. I was not a little amused last night at a conversation between the gents as to the practicability of teaching ladies to skate and the best means of so doing. Dr. F. dissuades me from even the attempt. Mr. C. seems certain I might learn and in his imagination has invented a frame such as children are taught to walk in. Oh, I am so sleepy and must positively write a letter to-night. I have just returned from a visit to Gen. M^cA.'s. [I] took tea there and had a cold walk home across the fields with Willy. Mary is a pretty girl and only wants energy to make a very useful woman—it is a failing in the family. Effie is a generous and amiable woman and has acquired energy by being obliged to act. Pity, but truth, that she will coquette. Surely. Surely yes, be deceived by vain hope again. Fools love folly. I dare na think of . . . it makes me sad and that I am too often—.

Adena, December 30, 1836

Friday. Mother spent the day at Ellen's. Willy went somewhere, as I thought, to stay all day. I was alone and gave orders, "no dinner" for me, but about noon Aunt Nancy and Henry came, and Mary M^cA. I went to the kitchen to see what could be done and found that Mother had by mistake carried away the key most necessary. However we "made out." I <u>knocked up</u> a pie, etc., Yankee [fashion]. I was too much pleased to see them to be very solicitous about the fare.[12] Wrote to Mary Tompkins and I. L. M.

Adena, December 31, 1836

     Sat. Alas, 'tis the last time I shall write that date as present—-in an hour and it will be—gone—the past. My employments have been varied to-day to an amusing extent, writing, sweeping, sewing, reading—making cakes and knitting. In this last, I have spent the last two hours to finish a pair of mittens, a New Year's gift for Mary W.[13] But half an hour yet remains of the old year. How many hearts are interested in the coming year—-some look towards it with painful anticipation—to others, it's the fruition of joy—with some, hope is just dawning to happiness, and alas, to others— 'tis vanishing—dying. All are hoping to be happier in the coming year even though in the depths of sorrow—"The saddest human look has hope in't—faint indeed—but still, 'tis hope."

     'Tis a most intensely interesting period—and I, where am I at the close of this year? What do I hope for? This time last year (oh, how time speeds), my hopes were <u>all</u> just where they are now. A new hope has arisen but I cannot bear that it should be realized—inconsistent, yet so. I must write no more of myself—but this I am sure of, that next year, if my life is spared at this time, my feelings <u>will, must, shall be</u> very different. To my dear friend Elizabeth, what a change will the coming year bring. I wish her to marry and yet I am selfish enough to wish the event delayed indefinitely.[14] If ever mortal women were sincere in a wish, almost a determination, not to marry, I believe those two were E. and myself and yet she will soon be married and I dare not say I shall not follow.

     'Tis twelve o'clock and I may write 1837—'tis gone, yes forever, and what record of me has this time borne to the eternal world? My heart aches—I weep—oh, how shall I express my sorrow for the follies of the past year? The sound of a cannon breaks on the silence of midnight—and yet another. 'Tis meant as a signal of joy—is it not, rather, a knell over past joys, griefs—all are buried now in the past, that word so full of meaning. Another gun, well I should, too, rejoice in the goodness of God who has continued me in the possession of such signal mercies. He only knows what is in store for me in years to come—-be it joy or grief, 'tis all well if I have but his favour to uphold me. Our family meeting will be on Monday, as to-morrow is Sabbath. Oh, the sad hearts, the disappointments this year is destined to bring! 'Twill be crowned with mercies which thankless mortals overlook in the contemplation of their selfish sorrow. If we could only remember that this world is not our home. One thing have I desired and earnestly prayed for, that I may be a more devoted Christian during the coming year, that all my passions and feelings, yea, though now they are as my life, may be brought into subjection to my Saviour. 'Tis hard to think of rending the heart from those about whom it has closely entwined itself but yet, "Sanctify me, though it be by fire" is my heartfelt supplication. I tremble to think how it may be answered—but it is "Our Father" who hears and will answer the petitions of his children.

Several times I have laid aside my pen—and again resumed it—'tis past one o'clock and yet I am not drowsy—I am so excited, so deeply interested by the time— the future, the future! I will to bed now—though sorely against my will. What right have I to give way to passions, be they love or hate, which are against the known will of God? I am not my own—I am bound to glorify God—shall I do it by marrying an unbeliever? Dare I do it? God knows I need one to urge and assist me on my heavenward way—not one whose influence will have a different tendency. Oh, pride, how much suffering it has cost me—I deserve it—'tis all right.

Part Five
"I would forget . . . I would form new attachments."
January 1 - February 13, 1837

Adena, January 1, 1837

Sabbath Morning. I am waiting for the carriage to take me to church. 'Tis a gloomy morning—a driving snow mingled with rain. The first Sabbath of the year—how full of interest to the heart of the Christian—a way mark for the pilgrim—a starting place for the soul refreshed by the retrospect of the goodness of its Creator, and animated by a zeal for the promotion of his glory. We are made to "glorify God and enjoy Him forever,"[1] did man but rightly understand the end of his being. Could he but realize that happiness alone can be found in the service of his Creator, what a different aspect would our world present. It is heart-sickening to look abroad and know and feel most powerfully impressed this truth of Holy Writ: "The world lieth in wickedness."[2] How long, oh Lord, how long till "the earth shall be covered with the knowledge of [the glory of] God as the water covers the seas?"[3]

Evening. Heard a very excellent, instructive and appropriate sermon from Mr. Peet from Ec. 1-4. "One generation passeth away and another cometh." I do hope I may be benefitted by it. At Sabbath School I was much engaged and interested in endeavouring to impress on my dear children the duty of improving the season. Received from "my friend J." a New Year's gift of a beautiful Paragraph Bible accompanied by a note expressive of gratitude for interest I had once manifested in his spiritual welfare. I well remember the time and the particular occasion to which he alludes and what chapters I recommended to his prayerful perusal. I thought he had long since forgotten it for 'tis six years ago, and nothing on his part has ever evinced his recollection of the event. When we are brought to yield ourselves to Jesus how grateful are the emotions we feel towards those who ever directed us to a Saviour's love. I do believe J. is a sincere Christian. May God bless him and strengthen him in the path of duty. I shall highly value the precious volume he has donated me, more so from the circumstances connected with it.

Adena, January 2, 1837

Monday. Julia came up with me yestere'en and last night Mother was sent for to go to Ellen's. J. and I have been busy all day preparing for company. The weather is colder than it has been this winter and I have feared our friends could not come. We had not as usual a family meeting. Mother was absent and James, Julia, Willy and myself surrounded the dinner table. In the evening, better than my hopes, several of our friends came: E. McCoy, Mrs. John Walke, Mary McA., Ellen S., Mr. Taylor, Mr. Campbell, Mr. Massie, Allan McA.,[4] John W[alke] and H[enry] S[wearingen]. We passed the evening merrily. A bet between Cousin H[enry] M[assie] and myself was opened and as usual I was the winner—also a small prophecy which Mr. Taylor delivered into my keeping one year ago. Surely he will gain a name as a prophet—for, of more than a dozen predictions, one was verified. He delivered to my keeping another important document of the same nature for '38. In what . . .

I have, too, "The Follies of Henry Massie," to be opened at the same time—it occupies three pages and I am [a] bit curious to know its nature. I sang a dozen or more songs, I do believe, and the whole company joined in "The Star Spangled Banner," and dear "Auld Lang Syne" with great appearance of enjoyment.[5] Allan McA. promises me a horse if I am not married by this day next year, and a match to it in case he himself remains unmarried at the same date. I perceive it is yet the prevalent opinion that I am to marry J. P. C. and (though it may be wicked to give the wish utterance in the present state of my feelings) I do wish it could be so. How some good folks would open their eyes did they know the real state of the case! I have a sincere friendship for Mr. C.—my esteem and respect increase with my acquaintance—more he has not asked and if he did I could not give it. This time last year John and Fanny Walke knew not of their coming destiny—could it, can it be that I shall be so surprised also? To my regret, Dr. Foulke was not here; I wished it particularly. Cousin Henry and Mr. Campbell remained all night—'Twas late ere we retired to our rooms and we bore with us, E. and I at least, many and almost oppressive thoughts of the future. I am almost tempted to wish for a "spirit of indifference"—I have such forebodings of the future—such sadness of heart at the prospect of the various changes which a single year now produces in the round of my friends and acquaintances. O, for the glad images of the happy future which joyed me when a child; ere I had learned the sad truth that "Hope's gayest wreaths are made of earthly flowers,"[6] or felt that "It was a fearful thing to love what death may touch." Ere the next recurrence of this day, there may be very material changes in even the small circle which met around our fireside—it may be for the happier and, if we are Christians, be those changes what they may, all will be well, yea, even though death claim some. James told me of the birth of a new member of our family—a daughter for Arthur and Ellen, a welcome and blessing for the little stranger. Wakeful, weepful, thoughtful and oh, sinful.

Adena, January 3, 1837

Tues. Julia and James left us soon after breakfast. Mr. Massie must have found a peculiarly amusing theme for conversation as he kept Lizzet laughing for two hours—he left before dinner. Mr. C. remained—gave me a lesson in chess. The youth seems grieved that I have not full confidence in his veracity and promises amendment and entreats my better opinion and advice!! (Neither of which I promised.) He dined with us—Willy was absent but came home sick soon after dinner. E[llen] and H[enry] S[wearingen] are with me too, and little Mary [Worthington]. In the evening I played "lots" of songs for Lizzet.

Adena, January 4, 1837

Wednesday. We went this morning to the pond, by courtesy the lake, to amuse ourselves on the ice. I put on skates and found I could walk tolerably—better than I had hoped. We slid and sported in various ways and then, returning, Lizzet and I separated from Will, Henry and Ellen and scrambled up the hill in its steepest part to look at a frozen waterfall which was beautiful, and to a rock which is one of the most retired spots in nature. Poor Lizzy toiled after me, much against her will, I fear, but I hope was repaid.

Mother came up and told us all was doing well at Ellen's; she only remained a short time and left us again. Dr. Foulke came up instead of Mr. C., but Elizabeth chose to remain as the weather was bad—snowing fast. The Dr. chose also to remain. How Nelly and Henry and Will were in my way that night—I did wish to have some private talk with Dr. F. but they would not go to bed. No letters yet. Why does not Sally write? A message [came] from Albert yesterday through Mr. Campbell pleading business as an excuse for not having written. Of what stuff is he made to suppose I will admit such a plea, in such a case, and to send such an apology to me by Mr. C., too? Unsuspecting youth—"ah little think," etc. Well what will the end be? 'Tis altogether probable that I will shew out a good deal of "human nature" if I have an opportunity. "Revenge is sweet" etc., said wicked Byron—and I'll be revenged—provoking fool that I am. We are surprised at the blindness of owls and bats but they are sharpsighted in comparison with me. Duty says—what I won't write—inclination says—the same.

Adena, January 5, 1837

Thursday. Dr. F. remained till afternoon hoping that E. would return with him to town. But she gave him <u>contrary</u> directions and he took leave accordingly. I had not expected company to dinner and had not made preparations—so was a little mortified as the Dr. is a stranger. Poor Bessie [Elizabeth McCoy] was so vexed with him for staying. William brought her Album home for me and the first lines that met poor Lizzet's eyes were some of her "elect's," of a most decided character, addressed to herself. She was ever inclined to be fastidious and her looks and expressions of amazement and displeasure were really diverting to me. "Oh—! did you ever—! Was he possessed! provoking! I'll pay him for it!" etc. And then she deliberately took the scissors and relieved her fair book of these precious evidences of affection—one she destroyed whilst I was out—another I preserved and shall produce one of these days. Lizzet and I sat till very late talking over the future and arranging plans for her wedding—she wishes to postpone it—but if Dr. F. is like <u>all</u> other gents—she cannot do it—why should she? She has not played the fool as I have done.

Adena, January 6, 1837

Friday. Elizabeth left me this morning. The prophecies entrusted to her, with those in my care, and one I had written for cousin H. M., we (E. and I) sealed in one envelope and endorsed and they are to remain in my keeping. Ah me, ere they are opened! And the one page I wrote—<u>can I change</u>? If I do, I will honestly make the confession. Oh, that I were sometimes less resolute and firm. Ellen and I spent the day very soberly; in truth, these two days my heart aches—and yet I could be gay if it were necessary. I am growing more deceitful because there seems to be more need of it to screen my feelings and thoughts from the prying people who have their own conclusions already made. Ellen [S.] left me this evening. I am becoming simple again.

Adena, January 7, 1837

Sat. Woefully out of spirits—rubbed silver—washed glasses, put the house to rights, etc. Bessie has complained of me sadly for withholding—how can I confess to her that which it cost me so much to admit to myself? Wrote letters till midnight—one to Ellen Irvin.

Adena, January 9, 1837

Monday. James has just been giving me an account of the passage through our town of the Mexican President, Gen. Santa Anna and his Aide, Col. Almonti.[7] There was an immense crowd (for a village) collected 'round the hotel as they were departing this morning and the Col. A., throwing up the curtain of his carriage, exclaimed, "You shall not be disappointed, gentlemen, I am aide," etc., bowing politely on either side of the carriage. This was received with cheers from the multitude. "That's good," exclaimed one with true American _feeling_. James says the Gen. S. A. appears in ill health and exhausted. He labours under great disadvantages from his inability to speak any language but the Spanish which is rarely known among us. Col. A. speaks both French and English and is very affable and intelligent. What an intense excitement there must have been in our little town—when exciting causes are so rare!

Yesterday, I received a letter from Sally—so the little lady thinks _maybe_ she will be married and have a little house of her own by this time next year. And who will command this castle?[8]

Yesterday, I took my first peep at the new little Watts—a very fine child—like Ellen. Mother has returned and next week, no, this week, I am to stay with Ellen. I am selfish; I do not wish to go away from home. I am here so comfortable, so snug and have all my fixments to my liking. I shall never love any other home, I fear, or be so free or so much my own mistress as I am here in Spinster's joy. Well, maybe there'll be "no occasion." I was wakeful last night—as I often am. "Alas, that dreams are only dreams." I had such a delightful one last night of (guess who)—just as I wished—ah me—like "little Bo Peep's," my dreams are fleeting.[9]

Eolia, January 10, 1837

Tuesday. Came down here this morning with Mother. Found Ellen only tolerably. I stopped in town and called with Lizzet to see Mrs. Eckert.[10]

Eolia, January 14, 1837

Saturday. Ellen has been quite sick for some days. On Thursday mor'g I walked to town with Ellen Watts [age 2] to execute some com[missions]. Heard from Julia that her father was in town and would remain but one day and was much engaged. I felt very desirous to see him, and Arthur walked to town with me. Found

Mr. G. looking very well and spent two hours in pleasant chatting. Oh, for my revengeful resolutions! I wrote to Sally—scolding her for a certainty; she, Amanda and Henry will be here in a few days, maybe, and Sally will stay a long time—what pleasure do I anticipate with her!

Yesterday, a snow of some three inches fell and this morning E. M^cC. and Mr. Campbell came down in a sleigh and made a long morning visit—asked me if I had received the letter yet? I said no, with apparent unconcern, and begged him in his next letter to say I bore the neglect very patiently. Oh, what a fib; how could I tell it so deliberately! And how responded my heart to that untruth? Its slow and heavy beatings did pain me, almost, yea, more than the tremulous fluttering which I sometimes suffer—yet I wilfully told that—lie. And to this youth, too. In the afternoon, I went with the children in a sleigh to town, took in Julia and called to see a new arrival, Master Fred Peet, and then <u>enjoyed</u> most bitterly a drive through a snow storm. Mrs. McCoy accompanied [me] as Lizzet was not at home. Returned sick, sad and disappointed. I don't like my symptoms at all.

Eolia, January 16, 1837

Monday. I have been reading, "The three eras of woman's life."[11]

> Yet shall the tale instruct, if it did me
> How <u>some</u> have borne the load ourselves are
> doomed to bear.

This afternoon, Lizzet came again and with her, Col. Taylor of the "Invincibles." He made a wonderful ado over the babe—for he is, or affects to be, very fond of new born babies. On New Year's day, I jestingly asked a New Year's gift and reminded the gallant Col. that he owed me one from last year. The simple man has mortified me by presenting an Annual.[12] I at first refused it, and felt strongly tempted to be very indignant—but he is Mr. Taylor. Lizzet is trying her poor betrothed sorely—he is ever urging her to fix a time for their marriage and she as often "puts him off." She told me this eve'g he was terribly out of patience—poor youth.

Eolia, January 17, 1837

Tuesday. A long visit from my friend, cousin Henry M.—what a gossiping pair we be. We crone like any old women—I am more at ease with him than any of our gents and like him better. Every <u>confabulation</u> suits. Just after tea, Mr. C. made his appearance to take me sleigh-riding. I—consented—the night was lovely—bright moonlight and brilliant stars—we called at Mr. M^{c}C.'s—and took in Lizzet and Dr. F. and rode round a bit. Disappointed that my Xenia friends had not arrived as we hoped. Letters [came] from Annie J. and Ellen I. Annie speaks much of <u>home</u>—I wish she was here. Ellen is to be married next month. Can I go to the wedding? She wishes it, and it might "<u>keep</u>" me—it would give me much pleasure and if possible I will go—she is a fine girl, if only not so formal—so artificial. Years will cure that I am sure, though 'tis not generally so.

Mr. C. came in and stayed till 11. And such a long, long talk about many things. He has much more heart than I once gave him credit for—he speaks so often and affectionately of his relatives. Again he reverted to the time when I had pressed on him his need of an interest in religion; and again and again [he] spoke his gratitude to me and said how much he had felt at the time and never had, or would, forget. Thank God, unworthy as I am to speak his name, if I have ever been the means of causing a fellow mortal to turn to Him. I have only one source of uneasiness. I fear—to express half the interest I feel for him, lest it may be misinterpreted, but why should I mind. . .

(In the midst of our confab Frank entered, greatly to my surprise, for I thought him safely in Cambridge where he would have been, had he received Mother's last letter. He looks well—made his disappearance supposing, I presume, he was an intruder.)

Of this youth—there is, I must . . . maybe not—yet so it seemeth. He has good feelings, and correct—he is very obliging—aye, and I owe him a large debt of gratitude, but yet . . .

> This is na my ain, ain lad
> Though good the laddie be.[13]

I am a coward, a very coward, for I fear to read my own thoughts, or rather, I fear to <u>see</u> them in writing. So much that now stirs within me I should like in time to come to recall for my warning and improvement. Often I have wished to write exactly my <u>idea</u> on a subject which has interested my <u>friends</u> very deeply; yet I have not courage. I am growing bolder though, and some of these times I will write just what I please—bravo! make good the threat!

How I wished during that long confabulation for one other, and that one "Nemo!"[14] 'Twas late ere I slept—and my rest was broken, and today, Wednesday [January 18] I have been quite sick—alas, mentally as well as bodily. As I wrote Lizzet, quite under the weather—literally as well as figuratively, for the day was doleful indeed—the snow melting and everything looking desolate and <u>dirty</u> below, and a villainous blue devil fog obscuring the blessed light of the sun. Ellen laughed at me—she would not if she knew my doleful condition. I have been patient—have I not? I have borne my spirits up by reason, assisted, I hope, by a higher power—I have framed excuses—and yet I am still suffering from bitter disappointment. Of late, only for a week or so, I have begun to be rebellious again—it must not be—but "it is no dream" that I am sad. It is meant for my good. Firmly believing in the particular Providence of God, I know that in this trial there are designs for my good—I have set my affections sinfully on the things of earth—my loved one, though I have had severe warnings—therefore, I need to have my heart chastened and elevated. Wrote to Lizzet to come and comfort me. Ellen is yet quite sick, confined to bed.

Eolia, January 19, 1837

Thursday. Lizzet can't come which is a disappointment to me, truly. She has company at home—I heard today that Wm. Allen had been elected to the Senate of the U. S.![15] I am not surprised—he has marked out for himself a brilliant career and will spare nothing in the attainment of his desires. Ambition, and St. Helena's prison rock![16] They are so nearly associated in my memory, and yet the aspirants for this world's fame think no more of the fate of Napoleon than if his career had ended brilliantly. I walked to town to breakfast this morning—at James's—all well—but the girls not yet arrived.

Eolia, January 24, 1837

Tuesday. This evening, Elizabeth McC. came with Mr. C.—soon after, came Col. Taylor and Cousin H. M. [We had] a pleasant evening; poor Mr. T., how painfully sensitive he is. I received this morning from Mr. Willock the bass (set for the voice) of "The Pilgrim Fathers" which we used to sing together—Mr. C. promises to learn it; L. T. will sing it much better.

Eolia, January 25, 1837

Wednesday. L. and I spent a quiet day. In the eve'g Mr. C. came by appointment—to walk home with Lizzy—I had agreed to return with her after tea. We had a beautiful Aurora Borealis—I never witnessed a more brilliant scene of the kind—after the color had faded partly, the light shed was much like the morning twilight; by the time we reached town, only a faint color tinged the sky. Dr. F. made his appearance soon after our arrival. I received a letter from Sally saying she would be here on Saturday; also, that she is to be one of Ellen Irvin's bridesmaids. Mr. C. left at a little past nine, and I went to Lizzet's room to write a letter enjoining the young lady to treat the youth well and give him a positive answer as to the wedding day. I wrote a long letter to Ellen Irvin declining her invitation—I should like to attend her wedding but 'tis too near Lizzet's. In the course of two hours Lizzy came, in a good humour; having had a comfortable talk and settled matters, she felt much more at ease. "The day" is the twenty-third of Feb.—just as the gentleman chose and the very day he fixed months ago. Thus and thus, do these gentles carry their point.

After breakfast, Thursday, [January 26] I called to tell Julia of Sally's letter and then walked home [to Eolia]. I stopped for a short time in the burial ground—it is at all times a melancholy spot, but oh, how much more so when the palings are broken, the tombstones thrown from their places and everything indicating, not only neglect, but willful destruction. It fills me with sadness to see the dwelling of the dead thus sacreligiously invaded. I marked the spot where lay the ashes of my beloved friend of long ago, Elizabeth Waddle.[17]—Oh, the hopes—the love, the idol affections that were buried in that small space, and who that loved her can ever banish the recollection of her lovely and endearing character. She was dear, oh, very dear to me. I came home sad—and indisposed, too. Julia and Lizzet are to spend to-morrow at Eolia—Wish Julia +++—Ellen is much better.

Friday [January 27]. They came—and Julia went home about dark. L. stayed with me. I hoped we should have had this evening to ourselves—for I was—wicked, but before tea, came Dr. F. and Mr. C. Well, I did feel mad, but tried to recover my equanimity and succeeded sufficiently to talk a long time with Dr. F. They departed about ten—then Lizett and I had to arrange wedding finery and I wrote a long letter to [sister] Lizzy giving directions about it. It was one and past and a lovely moonlight night—ere we retired. My head ached so that I could not sleep.

Eolia, January 28, 1837
Sat. Head aching all day—and not relieved by what would cure that of many

ladies—the reception of my new bonnet and cloak.[18] A letter from Lizzy—every letter I get, no matter how interesting, is a disappointment. Ah pride, my mountain pride, for once your monition should have been regarded—but why should I say so? I did that which I esteemed my duty. I acted according to the golden rule of doing as I would be done by. What possible excuse can be framed to soothe my wounded pride? All that my mind could imagine have been vainly exhausted. My heart leads me too often wrong—I, tender hearted!!

Eolia, January 30, 1837

Monday. Sarah, Amanda and Henry [Galloway] arrived on Sat. eve'g accompanied by Messrs. Tennant and Beecher of L[ancaster].[19] Sally looks very frail, dear girl—now I can imagine her sufferings—alas—she alone could tell a tale of disappointment that few suspect. How many times 'tis woman's lot.

Eolia, January 31, 1837

Tuesday. Rode up to James's to see the girls. 'Tis vexatious that I should be sick now—alas, for the cause. Henry is the same youth as ever—I would his stature increased in proportion to his—no, not self-esteem, but self-conceit. Yet I like many things in him—there is little about him to please a woman, though he seems perfectly unconscious of the fact. My life on it, he will live and die a bachelor, for all his protestations contrariwise. Whilst I was dressing, the Lancaster gents and H. called—saw Mr. Beecher for the first time. His manners are gentlemanly—rode up with me in the carriage—has a soul—.

Eolia, February 1, 1837

Wednesday. I have just returned (12 o'clock) from a party at James's— weary, heart-sick, disgusted, displeased with myself and feeling altogether more misanthropic than I like or have been for—how long? Have I a soul? a mind? capabilities for understanding and appreciating the wonderful things of earth, the mysteries of nature, and yet am I the being of to-night? The frivolous—irritable—selfish creature that I must have seemed—I am not myself—the bodily pain which I have suffered must surely have touched my brain—how many disagreeable things I have said to-night to gentlemen; quarreled outright with the Hon. Senator and wished all (except two) of the gents felt as irritable as myself, for then they surely would have left me undisturbed. Oh, fool—bitter fool that I have been and am—my self-control, where is it? Alas, if never before, now I should be humble—for never was the weakness of poor mortal more fully exhibited to herself than that which is daily, hourly forcing itself before me. I wish he was in. . . .

Eolia, February 2, 1837

Thursday. I rode home [to Adena] to prepare for the reception of company—and in truth I was much fitter for my bed than seeing or preparing for company. It was only the girls and their attendant gents, but yet I would rather indeed have remained at home [at Eolia]. We had a merry day, that is, considering all things. Mr. Beecher improves in my esteem—Mr. T[ennant], just as always—there is a *gaucherie* about him not to be overcome that makes him just bearable. Sarah and Amanda wished to call at Fruit Hill, so I offered Sally a seat behind me on the much admired and redoubtable Peter Pancake (she came up in the carriage with Julia). Amanda was on horseback and we set off, well escorted by five gents—made our call—and had a delightful ride to town. My head better, the evening mild and bright—and all uniting for our pleasure. I should not omit Mr. Beecher's dancing horse.

Sally promised to go to Eolia with me, but when we reached town Julia forbade on the plea that she was invited and expected by Mrs. Douglass. This was wrong and displeased me. Cannot Julia see how ill poor Sarah is? I hope I am wrong—God grant it may be so, but I greatly fear Sarah is—I weep to think so—dying; they told me she was better—how? I see it not in any way—-every symptom tells of a wasting of life—she looks, alas, she is so fragile. And yet she must dress, visit, see company, be gay, keep late and irregular hours—oh, 'tis a sin—a cruelty unpardonable, to ask it of her who seems to have so short a time on the earth. I do think a year's quiet, in my sense of the word, is the only thing that could restore her—and, if 'tis as I fear with her, even that would fail. Dear girl—oh, that her health could be again restored. Since I came here, my own health has been good for a long time; now I am really sick. The feelings, mental as well as physical, of months agone are taking possession—languor—palpitations, and for a week, a dull heavy pain in my head. I sent for an emetic several days ago, and to-night I must take it for I can bear this no longer.[20] Ah me! " 'Tis not wise to suffer mentally."

Eolia, February 3, 1837

Friday. Took my medicine last night and in consequence feel languid and weak this morning. I must have been exceedingly stupid on Wednesday evening—I remember Mr. Leonard asking me if I had read anything interesting of late and my answering no—when I was quite aware that I have read several works of great interest to me. I know I was unmerciful on our Hon. Senator and poor Gen., and was quite out of humour because I had to sing. Arthur has disappointed me—he has been absent nearly a week, and promised to return yesterday that I might go home. Lizzet wants me to be with her and assist her in the preparations and I greatly wish to do so, but I have been absent so long I know not if Mother will be willing.

Julia, James, Sarah, Amanda, their gents, Cousin Henry, Mr. C. and Dr. F., and Frank and Willy dined today at Eolia. Ellen did not make her appearance, and I graced the head of the table, James opposite me. After dinner, music and chat—I had a long conversation with Dr. Foulke, and I think we shall be good friends. He is almost too cautious, too guarded to please me entirely—'tis safest however. Lizzet is somewhat of the same character—may they make each other happy.

Eolia, February 4, 1837

Sat. I went up to town to attend singing school with "my friend J."[21] According to a promise of yesterday, called to see Mrs. James and heard a <u>quantity</u> of gossip in which I was interested most intimately. It seems I am to be married next week after Lizzet, wedding clothes purchased, and not only that, but a house in readiness, etc. Whew—much obliged, but I really cannot promise to fulfill all the wishes and engagements of the people; nay, nay, I am not quite so yielding. I sincerely believe that many marriages are brought about by this means. Fortunately for myself, and unfortunately for those who have kindly arranged this affair, I have a little will of my own which rebels most stubbornly against these arbitrary proceedings—would it were otherwise, yes—I say it sincerely, 'tis all in my power—poor fellow.

Called to see Martha Fullerton[22] who is dying of consumption, that relentless destroyer. A few days must end her career on earth—oh, how full of blessedness the assurance that an eternity of bliss awaits this dying Christian. What but this could support her in this awful suffering—what but this glorious hope could sustain her agonized mother who is soon to be twice bereaved. And her sister—her untiring, affectionate nurse—soon will she be left alone, the stay of her mother. There are brothers, but there is rarely that intimate association between mother and son as between mother and daughter. Margaret is in delicate health. Oh, should she too be taken—God in mercy forbid and spare her to her doting parent. I did not go to Martha's room—she is so ill that it would disturb her—her family seem to be in a most painful state of suspense—every hour expecting her death. In this ruthless disease, not the least distressing is the painful conviction—there is no hope. My heart sympathizes with the sufferers.

I took tea at James's and went with Mr. C. to the singing school where was assembled, I should suppose, nearly an hundred persons young and old. As usual, the singing master was a most consequential person of the Universal nation—I think he will improve the style of singing. I did not remain more than an hour—returned to James's and found some gentlemen and Miss Bond. No letters—no letter. Passed the evening pleasantly and at 9, Sally and I mounted Peter, with Henry as escort—and returned to Eolia. Sarah is much indisposed—I am in pain for her—she asked me of J[ames Campbell], and I asked her of P[atterson Brown], and we were equally satisfactory to each other. I wish I could tell her all—but no—mortal shall never hear it all, though my proud heart be crushed by the effort to retain my folly. I told her I was a fool—aye, that's the hardest—to know so well that 'tis my own folly that causes me such suffering. The devotedness of one and the negligence of the other! Oh, heart—ungrateful heart of mine, that will not return such true affection.

Eolia, February 6, 1837

Monday. Yesterday, I went again to see Martha F. and, as I fear, for the last time here—may we meet again in Heaven. Amanda stayed with me last night and this morning early, Frank came to ride to town with us—the fog was very heavy, and I feared to go out but I had promised and must perform. The girls were to leave at eight—so we, A. and I, mounted Peter (poor Peter, how he has been imposed on of late) and by the time we reached town we were nearly "dripping with dew," more beautiful in poetry than reality, I shrewdly suspect, from my little experience. Sarah languid—as usual, the party was detained by the coach and it was nearly ten o'clock ere they got off. Cousin Henry stayed and we had as usual a gossip of an hour—told him of Lizzet's approaching marriage, of which he had not heard. Jested about my own—ah me. After he left, I went to Mr. McCoy's, sent for Ellen Waddle, and consulted about and arranged our dresses for the important occasion. Lizzet talks of standing me with Jamie—I do in truth object.

Rode down to Eolia and was sick, heart and head, all day—I wish I could not feel—some women get over these matters just as they would take a stroll through the woods—avoiding the rough and disagreeable and enjoying the delightful. But I, fool-like, get into every difficulty of burrs—mud-puddles, and as though that were not sufficient, conjure up ghosts to torment me. I am sick—how can I be well? Glad to date—Adena.

Adena, February 7, 1837

Tuesday. Much to my satisfaction, Arthur returned last night—he has been at Cincinnati. [Sister] Lizzy and all are well. [He] brought me a beautiful silver buckle, for which I am doubly grateful as I particularly needed an article of the kind. I disliked to leave Ellen but surely I have been there long enough. When the carriage came, little Ellen would go with me—a rare thing for her who never will leave home. Called at Julia's—then at Lizzet's—then home—met Mother on her way to Mr. Jacob's. [She] gave me the keys, and when I reached home I immediately ordered a fire in my own room. Just as I had taken off my dress, the cook came to me in consternation saying some gents were below and the whole house was locked up and no fires—well, this was a predicament. She found the keys and when I had <u>re</u>-dressed I descended to the dining room and found Senator Allen and Mr. G. Scott by a newly lighted fire—gloomy enough. However, I did my best to make amends for the cool reception and I hope I was successful. The senator wants polish—'tis almost disgusting to hear him speak of himself—boasts at the same time of his susceptibility and command of his feelings. I am vexed with myself for caring about him one way or the other.

Adena, February 8, 1837

Wednesday. Cold—snowy and blustering. I would that my foolish hopes were dead and gone—my heart flutters whenever a member of the family returns from town because they have been to the Post Office and they may have letters for me. I am childish—irritable—wicked.

Adena, February 9, 1837

Thursday. I have been very busy sewing all this week, preparing to spend the next two weeks with Lizzet—this day, [in] two weeks, is the eventful day. Mr. C. came this evening—he is a clever fellow and I like him very well—more as I know him better, yet I wish I liked him better still. I fear me he is more in earnest than I had thought—passed the evening agreeably—put on his alarmingly grave face once or twice—that's all. Mother was sick—Willy absent, so we were "*tête à tête*," but I am used to that—stayed till nearly 11—he never used to do so.

Adena, February 10, 1837

Friday. Could not sleep last night for thinking of <u>one</u>, and <u>another</u>—in consequence of wakefulness and anxiety, felt wretchedly. What a marvel I am to myself, always seeking something to pain me—now I am framing excuses for . . . and then devising ways to prevent a declaration which I dread most terribly. My mind is illy at ease and my poor body sympathizes painfully. Oh, that I might love just whom I would—fool have I been. Effie came to spend the afternoon; we had some interesting conversation. She amused me exceedingly with an account of a visit from Messrs. Allen and Scott on the same day they were here—they missed their dinners!!

Whilst we were speaking of him, Dr. Foulke entered. Thanks to Effie, my spirits were much improved. I could not but regret the presence of a third person—for never yet have I had an opportunity of conversing with the future husband of my dear E. without a witness. There are so many things I should like to talk over—well, after they are married I shall have time enough. After tea (Effie and the Dr. both left before dark), I practiced some songs for the wedding but there was no melody in voice or heart so I gave it up.

Adena, February 11, 1837

Saturday. Still doleful—have I a right to thus make myself wretched, thereby unfitting me for duty? Before I rose this morning I came to a conclusion which gave me some relief and unless I see very good reasons to the contrary, I shall act upon it. If I get no letters or see not this youth by the wedding I shall request my last two letters to be returned to me. Why may I not forget? Alas, 'tis a frequent thing for a woman's affection to go out without return. But I, I, who have prided myself on my impenetrability, whose heart seemed cased in armour—that I should be led into this folly. I have been thinking all day of J. and my tho'ts were burdensome—head ached and I had taken medicine when the gentleman was announced. I could not—I would not see him, for in sincerity, I was too sick, yes, too sick. Elizabeth and Dr. F. have told him, so he told me on Thursday, that he is to be my bridesman. If left with me, it should not have been so, yet since they have so arranged it, so it must be—surely I can conduct myself so as to forbid any . . . till after that and then if he do not understand me, his be the fault. I have done my best to prevent what will be painful in the extreme to both. I wish—oh, I do wish I could—feel angry—then I might be cured, but this corroding feeling of wounded pride, alas, pained affection I might say, is far more difficult to bear and cannot be subdued. Aid me, my woman's pride—to feel resentment—but no—still that aching pain maintains possession and I suffer for the poor fellow.

How much I do wish Lizzet were here to-night and I would tell her all she has so often wished to know—yes, I will, the next opportunity, tell her all my silly tale with the hope, ah, maybe vain, of relieving my sad heart. She will give me sympathy, at least—and that I need. I am a burden to myself—oh, witless wight, I would forget—I would form new attachments. I wish, oh, I cannot write my fruitless wishes. Why did I not let it come to pass long, long ago—and now I might be at rest? It seems to me I have no right thus to put away from me a chance of happiness, and yet—"that way I cannot bear to look." Maybe I am mistaken, but I fear J. came with a settled intent to give me trouble as well as himself. All along I have thought, why should I be suspicious, when my strongest reason lies in this—the gossip of the town; yet since my return from L[ancaster] there has been a change in his manner I cannot mistake. I like him, oh, very well, but no more. Again I say, would that I did. I'll tell Lizzet—and what will she say, I wonder? He shall ever be my good friend and—I'll not marry at all.

Adena, February 13, 1837

Monday. I have been much better for two days, body and mentally—resolution has aided me in the latter case—took a long walk to the lake and through the woods which quite renewed me. The sun shone brightly and though 'twas cold I almost expected to see flowers looking out from among the leaves on the sheltered hillside. Dearly, oh, dearly do I love a walk in the woods with pleasant thoughts for company—to-day it gave me new life. Spent the morning in cutting out and fixing work. In the afternoon went to Fruit Hill—all well. Allan says he surely will be married soon but to whom he says not. Willy came over for me after tea and told me there was a letter at home for me—I suppose I shall be disappointed, thought I—if 'tis from any but one, I shall be. A lovely night, but cold. Walked home with my thoughts engrossed as usual of late. Asked for my letter and lo, it was from Nemo, and just such an one as I had expected, for I've given him no encouragement to write otherwise. Though the paper is white and the ink black, the letter hath decidedly a blueish aspect. Oh, how I will pay up this youth in time to come! "Forget that he owes me an apology"—no, not I—I have been too gentle, forgiving and yielding. I will <u>mayhap</u> shew out a little and yet <u>mayhap</u> it may be out of my power. I'll try, or I am not a woman—he has too sorely touched my pride to be easily forgiven.

Again, I am to leave my beloved home for some weeks—it appears an inconsistency for me to profess so much attachment for Adena and yet to be so much voluntarily absent—but how can I avoid it? Lizzet will soon have a nearer and dearer to claim her whole affection and whilst I can, I will assert my rights to her friendship. She has been sick for some days, poor girl; I hope she will soon be well. Dr. F. was here this afternoon during my absence. How very sorry I am that I did not see him.

And now again I am on the last leaf of my second volume and marvel on the follies recounted, yet—I shall go on in the same manner. If, as I ought to do, I wrote with care and were more general in my notes, it would be a profitable exercise to me but I write usually late at night and in the most hurried manner so that my faults of style are confirmed rather than corrected. I was not trained to think—whose the fault was I dare not say, for I do not know, but this I bitterly feel, that my total education has been a most faulty one—mind and heart, too; neither are they what they might have been under different culture.[23] My sensitive nervous temperament makes me a terror to myself—my irritability of temper and overbearing disposition are objects either of fear or dislike to others. Knowing my faults, why do I not set myself to amend them? Aye, do it! As easily bend the tree as once you did the sapling—the tree may be hewed but not bent, and such a moral hewing is necessary to alter my stubbornly fixed habits. Heaven aid me and it shall surely be accomplished but never by mine own unassisted efforts.

What fools we women folk are in matters of the heart—will take none other advice or experience than our own and dearly is the latter bought most frequently. Irving's beautiful reflections in his tale, "The Broken Heart," so often recur to me when I think of a matter of this nature.[24] How very few women have attained the mature age of Lizzet and myself without one or more affairs of this nature—what has been her conservation I don't know—but I am beginning to discover mine—and oh, marvel of marvels, that I did not make the discovery long ago. Would it were otherwise—I don't like the idea on more than one account—blinded creature that I—(we) have been. He thinks he has said and done all right—don't break or quail, heart of mine, and pride, thy staff if thou please (thank you, it's never wanting), and we'll look further into this matter before we make our decided observations. I could hide me whenever I think on it, for my shame of my weakness—Lizzet did not so— how happy she seems to be.

Interlude Between February, 1837 and July, 1838

Editor's Introduction to Margaret's 1838-39 Correspondence with Edward Mansfield

No diary by Margaret Worthington has come to light describing her activities in the period from mid-February, 1837 (the end of Part Five) to the first of her letters to Edward Mansfield on July 27, 1838 (the beginning of Part Six). It was to be a busy time at Adena. The women of the family, while mourning Mary's loss, were also very concerned about what would happen to the Macomb children. Eleanor wrote to Lizzy on December 21, 1836, that when she first learned of the death of her eldest daughter on December 3, she was too upset to write and had asked William to let Lizzy know. She continued:

> Mr. [David] Macomb wrote that Mary took a severe cold on her passage [from Florida] to Texas. Complications set in that could not be checked. She died on the 19th of October, perfectly in her senses, leaving directions for all her children . . . enjoining on their kindness and affection for each other especially in affliction. [She] sent her kindest love to her brothers and sisters requesting them always to show respect and kindness to her mother and left me [ESW] a lock of her hair and a breastpin and regretted that she could not see me and die under my roof. My loved Child, I trust she is now happy with her Saviour.
>
> 'Tis to me a sore trial, amongst the greatest I have ever experienced. Her desolate children, too. O, God, have pity on them for the great Redeemer's sake. Have written to Mr. Macomb to let me have the 2 Daughters and David—I know my time [is] short, but if the children were here they have relatives that would take care of them.
>
> Mr. Macomb says himself her married life has been one of trial and affliction such as would have laid many a woman of less fortitude in the grave long ago. [S]urely it was himself that caused most of them. I fear my poor Child was in great poverty and probably wanted not only the comforts but the necessaries of life far from all that could assist her and then taken to a land of worse than Hell, of Infidels, and sunk into her grave brokenhearted.[1]

On December 27, Lizzy replied, "I hope Mr. Macomb will send or bring Ellen and Mary to us. Texas is no fit place for them without a mother's care; he cannot be a proper guardian with his habits and sentiments, though he is their father."[2]

Later, the shocking news reached Adena that David Macomb, despondent over Mary's death, had committed suicide on February 10, 1837.[3] Eleanor subsequently arranged to have three of the orphaned Macomb children come north to Adena: Louis, age sixteen, Mary, thirteen and David, ten.

The three youngest Macombs had apparently been at Adena with their grandmother for about two months when Margaret wrote the letter to Lizzy reproduced below. Ellen Macomb had not come to Adena as Lizzy had suggested, because in May, 1837, she had married Joseph T. Harrell in Texas; nor had Thomas come to Ohio with his siblings. He was eighteen and presumably able to fend for himself.[4] Margaret's newsy letter also informed Lizzy about her active social life and some of the people mentioned in her 1836-37 diary.

To: Mrs. C. R. Pomeroy   Adena, January 4, 1838
Salisbury, Meig's Co., Ohio   [Postmarked January 11]

Is it not charming, dear Lizzy, to sit in January by an open window and enjoy the soft air and music of birds? I am growing young again [in] this delicious weather and can hardly realize that winter is really begun. Your letter I received day before yesterday, Jan. 2, being the eleventh day after it was written. Letters from Va. come in four days—we must certainly complain to the Post Office department at Washington and pray for redress. I have much that I wish to say to you, or rather, did wish to have said, but have now forgotten. I will write whatever I can remember that I think will interest you.

Have you heard anything of Sally's wedding?[5] I arrived a week before the wedding and had a very pleasant visit—both to Xenia and Dayton. I was too much vexed that you were not there with us—tell Charles, "I've taken a scunner at him" ever since, for not contriving to give you the pleasure of attending Sally's wedding. All the family so much wished for you. I should have remained longer in Xenia, but somewhat to my surprise, was summoned to act as bridesmaid to H. Madeira.[6] Tell Charles the full blown roses were much admired on that occasion.

Since Harriet's wedding, until last week, I had not spent a day in town nor even been there except to church. As you know, there was much to be done at home: carpets, curtains, etc., a quantity of sewing, teaching the children "and so on" . . . which gives me but little leisure time. Added to my multifarious and also multitudinous engagements there was a strong inclination and—positive determination to stay at Adena this winter. I have done so, thus far, and the poor people are this time sure the wedding they have so long predicted is at hand—but I guess they are farther than ever from the truth.[7]

Mary McArthur was married on Christmas day.[8] Misses Walke, Creighton, Morris (?) and McMahan, bridesmaids. There was not as usual a crowd, only selected friends. Mr. and Mrs. Trimble left the Wednesday after the wedding for Cincinnati via Hillsboro. Effie [McArthur Coons] accompanied them and has not yet returned. She was much opposed to Mary's marriage and did her utmost to postpone if not prevent it. She says if Mary is not happy in Cincinnati she shall not remain there. Mr. Anderson[9] thinks he will probably reside in Kentucky, and if so, Effie will be alone [at Fruit Hill]. Gen. McArthur continues in the same lamentable condition, but I think his health is failing. He came into the room on the evening of the wedding and looked about him as if he had no concern with matters.

Our meeting on New Year's Day was but small. Ellen, James and Julia with their children were all, beside our regular family. Uncle James's family did not come from some cause, I don't know what. Aunt Collins[10] is engaged all the time with her dying sister, Mrs. McLean. Arthur has gone to Virginia. We expect his return next week.

Mrs. Foulke[11] has a son nearly three weeks old as lovely and interesting as our little Mans [?] was at the same age. Elizabeth is (to use Albert's phrase) "as well as could be expected," and all the family are much pleased with their new relative.

Monday morning by candlelight. I wonder if you ever rise so early? I have been in excellent health ever since my return [from Xenia], and have always risen by candlelight (early). I always was fond of doing so and my health only prevented. I could not finish your letter the other night. My thoughts wandered away and in vain I called them back. I tell you this to excuse me for my disconnected letter. Everything this morning is covered with snow and out-of-doors looks like a magician's triumph, but so warm yesterday that fire was uncomfortable. "Alas, that dreams are only dreams." I dreamt I saw you all, both Ellen[12] you and Charles, getting out of a coach at the door and little Elly knew me. I was so delighted and scarcely could recover from my disappointment all day yesterday. I am afraid she will find a rival in Master Jacky Foulke.

You would be amazed to see me acting pedagogue. I sit in my room in great dignity and teach the "rudiments" and sometimes my pupils seem to dislike them as much as ever did Timothy. You can scarcely form an idea of their uncultivated state and 'tis with great difficulty I can explain their lessons to them so as to be understood. David is the quickest—poor Louis seems very dull; Mary, you know, is given to pouting—they have all difficult dispositions to manage, more from neglect, I think, than any unusual natural defect. I hope to be enabled to be of use to them in other ways than mere mental culture—they want Moral principles now; they have none other than—will.

Misses Waddle, Woodrow and Creighton[13] are coming to spend this week with me and we anticipate much pleasure . . .

Uncle, Aunt and Sally [Swearingen] are well and they, among others, make frequent enquiries for you. You know how they have been answered. The canal is not in use; of course we cannot send you anything. It will soon be spring, dear Lizzy, and you will soon come home again and then we shall have plenty of apples and I suppose they will be quite as acceptable in March as now. I would have had some sausages prepared for you, but your letter came too late.

Mrs. Luckett and Jane[14] send love. You ought to write frequently to me, for you know I am always punctual in replying. I will write to you soon, if you choose, and maybe a better letter. I am suffering from a violent headache and never wrote a letter with more difficulty than this.

Love to Mrs. Pomeroy[15] and Charles. Tell him I have not rec'd his letter yet; where did you put it? Ask him also if he be fully persuaded yet that I am engaged to Mr. Campbell? —Ah, Charly, you made a mistake once in your life . . . . Mother and Willy send much love. Mary Macomb says she is tired of not seeing Nelly. Tell Ellen she never told me how to make her gingerbread —pray ship me a cargo per first opportunity—Goodbye. Sincerely, your Sister.

[In the margin of page 2] Have you heard it? John Marye died of yellow fever. Also died, Oscar Craig a few days before.[16]

[Postscripts on outside of letter] The girls are with me and all send remembrances. We have heard lately from Sister Sarah; all are well and she says doing well.[17] Now, dear Lizzy, pray write often and not hastily. We have thought it unkind, your prolonged silence. Had you not said in your letter by Tom Williams that you would very soon write to me, I should have written to you long ago. Words, you know, must be understood just as they are. Goodbye, once again. Your M. W.

Do not blame the P. M. for not delivering this letter, for it has been nearly a week on hand. It has been finished two days, but I neglected to send it to the office. Today is Wednesday, 10th. Mrs. McLean, Aunt's sister, died yesterday. She gave such continued evidence of Christian fortitude and cheerful acquiescence [to] the will of God, that we can have no doubt but that she has made a most happy exchange.[18]

Again, no written record has been found of Margaret's activities in the period between her January 4, 1838 letter to Lizzy and a June 2, 1838, letter to Sally Galloway Browne, shown below. One assumes that she continued to keep house, teach the three Macomb children and to socialize with her friends. Willy wrote to Lizzy during that period, "Maggie is chief cook and bottle washer."[19]

Margaret's letter to Sally was written from the Cincinnati home of Edward Mansfield and his mother. She was there as Mrs. Mansfield's guest, having come down from Chillicothe, it would appear, with her sister Ellen and brother-in-law Arthur Watts.[20] Since her evening at Edward's home in the spring of 1836, recorded in Part One, his wife, Mary Peck Mansfield, had died from complications in childbirth, and their baby son had also died. Edward was left with two small boys, Eddy and Charley.[21] Elizabeth Mansfield presumably helped care for Eddy while Charley was in the care of his maternal grandmother, Mrs. Abel Catlin (formerly Mrs. Peck). It is unclear where Dr. and Mrs. Catlin were living in 1838, but in the 1840s their home was in Portsmouth, Ohio.[22]

To Mrs. R. P. Browne   Cincinnati, June 2nd, 1838
Dayton, Ohio   Saturday night [no postmark]

Your letter, my dearest Sally, was a most effective one, for it changed my plans entirely, and brought me to your way of thinking. I have no time to write a long letter now—to tell you what a pleasant visit I have had—but you are interested in the information that, nothing preventing, you may expect Mr. B. Drake[23] and myself on Wednesday or Thursday evening at furtherest, to make you a brief visit of a day or so. I wrote yesterday to Amanda[24] wishing to apprise her of my intentions with the hope that she would visit me at your house. Are you pleased? I hope so, for 'tis my earnest desire to give you pleasure.

Ellen and Arthur left on Thursday for home by the river boat. I am staying with Mrs. Mansfield and as pleasantly situated as I could possibly wish. And shall see you so soon you will excuse me for writing only one page? I will make up for it I hope [by] agreeable conversation when I arrive in Dayton.

I grieve to hear of your ill health—I have been suffering terribly for two days from nervous headache which is no small drawback on my engagements. I'll take laudanum to-morrow if it be not better.

My love to Patterson and tell him I could not slight or refuse his invitation. Good night, dear Sally. I hope in a few days to see you and—pray rouge a little in honor of such important personages as Mr. Drake and myself —

Sincerely your friend, Margaret

[Postscript] I have just returned from attending an address by Mr. Mansfield—excellent, instructive, interesting—but I dared not tell him I thought so—for [he] is a genius undoubtedly, no, he is far above what goes in the world by that cognomen.[25]

Sunday evening. I neglected to read my letter last night and this morning went off in a hurry soon after breakfast to attend Mr. McGuffey's lecture and have not been at home till now.[26] I dined at Mr. [John G.] Worthington's [27] and whilst I was there John Stearns [?] came in—said you were more indisposed for a few days past—now, dear Sally, remember you said my coming to see you would make you well and I hope you will keep your promise. I have not seen Mr. Drake today. We have not positively determined what day we will set out on our journey. I anticipate much pleasure—will it not be sentimental?

Elizabeth Worthington is forced to keep [to] her bed most of the time. I have only seen her sitting up once. She looks quite well, however. Goodbye, my own dear Sally—how happy I shall be to meet you in your own house.

Margaret[28]

The twenty-nine letters that comprise the rest of *Daughter of Adena* begin with Margaret's letter to Edward Mansfield on July 27, 1838, while he was on a trip to Eastern cities. From its tone and content, it is apparent that they had become engaged while Margaret was a house guest at the Mansfield home in Cincinnati the previous month. Margaret's 1838 letters explicitly confirmed their relationship as "match" or "engagement," and in her early 1839 letters she often sought Edward's advice about wedding preparations.

Only one letter from Edward to Margaret has come to light to include in Part Six. He wrote it from Cincinnati on September 9, 1838 after his return from the East. In it he expressed his great loneliness since his wife Mary's death and his anxiety about financial matters. Margaret's subsequent expressions of a desire to know more about his troubles and Edward's reticence in divulging all the details amounted to a lovers' quarrel on paper.

Throughout this correspondence, Margaret seems just as impatient with Edward as she had previously been with Sally and Albert Galloway because they did not write to her as often as she would have liked. Perhaps she needed constant affirmations of Edward's love. She probably longed for reassurances in regard to leaving Adena, the home she loved so intensely, and the mother to whom she was so deeply devoted.

Other issues loomed before her: could she adapt herself to Cincinnati's worldly hustle and bustle when her expressed preference was for a life in the country? Would she be adequate to the new relationships which marriage would bring her? She was not only about to marry a literary man ten years older than herself but would become step-mother to two small boys and daughter-in-law to Elizabeth Phipps Mansfield, an admirable but dominating woman. Margaret was accustomed to moving socially among Chillicothe residents whose elite status rested on political and economic achievement; in Cincinnati she would be joining Edward's circle of lawyers, doctors, educators and influential writers who were among the city's intellectual elite. Did Margaret's native intelligence, her education and the breadth of her reading equip her to mingle comfortably with her future husband's associates? Her family members and many of her friends were raised in the traditions of Virginia, while Edward's family and many of his friends were transplanted New Englanders, so she and Edward would have to accommodate themselves to cultural and regional differences. These questions are either explicitly addressed in Margaret's 1838-39 letters or are implicit in her situation. One wonders whether the emotional growing pains she suffered in 1836-37 were a necessary prelude to betrothal, the resolution of inner conflicts freeing her to make a good choice of marriage partner.[29]

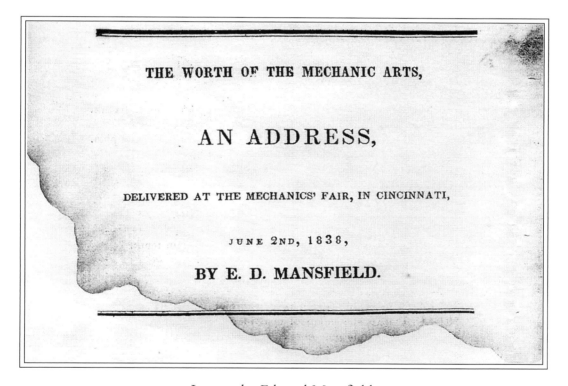

THE WORTH OF THE MECHANIC ARTS,

AN ADDRESS,

DELIVERED AT THE MECHANICS' FAIR, IN CINCINNATI,

JUNE 2ND, 1838,

BY E. D. MANSFIELD.

Lecture by Edward Mansfield
that Margaret attended
From the estate of Winston Mansfield Dudley

Cover of "The Western Patriot," Margaret's 1838 Almanac,
published by Peter Kaufmann. *From the estate of Winston Mansfield Dudley*

Chronology of Correspondence

June 2, 1838 — MW wrote to Sally Galloway Browne from the Mansfield home in Cincinnati where she apparently stayed most of June. During her visit, she and Edward D. Mansfield became engaged.[1]

July 13, 1838 — EDM stopped at Adena to visit MW on his way East where he would make stops in Baltimore, Hartford and New York City.[2]

July 25, 1838 — MW's twenty-seventh birthday; two days later she wrote the first of twenty-eight letters to EDM which, along with one letter from EDM to MW, form Parts Six, Seven and Eight of *Daughter of Adena*.

August 17, 1838 — EDM's thirty-seventh birthday; on August 24, 1838. MW expected EDM to be at Adena again, on his way back to Cincinnati from the Eastern states.

September 9, 1838 — EDM wrote from Cincinnati to MW; this is the only EDM letter in the collection that was written during the engagement period.

December 22, 1838 to January 3, 1839 — EDM visited MW at Adena for the Christmas and New Year holidays.

January 27 to February 10, 1839 and again, February 16 to 23, 1839 — MW wrote to EDM from Eolia, her sister Ellen Watts's home in Chillicothe.

March 23 to 30, 1839 — EDM visited MW at Adena.

April 20, 1839 — EDM arrived in Chillicothe for their wedding.

April 24, 1839 — On the evening of this date, Margaret Worthington and Edward D. Mansfield were married at Adena.[3]

(Compiled by C. W. Wells)

Part Six
"Your letters are <u>my</u> life."
Letters to and from Edward D. Mansfield
July 27 - October 31, 1838

Adena, July 27th, 1838
Friday

I received today, my dear Edward, your letter from Baltimore and, although your kindness is very gratifying to me, I must chide you for disregard of my injunction <u>never</u> to write when you were suffering from fatigue. Your letters are my greatest happiness now, but they are dearly purchased by your pain. The severest part of your journey being accomplished, I need not repeat my injunction, but I hope you will remember what I have already said on this subject—do not think me selfish, only anxious for you and I hope not unreasonably so.

I have been tempted to write daily, and you can scarce imagine my disappointment when three days elapsed without my receiving a letter from you. Your letters are <u>my</u> life—but do not write when you are sick, fatigued or engaged. I know you wish to give me pleasure—then care for yourself. Do you know I have wished a thousand times I had made better use of my opportunities of <u>talking</u> <u>to</u> <u>you</u>. I have so many <u>little</u> things to say that my pen cannot express as would my tongue. <u>We</u> are a most interesting theme for the good people here. I often wish you could hear what is said—this I will tell you, that the <u>match</u> receives general approbation. Mrs. Coons returned a few days since from Cincinnati.[4] <u>Your</u> citizens consider you irresistible—how came it that they are aware of your object in coming to Chillicothe? Mrs. Coons says she heard many speak with some solicitude of <u>my</u> decision—your intentions they <u>knew</u> and thought Miss W. could not do better (how I hate that calculating phrase) than to accept you. Further, we are to take your mother's house on Broadway, and I am to make my appearance in the city about the last of November. I have more, but that is sufficient. I have not told a single <u>fib</u> or equivocated in the slightest degree on the subject, but people have no idea of the relation we sustain towards each other—they only think such a thing may happen some time hence—on your return, maybe. I have not visited any since I wrote you last but we have had company almost constantly. What a consuming of time it is unless our hearts have choice.

With your letter, dear Edward, came one from your mother which I have been anxiously expecting. She expresses her pleasure but does not say as much as I hoped she would have done. I shall write very soon to her and hope she will in answer write more fully. She speaks of your boys [Eddy and Charley] and says I can make what I please of them both. I will do my best, dear Edward, and hope it is not presumptuous in me to undertake so valuable and responsible a charge. With your acceptance, and that promised from God to all who seek it, I hope to perform my duty.

Mr. [Ben] Drake and Harriet [Drake][5] reached the city the day before your mother wrote. Mr. Drake was quite sick at Springfield and on his return was not so well as when he left home. I fear he will never again have health. I hoped much from his journey and he certainly was much better whilst here. I received a letter from Harriet during her stay at Springfield in which she makes many enquiries, and solicits my confidences—she speaks as though she had intimations from you. I just wish everybody would interest themselves more in their own affairs and permit us to remain quiet.

You had best not allude so often to Col. Madeira,[6] my good friend—have you forgotten 'tis in my power to retort? For instance, only make a comparison between Miss C[atharine] B[eecher][7] and my humble self—think of her strong and cultivated intellect, ponder well upon the improvement you might have derived from her rational conversation—these and a thousand other advantages you slighted, and all for poor, ignorant, unpretending, rustic—me. I hope the recollection will not pain you severely, dearest, only sufficient to quiet your apprehension of the above-named gentleman.

This day two weeks ago you were with me all day—could wishes restore you, you were with me now. I have particularly thought of you today and desired your company, maybe because I am a little indisposed—four weeks will soon pass away, I hope, and then you will soon be here again. You will enjoy the remainder of your journey—tell me what Sister Sarah says to you. We were a little surprised to see Frank yesterday morning, but very much pleased—he is thinner than I have ever seen him and I fear not in very firm health. Since I wrote you last, our society has sustained a severe loss in the death of Mrs. Bussard, mother of the gentleman with whom you are acquainted.[8] She was a bright Christian and in the church and Sabbath School will be more missed than any other member would have been. I will talk to you of her, for she was one I highly valued.

Do you know that your last letter quieted some fears that you might not at some future day become a public man? You once, if I mistake not, said something of the kind, and it <u>grieved</u> me. We must both change, my own dear Edward, if the honors in the world's bestowal ever be the object of our desires or ambition. I have an ambition to make you happy and be so myself in the performance of duty—I am unacquainted with my heart if it cherish any other. Farewell now, dearest. Heaven keep thee and restore thee to thine own Margaret.

[Postscript] I am almost afraid my last letter wearied you, yet I am not sure if I were free from a headache, but this would be just as full. If I write next week I shall direct my letters to Hartford unless I hear from you, and then my last letter, two weeks hence, will meet you at New York. 'Tis a lovely evening and a walk through the woods with thee would cure me. Do you remember how you cured my head in Cincinnati? There is a tenderness in Mother's manner towards me since you left which deeply touches my heart. Sometimes, dear Edward, I think I ought not to leave her. She says "My Child" oftener and seems more than ever anxious about my health. I am a little disappointed today but hope my letter is not very gloomy. I hope to be better to-morrow. Have no concern on my account. Mr. Drake sent me last week's *Chronicle* in which is your first letter from Chillicothe.[9] Pray, in y'r second, did you gratify the public with a minute account of certain transactions deeply interesting to <u>certain</u> persons you wot of? Good-bye and soon come to me. You will, you do think often of me. Ever yours, MW

Cincinnati
Sept. 9th, 1838

My dear Margaret, do you think I was not disappointed when last night's mail came in and brought <u>no</u> <u>letter</u>? Indeed, I was in some <u>slight</u> <u>hope</u> of receiving one on Thursday. But <u>that</u>, I grant, was rather unreasonable. Still, I had no doubt of getting one Saturday. But, I will say nothing, for you have no doubt done right. Either you waited for <u>my</u> letter and had not time to put it in, or you were away, or something. But one thing, my dear, I wish you would remember—your letters are now, literally to be my <u>food</u>. I am far more solitary than you are aware of. In the first place, there is nobody at our place but Mother and Eddy who have any interest in me. I mean <u>at</u> <u>home</u>. And although I was very glad to see her, and although I am rejoiced in my little darling Eddy, yet, they are neither anywhere near my age, and cannot sympathize in the feelings of my heart. What I feel for you cannot be imparted to anyone, and if it were, would not be understood.

I feel a <u>loneliness</u> here, which you cannot imagine. My only sister[10] is far away, and brothers I have none. One of my two darlings [Charley] is also far away, and the house which was once my home is before my sight, to me, desolate. And <u>you</u>, who are the only human being who can talk to me in the language of the heart, or holds the power to restore my lost home, are too, absent, and can be spoken to only in these cold tracings of the pen. Ah! my dear Margaret, there is a loneliness which you have never felt—may, and I hope, never will feel. The loneliness of feeling that there is not one on earth to whom you can pour out the feelings of a heart, warm to all, that would receive it kindly. While I have you to speak to and write to, I can never feel this again. But something akin to it I do feel when I think how long I must remain <u>from</u> <u>you</u>, and when I look around me, and see many evidences of a bitter sorrow which is past, but not forgotten.

I confess I have hardly ever felt more melancholy than since my return. One reason is that I am quite dyspeptic, which of course colors my vision; another is that on my return I found my pecuniary affairs in more confusion than I liked,[11] and another is, that I have not yet settled down to a regular business, which with me is necessary to health and spirits.

Yesterday, I went out to the grave of poor Mary who, with her child, are buried in the Presbyterian ground.[12] I found the monument, which has been some time making, finished, and while it was very simple, it was, I think on the whole the most neat and architectural of any in the yard. Never was the past, present and future so blended and mixed up in my mind as they have been the past week. <u>You</u> will not think the worse of me that the dead is remembered when I stand in the midst of these memorials of the past. But if remembered, it is with warm hopes and ardent longings to fold <u>you</u> to my heart, never again to part while life remains, and with full knowledge that you can and will occupy my affections and fill all my desires.

Now, I suppose you want to know what folks say here. In truth, the people are so polite, or respectful to me, that they say very little to <u>me</u>. As Ben said, they do not jest with me. There has been much talk I know but exactly what I do not know. I think it likely some folks are <u>disappointed</u>, both for me and for you. But that is only to be <u>guessed</u> <u>at</u>. Dr. [Daniel] Drake says not a word to me. And, what do you think—the Dr. came over here yesterday to ask <u>Mother</u> when <u>it</u> <u>was</u> <u>to</u> <u>take</u> <u>place</u>, etc.—and <u>Mother</u> did <u>not</u> <u>know</u>, for I had not told her. I thought they might both of them have <u>asked</u> me. But in truth, everybody is very polite. Benny says he shall make out a regular <u>bill</u> against me for [a] 17- day detention at Springfield and at a dollar a day, etc.! He asked me how I came to take away <u>his</u> <u>sweetheart</u>, and I told him I had not meddled with <u>Mrs.</u> <u>Coons</u> whereupon he looked blank. Gen'l <u>Hodges</u> says I have taken his sweetheart, etc., etc.[13]

I called upon [the] Misses Galloway, etc., but did not see them.[14] I had no invitation to the wedding where I had intended going. I met Albert Galloway in the street. He looks well. But he turned quickly from me, I <u>thought</u>, a little confused. This may have been suspicion. But I thought he looked a little embarrassed, as one who is reminded of something unpleasant.[15] He is going in a few days to the West. Little Eddy is getting better. He speaks now quite well. But the dear little thing is as thin as he can be, pale and weak. Some of your friends I have not seen—but will soon.

I have formally declined going to the Legislature. Mother, I think, does not quite like it. She thinks I am made to be a statesman, etc., etc. But I am afraid I am made to be neither rich nor great, etc. If you have mistaken your own character and really <u>are</u> ambitious, and would like to live in style and be distinguished, I wish you would let me know in season that I may strive to attain it. My friends say I have talent, and if so, I may acquire wealth and distinction. But at present, I really <u>feel</u> <u>humble</u> and have small chance of distinction. So, make your choice, to be the wife of one who lives plainly, feels humbly and is contented with doing his duty, or of one who is engaged in acquiring distinction. The latter I may <u>be</u>. The former is what I <u>am</u>. I just saw a letter from Mr. [Charles] Davies[16] in which he speaks of me as being one of the great men out here, etc., etc., and of my constant improvement, etc., etc. The latter I am glad to know. The former is nonsense, although Mr. D. and Mrs. King say it.[17]

Elizabeth D[rake] congratulated <u>me</u> and <u>you</u> but chiefly <u>you</u>.[18] I was quite disposed to <u>resent</u> <u>it</u>, for I thought it would be more polite to flatter my judgement by praising you, than the contrary. But <u>here</u> it is with <u>me</u> as it is at Chillicothe with <u>you</u>. We are perfect <u>nonsuch's</u> at home, and I hope it may turn out to be so in fact, for then we shall be an extraordinary couple. You know I have tried to forewarn you of the uneven and uncertain currents of life, so that you need not be disappointed in me. In person and character, I am what I seem. But in the real business of life there is many a mishap; but that I suppose you know.—

Adena, Sept 14th, 1838
Friday evening

I did think, dear Edward, I would not write again to you this week, but this evening I have such a desire for your presence, for communion with you, that you must endure a letter as 'tis the only method by which my feelings can gain relief. I hope, I <u>know</u>, you will patiently <u>endure</u> as many epistles as I choose to inflict, for you said <u>I</u> <u>might</u> write twice a week. If I could only hear from you every day and see you <u>now</u> and <u>then</u> — I would be a <u>little</u> <u>happier</u> maybe.

Julia with her children and servants has been staying at Adena this week— though she is, as you know, one of the most amiable beings in the world, she is irregular in her ways, and so exceedingly solicitous about her children that I never feel quite easy with her—her constant anxiety is <u>painful</u> to witness. You know I have the misfortune to be nervous at times. The past week has of course been an unquiet one, and at its close I am beginning to weary of bustle—no, that is not the word— but you know what I mean. I feel all the while as though I ought to relieve Julia and so I would, cheerfully, were it in my power. [Her] little <u>Jim</u> is almost well but excessively fretful. Mother has been considerably indisposed but today is well again. I shall not have time to finish to-night as Julia wishes for the pleasure of my <u>charming</u> <u>society</u>. I would not for a pretty thing she knew I was writing to you—she <u>teases</u> me more than anyone else and though I try to look careless, she does <u>worry</u> me and in spite of my efforts my face will grow warm. Mother will be absent next week and I shall be <u>house</u>-<u>keeper</u>—will you come and see how I succeed?

Mr. Campbell spent yesterday visiting with us, or rather with me, for except at tea he saw none of the family. We had <u>long</u> <u>talks</u> about some of our friends—he speaks often of you <u>now</u>, and seems much pleased when I talk of Harriet [Drake]. <u>It</u> <u>is</u> <u>a</u> <u>match</u> <u>if</u> <u>she</u> <u>please</u>, I am certain. Mr. C. will visit Cincinnati next month purposely to see Harriet—he asked my advice and you know what I said. I hope it was right, and that the affair may terminate in the happiness of our two excellent friends. I should <u>grieve</u> if the poor gentleman should be disappointed, and I have <u>grieved</u> enough already for his past disappointment. I almost wish I could tell him how favorably Harriet has spoken of him, but not for the world would I intimate to him that I supposed she had the slightest preference for him—no, no, let him find that out for himself. I did not read the P.S., though Mr. C. asked me to do so. I wish you would tell me what you think are Harriet's feelings—<u>you</u> <u>understand</u> <u>women</u> <u>you</u> <u>know</u>. <u>One</u> you did, dearest—try again, but you know already to some extent.

I received a letter yesterday from a lady who was my room-mate at Mrs. Willard's—we have been separated <u>twelve</u> years, and yet have during all that time kept up a most interesting correspondence. She is one of the most warmhearted, ardent beings in the world—one of the <u>very</u> <u>very</u> few, dear Edward, with whom I have perfect sympathy and whose love has satisfied my heart. We have always been unreserved in our communication with each other, and I have written to her with more freedom than any of my friends. I wrote to her of <u>you</u>, dear Edward, and she expresses her pleasure and desired hers and her husband's remembrances to you. Unlike most ladies, Lucy has written to me more frequently since her marriage; she says her husband will not permit her to neglect me.[19]

Willy has been impatiently waiting an answer to his letter from Albert G. which arrived only this evening. Albert excused himself for not having written sooner, as he had not, till the day he wrote to Willy, formed his plans. He says he is engaged as an attendant at a wedding in Columbus on the 26th this month, and after that he will visit <u>Will</u> and <u>me</u> and set out on his <u>journey</u> <u>west</u> about the first of October. William cannot with safety endure exposure, especially to cold, and I regret that he must begin his journey when the winter is so near.

Should I write to Elizabeth Worthington, dear Edward, and <u>enlighten</u> her?[20] I shall finish this to-morrow evening, after I have read your letter that to-morrow's mail will bring me.

Saturday evening. No, there is no letter for me, and I did not positively expect one but I only thought, dearest Edward, maybe you might write. I had something else to say but I have forgotten it since I came to town. How is your health now? And do you keep your promise of rising early or have you begun yet to act upon it? I have not been up at night at eleven since you left, nor more than once or twice later than quarter past ten, but I assure you it requires <u>resolution</u> to make <u>myself</u> obey. I think of you and know you wish me to enjoy health, and though I think I might have an hour more, I will do as you wish. I am more precious to myself, my dear Edward, since I can make you happier—I would be whatever you wish me—for your sake, I wish I was <u>more</u> and better than I am—no reflections on your judgement, however.

Miss E[lizabeth] Drake was right—and I like her the better for her sincerity —she knows you, and—she does not know me. No letter till Tuesday!

Well, I am well and happy—should I <u>desire</u> more? How is dear little Eddy? I hope well by this time—it was partly on his account that I wished for a letter. Kiss the dear little fellow for me. Tell me everything when you write—I can understand maybe more than you think.

Will your mother come to Chillicothe? You owe me two letters, for this is the second since I received yours. In my first I urged your mother's coming and hoped she would do so and bring Eddy—do not let him forget me. Cannot Mr. Drake accompany your mother, should she think best to visit us? He told me that he would be here this fall. Good-bye—I hope you are well and patiently bearing your troubles. Wish it was in my power, dear Edward, to do <u>anything</u> for you. I shall not always be so useless, I hope. I am very seldom in town; the air there is <u>thick</u> with dust—the continued drowth [sic] is painful to endure—the effects, I mean. I am reminded of the Scripture expression, "The earth Languisheth."[21]

I have just remembered the concluding sentence of my last letter which was to this effect—that I would never write to you more than once a week and I did not think I should. We heard from Arthur and Ellen a day or two since—they will be home within a fortnight. Mother will go next week to the Madison place[22] and Ellen Waddle promises to stay with me.[23] She is with me now and I asked her if she would read <u>this</u>—"Certainly, with pleasure." But I said you had a right to the first perusal of your letters and then you would do as you pleased. You will not receive this till Tuesday eve'g. Write often next week, for I will maybe be alone if Ellen should fail to keep her promise. Cousin Henry Massie was at Adena this afternoon.[24] I think you will like him—he was absent when you were last here. I do not love farewells, but yet—farewell again.

Adena, Sept. 20th, 1838
Wednesday eve'g

Your last letter, my dear Edward, did not reach me till yesterday evening though 'tis dated only a week ago. I do not receive letters sooner by way of Columbus, indeed not as soon as by the regular mail. You have my last <u>precious epistle</u>? and do I not write <u>very</u> often, especially when I have nothing very particular to say? I would much rather talk, to say truth, but as I can't do <u>that</u>, my only recourse is to scribble a <u>few</u> of my random thoughts. Only think of my selfishness, to write chiefly for <u>my</u> <u>own</u> gratification.

An Excerpt From Margaret's 1852-55 Diary, *Courtesy of C.W. Wells*

West Point Sunday Augt 29th, 1852

      It is twenty six years since I paid my last & first visit here. I was then, fourteen years old, a pupil at Mrs. Willards & just recovering from a severe illness & Mrs. Willard kindly took me with her to New York for a few days & returning left me with Col. & Mrs. Mansfield—it was before my husband's first marriage. How little I thought then of the near relation in which I should be to him when I had not even seen him—nor did I think much more of it when I visited Mrs. Mansfield in Cincinnati twelve years later [in 1838].—Strangely are our destinies brought about, - truly I have been led in a way I knew not.

I have left Ellen Waddle and Mr. Massie in undisturbed possession of a certain large room you may remember and stolen away to write to you. Mother left home yesterday with William and will be absent probably till Friday. Ellen kindly kept her promise of staying with me and we have passed the time quite pleasantly. Somehow or other, we talk much of your own dear self. Ellen, I believe, <u>likes</u> the <u>subject</u>, and I am willing to gratify her innocent fancy, particularly when I can do so without a very great <u>self-sacrifice</u>.

Shall I thank you, my dearest Edward, for anticipating my wishes? On a former occasion you spoke of "difficulties," and in your letter preceding the last wrote something of having found your "pecuniary affairs in confusion," etc., so that I was certain you must have anxieties on the subject and in my last I told you to write me <u>everything</u>—not specifying, lest you might think me inquisitive. Why should I not know of any, every thing that troubles you? Have I not a <u>right</u>, Edward? The solemn manner in which you <u>ushered in</u> the subject in your letter very much alarmed me. I feared for your health, for Eddy, for your mother, and as rapidly as possible hurried over your <u>kind</u> scruples about troubling me to ascertain what calamity was threatened. You will believe me when I say that I was much relieved when I read what you scrupled to tell and am most grieved that you should have so much care and that I could in nothing aid you. It is not as you feared a <u>burden</u> to me to hear of anything which affects you painfully; therefore, my dearest, do not hesitate to communicate all that troubles you and you know assuredly I sympathize with you sincerely. Your health, I fear will suffer—do care for it, Edward. If you are like me, care and anxiety will have a most unhappy effect and scarce give you a chance of being well— therefore, 'tis your duty to keep your mind calm when it is <u>possible</u> to do so. Yours are troubles surely, but they are not the worst that could befall us. I trust in God our happiness is fixed too surely above this world to be materially interrupted by its many vexing cares. I fear much you are troubled on my account—dearest Edward, my greatest grief will be to see you unhappy. As I told you, I know but little of business matters, less than I ought. I know something of the difficulties attending a state of embarrassment from the experience of my brother James who has had the management of my father's estate which was left, as is usual with public men, deeply involved. I am selfish enough to applaud your resolution of serving yourself in preference to the public (<u>for awhile, you say</u>). I have seen and felt in my earlier life too much of the unhappy consequences attending a public life ever to have [a] very strong taste for it, even if I were ambitious.

I am distressed that our dear little Eddy has not entirely recovered; the city is not a proper place for him during the warm weather and I hope your mother will bring him to Adena. I will write to her in a few days—or, I will wait till Mother's return; perhaps she will write, as I know she very much desires a visit from your mother. But unless the river should rise, how could your mother perform the journey? Not in the stage over those rough roads—neither she nor Eddy could bear that. But you can arrange that matter; only I must have them here. Mother has wished several times she had Eddy here; all her grand-children are sent to Adena when they are sick and we have strong faith in the efficacy of the air and treatment which invariably restores them.

Ellen W. has been poring over your last _Chronicles_ and half read your last speech to-day, [when] company interrupted us. By the by, I must deliver Mother's message; she bade me thank you and say she was most flattered that you should send her your speech which she read with interest. She certainly does like you vastly, my own Edward, even though you had the misfortune to receive breath in New England.[25]

I hear very little about us now. Either the people think the matter too serious for a joke, or I look dignified, for they say nothing to me. Ellen tells me occasionally a little gossip. Benjamin has been a very busy person in serving us from the beginning. He told Mrs. Jesse Williams[26] that I need not deny or attempt a denial of certain reports, as our marriage was as certain as anything could be in this uncertain world. Now, 'tis nothing to me what they say—but Benny has not done right and has rather lost favor with me by his zeal in telling more than he knew. My love to your mother, to dear Eddy and to thyself, dear Edward. Good-bye—love always, your own Margaret.

Chillicothe Oct. 2nd, 1838
Tuesday eve'g

Edward, my own and best Edward, how could you be sad at anything I could say? I have this instant finished your letter and as speedily as possible hasten to reply. I am not sad nor hurt, but I am pained at the idea that you should think I could mean anything but affection for you. What if I did say I loved flowers, my home, etc. Would I exchange you for aught on the earth? Are you not dearer than a thousand homes, flowers—and surely, I need not tell you so. And what if I did say I might be a burden to you—I may be yet, dearest, though I do hope not—won't you let me jest? May I not love and praise a flower? You must be, indeed, as you said you were, a very jealous man. I grieve to admit that I am a little mortified by your last letter. I did think you better knew me. I don't know that I ought to answer your <u>unpleasant reflections</u>, for doubtless the fit has passed away. Indeed, <u>you</u> must not <u>indulge</u> in gloom—take to yourself what you said to me, now, my own dear Edward. I have at times awful seasons of depression, but I know I shall live through them and generally what is the cause of them. I had one day of real self-torment last week and even a letter from you did not remove it. I thought you had not said half as much as you might have done; then I remembered that I was not myself and laid your letter aside till night when I went to my quiet room and read it again—having come to my right mind again. 'Twas your last, dearest, before this evening's, and as kind, as warm as it could be, and the second reading made me happy.

Dear Edward, why will you doubt me? I came to town this evening, certain of getting a letter and so well pleased with the anticipation that my spirits rose higher, higher, so high, I am glad to say, that even your chiding letter cannot quite depress them. The truth is that I am perfectly assured of your love for me, and so calmly happy in that confident assurance that it must take more than one expression of gloom to destroy my happiness. I do grieve that you have not, as I thought, the same confidence in me. I cannot thank you for wishing yourself richer, or that your house had grounds about it. You owe me amends for that—for it implies I should love you better if . . . Edward, you did not, would not, mean that; if I thought you did, we should have a quarrel outright, but I know better and shall not indulge <u>you</u> by permitting you to indulge yourself in gloomy fancies—you have no right to do it. If you ever have had, I have taken it from you, and unless you wish to <u>bless</u> me with <u>misery</u>, you must overcome it. I read your letter so hastily that I may (as you have done mine) have caught a wrong meaning. The first half page told me it must be answered immediately and I am in haste, hoping this may go in to-morrow's mail. Write to me immediately. I shall scarcely, I fear, be happy till your next letter comes.

I have come to town for a week to visit my friends and <u>be happy</u>, but unless I can believe you are at least comfortable, I rather fear a small measure of <u>content</u> will be mine. Now I feel much more grave than when I began to write and if you were here and we were talking the matter over, I fear I might be baby enough to cry—so I will hurry and go see Ellen Waddle, for I am to stay with her to-night. I walked in the garden last night with the very best of good company—sweet thoughts of you— and by the bright moonlight pulled a rose which I will send to-night in <u>this</u> to you. I had thought I could send it whole but you shall [have] the leaves only. I might chance with the stem to send you another thorn—for my life, I would not do that— and yet you think I did, willfully, Edward.

I wrote to Elizabeth Worthington a day or two since. Go and see her—I love her—she knows of our engagement. She is too partial to me, but you need not believe what she says. I will love you better if you will tell me everything that troubles you, even though it be my own errors. Write freely, dear one, even at the risk, as you seem to think, of making me unhappy. I tell you, you cannot do that unless you wish to do so. Do not count this as a letter—I will write soon again. I have written this as hastily as my pen <u>could</u> do my bidding. Your mother's letter came with yours—I will tell you of it again. Now farewell for a day or two—you have this evening received my last letter written on Sat. I shall receive an answer on Thursday. So good-bye, my best, but naughty Edward. Good-bye—do you love me?   Margaret

Adena, Oct. 12th, 1838
Friday Evening
[Postmarked Oct. 15th]

Your last was a very dear letter and gave me great comfort, my own Edward, but I greatly fear <u>my</u> <u>last</u> was anything but a <u>comfort</u> to you. I could not help writing it, for I was oh, so unhappy and most grievously disappointed that I did not receive another <u>comforter</u> at the time I hoped. I tried very hard to elicit a cheering influence from your <u>grievous</u> letter and kept it by me constantly for many days that I might read it whenever I was <u>most</u> <u>sad</u>—but you who wrote it, dearest, can judge its effect on myself. I almost fancied I deserved your contempt though nothing told me in your letter that you had awarded me my deserts. I like your <u>last</u> very well—it may be often read without depressing my spirits—it was, and is, dearest, a great comfort to me.

Just think of me visiting about, making calls, spending "sociable evenings" etc. all of last week and I just about as anxious as I could be and grieving lest you were quite as much so. Now, if I had not been a <u>simpleton</u>, I would have remembered that gentlemen do not break <u>their</u> hearts about such matters; nothing could for a moment banish you from my heart, let me be ever so much engaged— well, it is right, I <u>reckon</u>. I give myself <u>due</u> importance, you will observe. I commenced my letter to-night, for I shall be busy to-morrow as we have company and I shall not have time to write a whole letter.

I received a letter from Amanda G[alloway] yesterday; don't tell her secrets, but I must tell you—she is to marry Mr. Trotter[27] in <u>June</u> and recommends May to me, no you—<u>us,</u> <u>that</u> is right. We shall talk of that matter when we meet again. I wish to do, my dearest Edward, whatever you think will make you <u>happiest</u>. If you know as much of me as I do, you would be so patient. Sometimes I am impatient that I cannot see you—so many little matters occur that I would like to tell you and so many thoughts, too. For several days I have been thinking a great deal of your boys, and how much responsibility I should assume. Sometimes, Edward, I fear I am presumptuous in undertaking to perform the duties of mother. I can but do my best [that] God requires, and you, my dearest, ask no more. You have said I shall not have very much to do for them, but I know, and you know, otherwise. It is best I should think of it —I shall be better prepared for my <u>office</u>. Do not mistake me—you will not.

Mrs. Galloway has been in town a week—she is <u>exceedingly</u> gratified by our arrangements. Mr G. arrived last night[28]—and almost his first words to me were, "And so, Miss Margaret, I understand you have been studying Constitutional law, political economy, etc., and how do you like it?"[29] To which I made reply that I had found the study far more interesting than I had ever thought possible. He laughs at me <u>prodigiously</u>, but so very pleasantly that 'tis no way annoying.

I am so delighted that I have discovered a way to stop Julia. I must tell you — I have only to revert to the time she <u>listened</u> to your conversation with James and she instantly becomes <u>quiet</u>. James and Julia expect to be in Cincinnati, I think, about or soon after the twentieth of the month. They will stay at Mr. [John G.] Worthington's. I asked Julia what pretty thing she would bring me from the city, and with the most ridiculous mock-sentimental air she replied. "A lock of dear Eddy's hair," meaning <u>you</u>, you know. There is a hint for you. I had a letter from sister Sarah last week but she does not say much beyond expressing her pleasure. I told you what she said on one point. Willy has been compelled to relinquish his Western trip on account of the river being unnavigable.

Sat. night. Mr. and Mrs. Galloway are with us tonight. We all sat talking so long that I have but little time to write—'tis past ten now and I must finish tomorrow. I received your last letter—do tell me what you were thinking of when you wrote part of that letter? Not of me, my precious—I do love to laugh at you some times, and wish you were here this <u>very</u> <u>minute</u> that I might have that pleasure. About my faults, poor fellow, you will one day say I was right, though you now say I <u>can't</u> frighten you.

I am much gratified, dear Edward, by Mrs. Catlin's approval, and thank you for telling me.[30] I wish, oh, how sincerely, I was better capable of fulfilling the very serious duties which will soon devolve upon me. Sometimes it makes me sad, the fear that I should fail to fulfill your expectations, for I know you think better of me than I deserve. How I long to talk with you sometimes—I ought to see more of you— won't you stay two weeks when you come?

Do not ask me to prescribe for your health lest I fall into an error common with physicians, that of prescribing, or at least <u>recommending</u> what is most agreeable to themselves. I grieve that you should suffer so much—do you not think you might be cured? You prescribe for me, and one of these days, I shall I return the civility. Indeed, you are not prudent in many things—I know better than you. I shall anticipate Christmas as eagerly as, when a child, I used to count the days, almost the hours, for half the year beforehand.

Mrs. Douglass[31] is very undecided about going to Cincinnati. She wishes to go but thinks it will be impossible, at least for awhile. She has two nieces visiting her.

And so you really accuse Harriet of being in love—well, the nameless person will present himself, I <u>think</u>, very soon in your city and throw himself on her <u>tender mercies</u>. I hope she will not be hardhearted. There was a very pleasant party at James's on Thursday and Mr. G. and I had a great deal of talk. You will be much pleased with Mr. Galloway's family and of them, I think you will like none better than Sarah and Patterson Browne.[32] Sally says she will love you very much though she used to be almost afraid of such a demure-looking gentleman. I hope Amanda will be happy, she seems much attached to Mr. Trotter. O, dear Edward, the woods are so beautiful! How I wish you could look on them with me.

I received a letter from Anne James[33] yesterday; you remember she is in Lexington. She gives me a downright scolding for having been guilty of the indiscretion of giving <u>heart</u> and <u>hand</u> to a <u>stranger</u> and all without her advice or even consent. She says Mr. Chase was in Lexington some time since but she did not see him, which she much regrets as she wishes to talk with him about <u>Mr. Mansfield</u>.[34] I shall write to her and tell her <u>part</u> of the truth and the remainder when she returns home. I have a <u>heap</u> of letters to answer. I cannot write now as I used to do when I sat up as late as I pleased. I am much engaged during the day and have always preferred writing at night.

I did not think Harriet's a wicked letter—not quite so amiable as her last, but I attributed that to something I had said, but I cannot imagine what it was. Now as I am about closing, do let me beg you to be as patient as possible and not give way to depression of spirits. I do not mean on my account, but in all circumstances in which you may be placed. I know you have much care and trouble and regret more than I can say that I cannot relieve you. I do wish you to be happy. Harriet tells me you have had a "terrible fit." I can sympathize sincerely with you and maybe, if I were with you, I might do you good. I rejoice to hear that Eddie is well again. I am, and all are much disappointed that your mother did not visit us. A gentleman preached to-day who reminded me somewhat of you. Give dear little Ed a kiss for me.

Good-bye—always love, your own Margaret

[Postscript] Amanda says she envies me my residence in Cincinnati, where of all places she would prefer living, but she says she does <u>not</u> envy me <u>my</u> <u>boys</u> that seem to make me so proud. Now she is wrong—I would give her what she covets, but not our pets.

Adena, October 19th, 1838
Thursday Evening
[Postmarked Oct. 20th]

I was in town to-day, dear Edward, and received from our kind friend Mr. C. a present of some very nice pens which tempt me to scribble. I have been thinking to whom I should write; my <u>conscience</u> told me to answer a <u>quantity</u> of letters I received last week, but somehow, when I seated myself <u>pen</u> in hand, it just occurred to me to write to you to-night, though I did not intend so doing till—<u>to-morrow</u>.

James and Julia will set out for Cincinnati on Wednesday in the stage— several days later than their first intention, but the court is in session this week and James cannot well leave home. Mother sent me shopping (a detestable business) for her to-day, but the rain came on before I had accomplished my purchases and so I spent the day with Julia. I looked into the post office box no. <u>119</u> thinking maybe <u>somebody</u> might have written to me—but nothing but newspapers were handed to me. I never in my life went myself to the office until since I have had the honor, dearest, of your correspondence. Julia really amuses me by her ideas of propriety with regard to <u>engaged</u> <u>people</u>. She has no idea, I presume, how often I write to you. I don't care that she should—but indeed, to me her opinions of such things are quite too overstrained for nature. I remember to have given you some of them. They exhibit a great lack of confidence in the parties toward each other. It may be natural to Julia, but it would be downright affectation in me to act according to her rules of propriety.

Did I ever tell you what Elizabeth Worthington said of you? It amused me so much that I will extract a <u>little</u> for your benefit. After speaking of <u>us</u>, she says of you,

"I have seen the gentleman since my return and indeed he is a very altered man—so gay (!) and so very affectionate in his manners. I understand he is just so to every one he has ever seen you with—indeed, he met me as a relation, and I could not help showing him my satisfaction," etc., etc. What business have people to make remarks?

I am very glad to hear of your intention of going into society this winter, on my account as well as your own, for you know, dear Edward, I shall need your aid in the selection of my friends, even my visiting acquaintances. I have but few now in the city and I am not sorry.

How do you progress in your habits of order, and the reformation you spoke of some time ago? I intend to ask Harriet some of these times if she has seen threads on your coat of late—that was a scandal of Benny's—he and I will have a settlement some of these times, and I'll not forget that.

Do you know that some of the friends of Athens College[35] expect Mr. McGuffie [sic] to accept the Presidency of that institution? They do, and amongst them none seem so sanguine as a Mr. Stone who was in Cincinnati some short time since; he told me it was his opinion that if Mr. McG. were not under personal obligations to continue in Cincinnati, he would unhesitatingly go to Athens. What do you think of it? Mr. McGuffie said positively to me last spring he would not leave his college—James too, thinks with Mr. Stone.[36] By the way, Mr. Stone said he had seen a Mr. Mansfield in Cin.—dined with him at Mr. McGuffie's and was much pleased with the remarkable simplicity of his character and manners. [He] asked me if I had ever seen him, if he had ever been at our house, what was my opinion of him, how he stood in public estimation, if he was a married man and a thousand other questions—looking intently at me all the while. He had evidently heard rumours and was trying what he could get from me, for he brought up your name whenever he could. I perceived his design, and my pride aiding me, answered as calmly as though you, my dear Edward, had been a mere acquaintance. I am sure my entire self-possession punished my inquisitor; he told me amongst other things that you had invited him to see you but said you were either building, or removing to a new house, which was the reason he did not accept your invitation.

Are you not fearful that I shall forget you? You had best write often for many reasons, amongst them this—your last letter is always read every day till the next one arrives; now, you know, if they are too "far between" I might weary of many readings of even a most interesting epistle—do you think I should?

I think I never before looked with so many sad thoughts on the fading of summer's beauties, not fading, but decay. The woods are beautiful, but they do not inspire the "sweet sorrow" of past seasons—can't. I wonder that I need your presence? O, is it the thought that I shall not again, as I have done, watch and admire the brilliant hues, the bright decay of my native woods? I don't know what the cause is, but I wish you were here to talk with me about it. Thank you for your hint about "roving imagination." I need it, dearest, more than you may be aware. If you do <u>your duty</u>, you will find and strive to correct many, very many faults in me. I only wish you knew how many, that you might nerve yourself to the task. I am afraid you will overlook them, and my <u>lamentable</u> deficiencies in every respect. I hope not for I expect you to do much for me—as much as for Eddy, and truth be, a difficult matter, too . . . <u>How</u> <u>is</u> <u>Miss</u> <u>Beecher</u>? . . . The rain is falling almost in torrents, I hope your river will be benefitted thereby. What if your mother should return with Julia? Love to you and little Eddy. I continue to keep <u>good</u> hours. Good-bye, dearest Edward.

Margaret

[Postscript] Mr. Galloway told me I must be very particular in my style and manner of writing to you, as you were a writer and nice judge of such matters—thinks I, if he did but see my <u>slovenly</u> letters.

Julia says she expects to be weary of your affectionate attentions—she said that, dearest, to tease me, in which laudable effort she is often engaged.

Adena, Oct. 31st 1838
[Postmarked Nov. 2nd]

I knew another letter would come to-night, Edward. I was sure you would write as soon as you received my letter by Julia. Thank you for it, dearest. I have had three letters in the last week and they have been precious letters all, and made me very happy—you write as though you were well and in good spirits. What, than that intelligence, can be more pleasing to me? And you got the flowers— but I did not send them to you—<u>remember</u>—they tell <u>you</u> nothing—well—if they stirred one pleasant thought of me I am repaid. I thought you would like to see some flowers from Adena.

Thank [you] for your kind cautions about my health, but they are needless now, for I am quite well. No sooner did I pronounce my cold <u>obstinate</u>, than it left me and for a week I have been better than for a month. As a proof, I will tell you that I <u>walked</u> to town to breakfast yesterday, spent the day at my uncle's, and <u>walked</u> home in the evening, bringing my cousin Virginia with me. Did I not tell you I was becoming more than ever precious in my own eyes? I promise you I shall take the very best care of <u>everything</u> you value. You say you love me, and—I, of course, believe you in part. I <u>do</u> believe you speak truth. So, for your comfort I'll tell you I am well, happy, and love to think of you. I have suffered very much from a severe cold, but thought 'twas not worth while to tell you, for I hoped it would soon pass away. It did not, however, but it has quite left me now—and I had no <u>cough</u> <u>at</u> <u>all</u>.

Today is [the anniversary of] Sarah [Galloway] Browne's wedding day. Dear Edward, how little did I anticipate my present engagements on this day a year ago—it seems but a little while, and how plainly is the scene of this eve'g last year before me.

All the years of my life have been filled with the mercies and blessings from my Creator, yet surely, dearest Edward, the last year has brought me the richest, the most precious. I wish I could talk with you of what now is in my heart. I had a letter last night from Amanda G. She, too, expresses herself astonished beyond measure at the <u>chances</u> which have befallen her since Sarah's wedding day. She first met Mr. Trotter in Lexington whither she accompanied her sister on a bridal visit. I do hope Mr. Trotter is worthy of Amanda. She says Mr. T. much opposes deferring their marriage till June and hopes my plans will just suit to aid her in mounting the opposition. She is quite willing to be <u>bridesmaid</u>, and if she is engaged to be so, of course the gentleman will be forced into acquiescence. I do think gentlemen are <u>exceedingly</u> unreasonable sometimes. Not you, my dearest— you knew it was best— but they all are so hasty. Does it argue vanity by the supposition that they can supply so much more than home? I know that is not the motive, but I do not like the way these things are arranged usually.

With your letter to-night came one from Anne James. She says, "<u>Can</u> it be? <u>Is</u> it so? What a change must have been wrought in a few months, when Margaret Worthington consents to leave her much loved home, become a city lady! And with a citizen, too, of Cincinnati, a place for which I know she has not much partiality. Truly, Maggy, I shall be forced into a belief that love is all powerful," etc., etc., to the end of the letter. Should I feel gratified by the regret my friends express at my leaving Chillicothe? Is it not selfish? Yet I do not wish to give them pain; it is only the regard evinced by the regret which is pleasing to me. Many ask if you could not, might not, be persuaded to come here—to which I answer, decidedly no. I have not tried my powers, for in truth I should not like to think you could be so easily moved. So, you do not like scolding—-very well, sir, take care not to deserve it, for I promise you shall have your <u>dues</u> in that way.

Thursday. My "hour for retiring" stopped me last night—thank you, dearest, for the kind things you said of me, but indeed I do not deserve them. I am sure 'tis for my good—in spite of Caleb Atwater's information, I am not out of health—how came he to know so much of me?[37] And in wonder's name, how is it that <u>everybody</u> is so well acquainted with our affairs? We have the full approbation of <u>Jesse L. Williams</u>. Mrs. W. was formerly Miss Creighton and one whom I love very much. She is now here on a visit. I went to see her a day or two ago and she asked me when I would keep my promise of visiting her at Indianapolis. I hoped sometime. "O yes, she said, I shall hope to see you <u>now</u>." Then Mr. W. complimented us <u>through</u> <u>each</u> <u>other</u> and Susan said she was well <u>acquainted</u> with you by means of *The Chronicle*. I did not, for I <u>could</u> not deny, and so I <u>looked</u> <u>simple</u> I suppose, much to the amusement of my friends. You would be much more interested in Mrs. W. than her husband. I always marveled <u>why</u> she fancied him—but you know there is a mystery in these matters.

I do not remember what I said to your mother of my faults, and what right, sir, have you to see her letters? Be content with your own. I <u>might</u> choose to say something to your mother of you, which you <u>might</u> not like. I think we had as well let the subject of our mutual faults rest, for the present at least. There seems to be a most unworthy desire <u>to</u> <u>outdo</u> each other in exposing ourselves—that is rather unusual I think. So I'll confess to you that I am satisfied that you <u>are</u> very bad indeed sometimes, and you need say no more about it.

What can you tell me of Julia? [Her] little Tom is a dear child—I love to have the care of him. I wrote to Julia, but she has not answered my letter. Not a word have you said of Eddy for <u>three</u> <u>letters</u>. I shall have another letter on Saturday and then I shall not expect many till you have leisure. I promise you not to be troubled. Matthias is waiting for my letter, so, my own Edward, good-bye. Mother, Willy and all are well.   Your own true Margaret.

[Postscript] How do you like my last letter? I have not seen Ellen Waddle for two weeks except in the streets. Willy says you and I carry on a very extensive correspondence—he has brought me your three letters in the last week—<u>but</u>—<u>he</u> does not take mine to the office. I never say to you half I wish but you know to-day is November, and in December you will be here and then if I <u>do</u> <u>not</u> <u>forget</u>, I can talk to you. The last few frosts have robbed the trees of their beauty, but the ground is most beautifully carpeted—oh, so beautiful. 'Tis a good time for the robins to perform their benevolent offices of sexton. Good-bye. Do not I make sad blunders some times?—

Margaret Worthington Mansfield
(1811-1863)
Courtesy of
Mrs. Edward Mansfield Swiggett

Edward Deering Mansfield
(1801-1880)
Courtesy of
Edith Dudley Sylla

"April 24. Our memorable day [thirteenth wedding anniversary] & this time Edward did not forget it. I have been sitting for my picture to [Thomas Buchanan] Read and he has made a very satisfactory likeness & good picture my friends say — he is now painting Mr. Mansfield & I hope will be even more successful." (MWM's April 24, 1852 diary entry).

Part Seven
"... love and fear so closely by each other"
Letters to Edward Mansfield
November 10, 1838 to January 29, 1839

Adena, November 10th, 1838
Saturday night
[Postmarked Nov. 12]

It is only a week, but indeed it seems much longer since I wrote last, dear Edward. I have been expecting the letter you said I should have on Thursday, but I suspect you intended your mother's should supply your <u>short</u>-<u>comings</u>. Well, I do not complain, I know I make large demands, and you have many engagements. Do you know that I have <u>half</u> <u>an</u> <u>idea</u> that I need not write so frequently? A day or two since, I asked Elizabeth how often Charles <u>used</u> to write to her. "Oh, <u>very</u> often." "But <u>how</u> often?" She said, generally twice a month, and she wrote <u>once</u> in the same time. Now Lizzy seemed to fear I should think <u>that</u> almost too much, and asked me how often <u>you</u> wrote. Most fortunately for <u>us,</u> a servant at that instant came into the room and addressed a question to me, which prevented a reply. I have no idea how other persons manage their <u>affairs</u>. I only know that I love to write to you, and that your letters give me more pleasure than anything else, and therefore <u>I</u>, and you, write very frequently. I believe—nay, am sure that I have written every week since—<u>July</u>—except whilst you were with me, or on your journey. Lizzy said she thought it right there should be frequent communications, when there was a <u>reasonable</u> prospect of a consummation of matters, and persons had confidence in each other. So, for fear we may quarrel, pray promise me in such a case you will return all my interesting communications. Twice a month! Dearest Edward, I must, I <u>will</u> hear from you oftener than that.

Your last letter came with more speed than usual. I received it on Monday morning—thank you for it a dozen times—your name looked so pretty on the seal. Are you <u>particularly</u> discontented in the winter? All your pictures of discontent are winter scenes—"by the fire"—so we shall have the whole summer without a cloud, for I, too, am usually most happy then. Oh, dear Edward, it is winter now with us—

the flowers are all frozen to death—the beautiful foliage of two weeks ago faded and scattered, and the wind whistles in true winter style through the sorry looking trees. Now is the time to feel the beauty of Brainard's beautifully appropriate lines—do you know them?—commencing thus—"The dead leaves strew the forest walk and withered are the pale wild flowers."[1] But ah! poor man, you are in a city, and so engrossed in the world's duties that you maybe scarce note the change of seasons. I do dearly love the woods in the Autumn, and have almost grieved, and thought it hard, that you could not at my most favorite season take our ramble through the woods with me. I think a year with the Indians would be of service to me—can you guess how?

I am glad I am in any manner a consolation to thee, dearest—may I never be otherwise. And so you were by your own admission <u>very</u> <u>friendly</u> with Julia. I have not seen her except for ten minutes since her return, but she sent me yesterday your pretty "Gift"—for which, my thanks. I opened the envelope, and looked carefully through the book for—what I did not find. I will tell you about it when you come. Julia will doubtless have much to tell me of you. Pray, did you remember to modulate your voice to her delicate ear?

Elizabeth has been with us for a week—last Sunday was the third anniversary of her wedding day. I should not like to think, Edward, that three years should so change me as the past three have changed my sister. She is not the same being—it is a painful change to me—I do not know whether she is sensible of it—but she must be. You have seen Charles, of course—and Arthur—and did you laugh at my present? All Chillicothe seems to be moving towards Cincinnati—have you seen Mrs. Coons?[2] She will seem wondrous wise to you. She asked me if she met anyone very anxious to come to Adena should she bring <u>them</u> or <u>him</u> with her. I told her she would find none anxious to come <u>now</u>—that matter was all arranged—which she said was very strange—wondered how many years such mutual good understanding would continue.

I had a letter day before yesterday from Amanda. She says Mr. Trotter urges her not to defer their marriage till June, and she wishes to know definitely our plans, which advice I cannot give her. Maybe I may be her brides-maid. She is very unwilling to be married before I am and I think the gentleman is unkind to urge her doing so—do not you? I wish all were as kind and considerate and good as you, dear Edward. Amanda does not know what to do.

I received by Julia a letter from Albert [Galloway] which made me sorry, and I answered it immediately. He wrote me three weeks ago and I did not reply to his letter—from which he infers that <u>other</u> <u>correspondents</u> claim all my interest. He is not happy, for he is engaged in no business and feels that 'tis quite time he was settled. I am so glad my flowers reached you ere they faded. Your mother's letter was very kind, and pray do not forget this time to thank her for me. I am afraid I shall be afraid of you some of these days from what you tell me of yourself—'tis what I have never yet been. Are you not forgetting me? Dear, dear Edward—no—I am well—very well and doing my best endeavours to be useful. The folks think we are to be married in a very few weeks. Good-night—good-bye. Your mother said you were in very good health.

Margaret

[Postscripts] I [love] long and frequent letters. Ellen Waddle says you have won her heart, you write so often. She has a mind to rival me—in your good estimation. Lizzy is writing to Charles to-night; I asked to be remembered to my friends in the city. Mr. and Mrs. Peet will be in Cincinnati next week.[3] I have not seen Mrs. Douglass since her return. Again, adieu—may the blessings of God be with you, and by it may we meet soon in health and happiness. Good-bye, love me always.

Margaret

How is Harriet Drake? She will think me a long time in answering her letter but I am waiting Mr. C[ampbell]'s movements. I told him he should take my next letter. Tell Harriet he spent Monday evening with me, and looked well and in good spirits. I do hope Harriet will smile upon him. Your mother always praises dear little Eddy—says it seems impossible to spoil him. Thank you for the manner you wrote my name in the Gift—it pleases me. Lizzy, too, admired it greatly and said Charles would never write her name with his before their marriage for fear, I suppose, some one should see it—well, what if they did? Charles is as timid as a young girl about many things.

Mary Macomb is much pleased with her present[4] "Only see, Aunt M., what Mr. Mansfield sent me." I wish you would let Mr. Thatcher know that his ink is too pale—people do say he will be a cousin of ours sometime.[5] I don't know—I think otherwise. He is not to Sally Swearingen's fancy.

Adena, Nov. 14th, 1838
Wednesday evening
[Postmarked Nov. 20]

It is not very often that I wish so very much to see you, dear Edward, as I chance to do this evening. I don't know why, but I can't banish the vain wish and so I will just write and <u>thus</u> accomplish my purpose. I shall not finish to-night I know for 'tis late, but I have engagements for to-morrow and the next day in town, and shall not have leisure even to write to you. I like best to write from home.

There are two parties in town to-night which we have declined attending. We have two invitations for to-morrow night, only one of which we can accept. Aunt Swearingen gives <u>Lizzy</u> a party—I shall feel almost strange in the <u>world</u> again, but if I have good health I think I shall make my appearance quite often in public this winter, and prove to my friends, "How blessings brighten, as they take their flight."[6]

I learned a secret to-day which, of course, I must tell you, the lady not objecting. Well, Mr. Thatcher <u>is</u> going to be our cousin, though I did say I thought not. Sally Swearingen and Mr. Campbell came out to breakfast this morning and S. stayed all day. I <u>spied</u> a new ring on the young lady's finger and a single question gained me the fact that she and Mr. Thatcher were on <u>very</u> <u>good</u> <u>terms</u>. It has happened very lately—for when I last asked her of the matter she seemed very doubtful, and to-day she told me Mr. T. had not then <u>opened</u> <u>his</u> <u>mind</u>. She says they have not even talked of <u>marriage</u>. Mr. Thatcher must be fifteen years her senior— rather more than you can boast. So now, what do you think of the match? Mr. T. came up just before night to walk to town with Sally; the <u>poor</u> <u>child</u> was in a tremor all the while he was here. I gave her some sewing, but she could not thread her needle—wonderful!—is it not? Sally has not told her parents, even—nor will she permit Mr. Thatcher to do so, so don't you be <u>too</u> frank.

I received your letter on Monday and should have written immediately to quiet your apprehensions of my health, but my last letter had done it in the meantime. I have not seen Mrs. Houghton for weeks—she is not to my liking, and I never visited her. I am well, dear Edward, as well as you would wish, I think, and hope for both our sakes I may always be in as good health. Your letter quite comforted me, and I will tell you why—you know I can't help thinking of you, and on the very day your letter came I was wondering if it were <u>possible</u> that your thoughts could be with me, a <u>thousand</u> times as often as mine with you. I concluded not, and yet I sighed, too, at my conclusion—and I don't often sigh. Then came your letter saying you sometimes thought <u>too</u> <u>much</u> of me—I hope not, but do you, indeed, think it such a trouble to send your thoughts to Chillicothe? Mrs. Douglass was here to-day with some other ladies. She casually mentioned that "Mr. Mansfield said he would <u>pass</u> <u>through</u> Chillicothe the week between Christmas and New Year and she hoped Miss Drake would accompany him." I shall talk to you about your frankness when we meet. Good-night and adieu till Saturday.

One thing I must say lest it be forgotten—I must take the liberty to countermand Madam [Julia] Worthington's orders, and beg you will have nothing to do with my dress. I <u>do</u> <u>not</u> <u>choose,</u> dear Edward, that <u>you</u> should bring it to me—there will be other opportunities, and even should there not, I would rather do without it all winter than that you should have the care of it. Julia was here to-day and I gave her a rare scolding. She told me she thought I had given her directions to have it sent by you—wonderful, again. Mr. Campbell made the pen I write with—pray, dearest, blame <u>him</u> not me—he took especial pains making one, for the special purpose of my writing with it to Harriet—marked her initials on it. Have you seen Charles? Lizzy has not heard from him and she is anxious. Elizabeth has a most particular desire to see one of your letters—and so has Ellen Waddle but unless you take a new pen and write a letter expressly for exhibition I fear they will remain ungratified. Elizabeth does not know you at all, dear Edward—thinks you can talk of nothing but philosophy, politics, or the common occurrences of the times—says you always wearied of talking to her. Good-bye, now. I have had sad thoughts of parting from home, and when <u>they</u> come, I wish most for you.

Monday, 19th—I went with Elizabeth to town on Thursday and most unexpectedly remained till Sunday evening. She wishes me to stay with her. I hoped for a letter on Saturday, dear Edward—you have spoiled me and must now indulge me in consequence. I am writing to you by candlelight this morning, and you are at this same time enjoying a <u>nap</u>. I rise now always before daylight. Last night I scarcely slept and was glad when the morning came. I had Ellen Pomeroy [7] with me and the poor little thing was sick all night. I am glad her mother is not here—she is so very easily alarmed. Charles arrived on Saturday, and Elizabeth will leave us, she says, to-morrow. I am hardly willing she should go, but it must be. Charles merely said you were well; oh no, he said you looked better than he had ever seen you—but did not talk very much about you.

You please me greatly, dearest, by the "prodigious efforts" you are making to attain a most desired end—surely you will succeed—no fears—and what a neat, orderly person I shall see you one of these days. So I must compromise with you about neatness—it may not be necessary, for I assure you I am not, as you say of your mother, the <u>very</u> neatest person in the world. I used to be <u>very</u> <u>particular,</u> but have lost <u>much</u> in that way since my health has not been so good as formerly. If you will make me <u>amiable,</u> I will make you orderly—is it a bargain? It seems a long while since we parted, dear Edward—it will not be very long till you are with me again. We are all engaged to spend to-day with [my sister] Ellen Watts, but little Ellen P[omeroy] seems so sick I shall stay and nurse her. Lizzy does not know it or she would come immediately home. I was at a large party on Thursday night and was congratulated on my re-appearance. I do not like myself in <u>full</u> dress at all. Good-bye, dearest Edward.

Ever your own Margaret

[Postscripts] Do you see Mrs. Coons often? Can her <u>captives</u> be numbered? 'Tis Effie's greatest, her only great fault that she will "stoop to conquer"—so I think.[8] How long will you stay, and when will you come? And will you tell everybody just precisely what you are coming for? Pray leave a little to the imagination, dearest. You are an <u>odd</u> one and I shall have trouble with you. I am glad I know some of your peculiarities. Is your health still good? and your patience unmoved? How many <u>little</u> questions I have to ask you. How is our little Eddy? Ellen Pomeroy is one of the loveliest children I ever knew. Good-bye, and may our God always give us his blessings.   M.W.

Mother is exceedingly pleased with your lecture on the qualifications of Teachers which you sent her some time since.[9] She has a strong inclination to send it to <u>Mr. Bussard</u>—he is an excellent man but has <u>no</u> energy and therefore can be of but little benefit to society—he is very agreeable and interesting in conversation. The gentlemen are <u>amazing</u> civil to me. Poor Col. Taylor[10] is sick and I am going to send him some <u>nice</u> <u>things</u>—is that right? I wish I had your letter which is in the office for sure to-day—but I can write again. I feel now as though I must write again in a few days. What are you about? I wish I could imagine. I'm right glad that people remind you of me occasionally. I hope they will continue their <u>kind</u> <u>offices</u>.

Chillicothe, Nov. 21st, 1838
Wednesday night
[Sent by Arthur Watts]

Did you for a moment, dearest Edward, suppose I thought there was the slightest impropriety in my writing to you very often? I can scarce think you did and yet certain passages in your last letter which I have just received would seem to imply such a supposition. So you will take me in earnest—I fear you were a little out of tune [?] by the grave tone of your letter—I hope not indisposed. But pray thee, dearest, let that matter of propriety rest, and to aid you, I do assure you I cannot believe there would be any impropriety in my writing to you every day—<u>hour</u>, if I pleased so to do. I cannot be made ashamed of that which I am convinced is right and if my frequent letters conduce at all to your happiness I am doing my duty and making us both happier. I will be candid with you, dearest—my only fear is that I might possibly weary you, for I am well aware I do not write very interesting letters; at the same time, I do hope they are always acceptable to you as evidence of my affection for you. Again, I do not choose that others who hold different opinions from mine should laugh at us as being too very <u>affectionate</u>, and therefore do not care about saying how often I write.

I do wish to see you, Edward—so many things I wish to say that may not be written. I must say good-night, for 'tis half past ten, and though I would rather write than sleep I will stop, and rise betimes in the morning and finish. I was at a party last night till nearly eleven. If it would do any good, I could <u>cry</u> to see you—to-night, but it is no use, so good-night.

Thursday Morning. Give me credit for patience, dear Edward, for I deserve it I assure you; although you promised me another letter last week, I most patiently bore my disappointment. I sent <u>very</u> <u>often</u> to the office, surely, but I know you must be much engaged or you would have kept your promise. I fear something troubled you or you were sick. I wish I could always be certain of your health. You will always tell me, Edward? Do not keep any thing from me. The last *Chronicle* has not yet come—I shall read and give you my thoughts as you requested. Sometimes you misunderstand me very much; I cannot express myself with perspicuity or else it is that you do not know me very well. I fear I often pain when I mean to give you pleasure—if my heart could but talk to you without the aid of so many artificial mediums I should have no such apprehension. It has been a right long while since you left me. I do believe I shall like to see you.

[My sister] Elizabeth has been waiting in town two days for a boat—ready to start at a moment's warning. I have been with her. She hopes to get off this morning and I hope she may; such a suspense is anything but pleasant or profitable. I do wish from my heart, Edward, she had never left home—to you and none other I say it. I fear she is not happy and that she now for the first time discovers in her husband the want of energy, decision and, I fear, industry, which must pain her heart. I will speak to you about it—perhaps I ought not to have written so much. I did not intend it— 'tis but [to] you, dearest. I thought I understood Charles's character before they were married—and alas, I fear I was more correct than hope flattered me I should be. My sister is not happy, Edward, I do greatly fear, and she deserved to be.

I am always glad to hear from [your boy] Charley but I cannot feel quite the same interest for Eddy. I wish I knew the little fellow. I wanted to find a book for Eddy but could not and so have sent him a pair of gloves to roll snowballs with. I used to be fond of such sport myself and Mother always allowed me woolen gloves for the purpose. I sent last night by Mr. Campbell some flowers for Eddy which you may look at, and think they came from me, if you please, dearest.

Mr. Campbell has really gone on a visit of observation—he told me he had come to no positive decision and said when Miss [Harriet] D[rake] was here he had not the most distant idea of being particular, nor, till I put it into his head. The truth is I believe you, yes, you sir, are the cause of the whole affair. I hope matters will come round as we hoped, provided it be for the happiness of the parties—but they must do as we did—judge for themselves. Mr. C. is quite cautious, and has not a quick insight to character. He would not consider himself acquainted under a year's communion. Arthur will give you this.

I do not think you will need fear so much as you do that I have unreal views of life. Five years ago it was perhaps the case, but five years have brought me too much sorrow, too many sore heart-aches, and forced too many of the sad realities of life to allow me to remain under very false impressions. I endeavour and pray for, dear Edward, a habitual state of preparation for whatever the Providence of God may inflict of pain, and gratefully enjoy my many, many blessings. I have always feared, as I told you, I was not capable as I would wish of making you happy, and that I was not meant for married life. I wish it had been more a subject of my thoughts—I do distrust my powers.

Thank you for your very satisfactory answer to my query of "What are you about?" Elizabeth was with me when your letter came and insisted on my passing it to her when I had read it. I did not like to give up my rights, but indulged her curiosity by reading most of the letter to her, with which she professed herself much gratified. I wonder if Mother will be as good to us as she is to Lizzy. She always leaves home well supplied with all sorts of notions.

I am glad Master Ned [Eddy] is pleased with his Marmalade. I have a jar of something rather better for your mother which I shall entrust to your care. I have requested Mrs. Coons to bring the dress which Julia left for you—I did not like that—I wonder you have not seen Mrs. C. often. She is always much pleased by her visits to Cincinnati.

The weather for two days has been most delightful. I wish you were here to ride with me—do ride often in fine weather. You will become fond if it and I know it will be very beneficial to your health. You had better practice <u>now</u>. And do you ever touch your flute? I shall try and be in good practice in my music when you come. I shall stay next week with Ellen. My piano is out of tune and I dislike to use it. Ellen's is a very fine one and will tempt me to play. I am in excellent health—I hope you are as well. How I should like to <u>see</u> and <u>hear</u> one of your merry <u>laughs</u>.¹¹ Do not be sad when you can avoid it, dearest. If you are very much engaged I shall not expect such frequent letters, but know you will write as often as you can, because you know what a source of comfort are your letters to me. Good-bye and be happy, dear Edward.

Your own Margaret

[Postscript] I have just returned from the canal boat—Lizzy is gone. I wish I could spend a month with her this winter. I hope you can write soon again. I cannot but fear you were not quite well when you wrote last and shall be happier when I hear again. I shall write very often. I have told you I hoped you would not weary of my letters— indeed, I do not think you will. I don't know what made me think so. Mr. C. asked if I had no letters for you but I preferred writing by Arthur or the mail. Good-bye once more—I do not like to lay aside my pen—it seems like parting and that is not pleasure.

Arthur says Ned is a <u>very</u>, <u>very</u> smart child and repeated some of his <u>sayings</u> to me. I hope you visit Mrs. [Elizabeth] Worthington sometimes. I do not think Eddy would like her Charly, they are so different.

Eolia, Nov 28th, 1838
Wednesday evening
[Postmarked Nov. 30]

I went to town to-day fully determined if I did not get a letter from you, dear Edward, to write <u>a</u> <u>scolding</u> to you. Your last was a <u>little</u> colored with sadness, and consequently communicated a <u>wee</u> <u>bit</u> of its little <u>color</u> to me, as <u>my</u> last may have already told you. No wonder then, that I should anxiously expect a brighter one. You <u>must</u> write often—for though you may think me foolish, I cannot feel happy unless I hear from you every few days. I have been with [my sister] Ellen since Sunday. If I had been at home, I should have written two days ago, for there, my own dear quiet room and a good fire therein is always at my command. So it would be here if I chose, but it would seem selfish, and in fact is so. I am glad I did not write sooner, for I was a little indisposed, and <u>I</u> might have written a gloomy letter. O, I have so many things to say, I hardly know where to begin, and yet nothing of any importance either.

Your last is a very good letter, I think—at least, it had a very pleasant effect on me, if I be allowed to say so. I do not pretend to [have] much knowledge of <u>the world</u> but, so far as I have had opportunity of judging, I concur in your animadversions of "men and women, too." It is a very great happiness to me that my opinions agree so often with yours. I believe it makes me think better of myself (and that, you know, is pleasant) because your opinions are of course more the result of thoughts and experience than mine. Doubtless we shall find enough of dissimilarity in our characters to prevent <u>entire</u> <u>monotony</u>—trust my <u>amiability</u> for that. No, dear Edward, I am far from amiable, but I must think 'tis more the fault of education than my natural character, and by grace may be amended. I am conscious of improvement in the last few years.

The essay on married life you recommended to my perusal I read some months since, before I had any idea, dearest, that I should so soon <u>perhaps</u> require the advice. 'Twas published in a Philadelphia paper, and I then thought them the best <u>rules</u> I had ever read, and a second reading, and by your request, has not altered my opinion. Most of the advice and rules, etc., on that subject are, as Cary says, very <u>objectionable</u>—that is too <u>easy</u> a term to apply—they always made me feel indignant, and the idea of being a wife on such terms as are usually proposed was revolting to my woman's pride. So far as I may judge, Mr. Cary has properly touched the springs which oftenest operate for and against the happiness of married people. However, I can only speak from observation, and that limited, but yet I have, and always had, my own thoughts on those matters, and I have seen but <u>very</u> few, either husbands or wives, who were to each other just what I thought they should be, and what by the exercise of forbearance and confidence they might have been. If my practice be but conformable to my opinions, my dear Edward, I shall never give you pain, but I have many fears for myself, and pray you, as I have often done, be very patient with me. I do think I should have been a better woman in a thousand ways if I had been so happy as to have been with those who understood my character—even my own family did not, and it has pained me to my heart to know it—to feel that my motives and actions were misapprehended by those who of all the world ought to know me best.

I suppose you have seen Arthur often; he is a warm-hearted, generous man, as you will find on further acquaintance. Julia was in good earnest about <u>writing often</u>

as I could prove most clearly—why, 'twas only the last time I wrote by Arthur, that she came into my room just as I had directed my letter and, seeing it, asked if I had spoken of the <u>dress</u>. I said I had done so in my last letter. "What, is it possible you have written two letters since my return?" Very true, answered I. She actually <u>blushed deeply</u>, for [you?] I presume, or in surprise, I don't know, and said, "I do think, Margaret, it is the most <u>imprudent</u> thing for you to write so often to Edward Mansfield; I do not know how you <u>can</u> do it," and then a repetition and enlargement of former expatiations on propriety. I did not say it, but I thought she had been guilty of one <u>equally</u> <u>great</u> in the matter of my dress. I cannot consent that you should take Julia for a model (if you are seeking one) of propriety. She is one of the most amiable and loveable women in the world, but at the same time a most inconsistent character. I wish I could be as amiable, but aside from that, I would not change characters—it is to you, dearest, I <u>think</u>.

I am so much engaged in various ways I have had little time just now for reading. I have tried to get "de Tocqueville" but cannot.[12] You said you left it with James, but you know I do not read French and 'twas a French copy. I wish I did read French; very foolishly, I discontinued my study of the language, or rather, I changed my school and had for awhile no teacher, and since I left school have had no opportunity from my country life of resuming. Jones, our bookseller, has brought just about nothing, though he made large boasts to me.

About the time of your coming, do what will best suit your plans. Our family meeting is on New Year's day and unless you choose you need not <u>dine</u> with the whole connexion and [guests] usually <u>leave</u> us before the evening, except our own family. I think I should love to have you. Julia anticipates with much satisfaction having you at dinner on Christmas; she and Ellen have us all at their houses alternately and 'tis Julia's turn this year. We dined with her yesterday—she is so good and so kind. I love her dearly, I think more than James.

Sally Swearingen and I had a wild drive yesterday. Ellen's buggy and the renowned <u>Peter</u> <u>Pancake</u> were at the door and we took the <u>whip</u> and <u>reins</u> and drove through town in high style, much to the admiration of our acquaintances. 'Twas not without an object, however, for I had shopping to do and Sally wished to enquire at the Post Office. We were not disappointed—thanks to you.

Do not be discouraged about rising early—as a precedent I instance my sister Ellen who all her life has been a very late riser, as fond as you could be of a morning nap. Now she rises before the sun—if I did not witness it I could scarce credit the change. I do wish I wrote better for both our sakes—for yours particularly just now. Do you not think I might mend? Ellen says she will write a postscript to you some of these times. She sends her love now, as also doth Sally S. who was much pleased with what you said of Mr. Thatcher. Adieu for awhile.

I excuse the wafer[13] for <u>once</u>, and the ink and the printing office and all that. You may write them every day if you wish, but I confess the idea is not the most beautiful in the world.

Thursday Mor'g, 29th. I rose at half-past five, and have been writing an hour— the sun has not yet risen but all the three [Macomb] children have come down, and <u>such</u> a noise as there is around me. I will just say that you had better write often as you can, for in truth I need your letters more than I did two months ago. I seem to have become impatient and without cause, too. How long will you stay? And what <u>day</u> may I probably expect you? O, you have seen Mr. Campbell and been very good to him, I know, for he deserves it. I ought to have given him a letter to your mother but did not think of it till he had gone. I am quite curious to know whether he and Harriet will fulfill <u>everybody's</u> expectations. I heard incidently [*sic*] that Harriet had <u>too much</u> temper—is it so? Now, that would be a pity, for <u>Jamie</u> is quite amiable. Did you get the flowers? Do you know that to-morrow is December? Write soon—<u>directly</u> and very often. There is such a noise about me that I must stop. Ellen Waddle says she will be very glad to see you. I am sorry Mr. Massie missed you. Good-bye, dear Edward,

Margaret

Eolia, Nov. 30th, 1838
[Postmarked Dec. 5th]

I have just made a discovery which is quite satisfactory to me, and what, dear Edward, to you think it can be? Only that your last letter was dated incorrectly—and you can't tell how I was puzzled, yes troubled, by it. I received your last, dated the 26th, which was Monday; yesterday, Ellen brought it to me from the office and I opened it, expecting to give her some news of Arthur—but no, not a word of him or my letter though we calculated he must have arrived either Saturday eve'g or Sunday morning. We both felt some anxiety which on Ellen's part was relieved by Arthur's return this morning. He said he gave you my <u>package</u> the morning after his arrival which was Monday. You spoke of Mr. Campbell's having dined with you the day you wrote, and it but just now occurred to me that you made a mistake in your date.

Ellen said you did not <u>wish</u> <u>me</u> <u>to</u> <u>know</u> <u>you</u> <u>wrote</u> <u>on</u> <u>Sunday</u>. You can't think how I am relieved by my discovery for I thought it so very strange you should not have spoken of Arthur. You said you would be very busy this week, but yes, I rather think I shall get a letter to-morrow night, or I don't believe I should write to-night.

And so your mother <u>does</u> <u>not</u> <u>know</u> but I have made a mistake—yes, dearest Edward, I think she <u>does</u>. Mr. C. <u>is</u> handsome, amiable, pious and has many other excellencies of character but I should have been a most <u>unprincipled</u> woman to have married him. I am very certain, also, that he loved me most truly and would have made me a devoted husband, more of a <u>pet</u> than I expect from <u>you</u>, and moreover, he will be very wealthy one of these days, <u>everybody</u> <u>says</u>—but what of that? All and more than he could offer failed to win my love and unless <u>you</u> blame me, I shall not think I have made a mistake.

I have received two letters from you this week, and like prosperity and adversity they were set "one against the other," for one made me very glad, and the last one very sad. Would you know the cause of the latter effect? "Everybody from your town speaks so highly of you, and your own home is so delightful compared with this dull town, that indeed, after all, I do feel sometimes as if I should fail in making you happy." Now, Edward dear, I have scarcely felt comfortable since I read that—even Ellen perceived something troubled me, and asked if I had any news from Cincinnati. Do not talk so to me—you do not mean it, but it pains me. I have been sad all day, against my reason, too.

Cousin Henry Massie has just left me—he came to tea, and we had several hours pleasant talk and that, with the resolution I am now carrying into effect, has restored my equanimity. I am sorry he did not see you, and he regrets it exceedingly—he says he wished to see you to give you warning of my many faults, etc., but I boldly told him he would tell something very different. It troubles me that people speak so well of me—they do not know me as I know myself. I do hope you may not allow anything that can be said to make you believe I am anything but just what you <u>ought</u> to know. I have too much confidence in your judgement to suppose it will be influenced by common talk. Why, <u>who</u> <u>would</u> say to you anything to my disparagement?

Do you know I love you better for your confidence in me? I wish, oh, how earnestly, I was better fitted to fulfill the place of mother to your dear little boys—it is a high and honorable trust which I hope God will enable me faithfully to discharge. The responsibility is very great, and I assume it with many fears, but yet a consciousness that I am doing right—I can but try, dear Edward. I am not required by my own strength to perform every duty—it is promised those who ask it. Shall we not ask it for ourselves and for each other? Now, good-night—I shall finish to-morrow, probably, for I think even though you were busy, you would answer my letter. A little while, and you will be with me.

Saturday night. There came no letter for me, dearest, as I hoped and I shall defer finishing my letter till Monday. To-day is the first of December, and Christmas sometimes comes in this month—good-bye again, till Monday.

Adena, Monday evening, Dec. 3. How glad I am, after a week's absence, to be at home and writing, dear Edward, [to] you. It gives me so much satisfaction to take my seat in my most comfortable rocking chair by a bright fire and feel at home. I do love my own room—'tis the envy of all my young friends who visit me and a dozen have spoken for it long ago whenever I should be so foolish as to leave it. I have everything to make me happy to-night but a letter from you, which I own I did expect even though you said you would be much engaged. I do not blame you, my own Edward, for not writing, but myself for expecting too much.

Now I wish to touch upon your last letter. I have not in a long while been so much vexed by a trifle as by Mr. Charles Pomeroy's unauthorized invitation to his friends. I never mentioned the matter to him; indeed, I did not see him for more than three months before he went to Cincinnati, for I was in town when he and Elizabeth arrived, and he set off for Cincinnati without my knowledge. I asked Mother to-day if she had sent out invitations—she said she had not spoken of you to Charles, much less appointed a time for us, as she did not know herself—so, you see, it is Mr. Charles's own doings. I do assure you, unless it be your wish, I have not the remotest idea of inviting Mrs. Wyllys P[omeroy] and I will tell you why.[14] About the time, we ought, I think, to arrange our own affairs and so if you please, dearest, we will question Master Charles's right to interfere—and plan for ourselves.

Arthur told me you had a "mighty nice new coat." I received your two last letters whilst I was at Ellen's and she and Arthur laughed at me because you wrote so often. Ellen told him she believed I wrote just as often—but she did not, as Julia, remark on the impropriety, for she said 'twas all right.

Poor Julia is suffering tortures from a return of her former disease, inflammatory rheumatism. I fear she will not recover for a long time. I intended staying to nurse her but when I came home this morning I found Mother quite sick and requiring all my care. I could not but think, dear Edward, she would miss me in sickness even though in health she could do very well without me.[15] Oh! it makes me so sad—I almost doubt my right to leave her. It is not with me as with my other sisters. I have always had the most active and sometimes really laborious duties of the management of the house, and for so much longer than they, that is pains me to think my cares must devolve upon my mother at her time of life. I am trying to supply my place in that way by a housekeeper, but as yet have failed in my wish.

I asked Mother to-day when she would rather you should come and she says just when you please, but she would like to have you here on New Year's day. I told her you should not come to dinner—she said you <u>should</u> by all means. Though you do not know it, it is no small compliment from Mother to wish you with us at a family meeting for she has a great dread of strangers.

Let me know when you <u>can</u> come, for the time is not very far off and you must have made your arrangements—just three weeks till Christmas. Will Elizabeth Drake accompany you? How is Harriet?—and has Mr. C. come to a <u>decision</u>? I should not like to be the object of such a visit of <u>observation</u>—he does not love Harriet, he is only <u>trying</u> to do so. My pride!! If it were my case and I knew it by any possibility . . . . Sometimes I am startled to think how little intercourse we have had with each other—we are, comparatively, strangers—<u>three</u> <u>weeks</u> comprise the whole time of our actual acquaintance. Truly, as Anne James says, I have been <u>indiscreet</u> or else maybe you are a very irresistible gentleman. I hope you have succeeded in persuading yourself that you are <u>very</u> charming, but I don't believe it will be as you, (modest gentleman!) aver, against your feelings. Good-bye, my dear Edward.

Your own true Margaret

[Postscript] Tuesday Mor'g. I wonder what mischief you are about this beautiful, mild fourth of December—be a good boy, and do as you are bidden. It is a comfort that I am not at all afraid of your doing anything wrong even though I can't watch you. I have not heard from Amanda for some time; all my correspondents are in arrears to me and I am not sorry for I have more leisure to write to you. Do not expect me to abide by Charles's arrangements—we will do just what we please, <u>will</u> we not?

As the time is so very near when you will see me, I suppose I need not write more than once again—need I? But as for you, sir, do you write twice a week or fear my severe displeasure—unless you do as you are bidden, I will give you both <u>ocular</u> and <u>auricular</u> demonstration that I am not amiable. Do, dearest, do write. I almost expect a letter every day and you know I do not get it.

I grieve to learn your mother is so much indisposed. My warm love to her and a kiss to dear little Eddy. Mother had letters from Frank and sister Sarah. Sister complains of the climate [in Massachusetts]—she is going to visit some friends in Philadelphia in January. I think she will not be out next summer, but she says very little of <u>us</u>.

These bright moonlight nights, do you think of me? I hope so—but I do not love the winter moonlight as I do the summer—it looks so still, so cold, as if it were not of the earth—the shadows of the bare trees make me melancholy and I miss the cheerful hum of insects. Nothing can be more beautiful than a moonlight snow scene, but yet I only <u>admire</u> it.

Adena, Dec. 13th 1838
Wednesday evening
[Postmarked Dec. 15]

Dear Edward, I received your most comforting letter yesterday morning and wished much to reply to it by to-day's mail as you requested, but I <u>could</u> <u>not</u> do it. My last was not a <u>very</u> <u>delightful</u> letter, but I will not apologize—for you did deserve all I said.

I have been staying in town for some days nursing poor Julia who is suffering dreadfully, and with but little relief from pain and I fear a prospect of its continuance. When I went down on Sunday I did not mean to stay, for I was not well, but Julia needed me badly and I remained till to-day with her—I should have stayed longer but I am not well enough to perform the office of nurse day and night, too. Julia requires more attention than any one I ever was with in sickness. I have been with her often and almost always made myself sick attending her.

May I think to you again? Well then, I do hope to find in you a more tender and sympathizing nurse than Julia has in James. He is too severe, too <u>stern</u>, kind when there is <u>absolute</u> <u>necessity</u> for his services, but you know, dear Edward, that is not all we require in sickness. I have not had a good night's rest this week and shall suffer unless I get it to-night, so good-night and I will rise and say my say to-morrow early, whilst you, shame! are sleeping most <u>profoundly</u>.

Thursday mor'g—I rather think this is the last letter I shall write you till you come—letters travel so slowly at this season over our <u>good</u> <u>roads</u> that were I to write by Monday's mail it would scarce reach you. Mr. Peet returned on Tuesday and brings "confirmation sure" of certain reports which have been circulated amongst our people about Mr. Campbell. Certainly he copied you, dearest; I told him if he were in <u>real</u> <u>earnest</u> 'twas the best thing he could do. I will tell you some of the long talks Mr. C.

and I had on the subject. I am glad he has decided for himself, but it makes me afraid when I think he was much influenced by me—not by anything I have said lately, but last summer—for of late, when I observed how seriously he took me, I was very careful. I used to think—I <u>knew</u> <u>it</u> <u>then</u>, that he would do <u>any</u>, <u>everything</u> to gain my approbation, and I know now that my opinions have yet great weight with him. But no one influenced Harriet—she loved very <u>innocently</u> and undesignedly—you say if she be not conquered she is incorrigible. Alas! for guilty me, how you would blame me if you knew how much more so I was—I used indeed, Edward, to think it was almost a sin in me not to love one so entirely devoted to me. I am sure of this—Harriet has gained a most excellent husband, one who will make her happy if she will be so—and I do hope she may make as good a wife. I want to see Mr. C.; he will come immediately and tell me all. <u>Everyone</u> <u>here</u> <u>says</u>, "Harriet <u>will</u> <u>marry</u> <u>Mr.</u> <u>C.</u> <u>if he</u> <u>courts</u> <u>her</u>." How angry I should be to have heard that said ever, my own Edward, of you.

I am so glad you are not coming with all those ladies. I once asked you if Elizabeth Drake was coming with you, but I could not in truth say I wished it. I wish they would all come some other time, for, like you, I am very selfish, etc. [and] don't want the trouble of paying them much attention whilst you are with me. I <u>won't</u> <u>do</u> <u>it</u>—now it is said. I <u>ought</u> to ask Miss Warden to stay with me, and if she remains longer than you, shall do so, but not else. You will be here on Saturday night, I hope. Mr. Woodrow will not be here to meet you.[16] Nobody teases me, now the matter is settled in the minds of the community, only they cannot fix upon the time precisely.

I fear we shall have but a small meeting on New Year's day, maybe none but our own family. I do not love to think it the last I shall be at home—I do not love to think of leaving home, and as the time approaches the more painful does it become. To think <u>this</u> is not my home—I do not know how I shall do it—it makes my heart ache, Edward. Come and talk to me and then I shall forget it. I do not feel as though it were worth while to write a long letter—I shall see you so soon and would so much rather talk—I have not half as much to say as usual and all because I am to see you next week—only a few days, you know. I have received the dress which was to have been brought by you. I will <u>shine</u> in it if I have opportunity whilst you are here, though it is a plain dress.

I much fear poor dear Julia will not have the pleasure of giving you a good Christmas dinner—she is confined to bed and utterly unable to use her limbs—as helpless as an infant. I wish I <u>could</u> stay with her as I have always done, but now I cannot and it grieves me to think she needs me. How is dear little Eddy? and your mother? I had a letter from Mrs. Worthington yesterday and she wonders why you are not more sociable during her husband's absence—remember, dearest, to make her a call before you leave the city—invite yourself to take tea, and show that you are not troubled with a certain <u>annoyance</u>. Good-bye, and if you get this in time, write to me. I expect letters every day, but 'tis a vain expectation. I can't think now of half I wished to say in my last letter but, no matter—I shall go to see Mrs. Coons this evening and hear what <u>she</u> has to say of you. How does that most incorrigible gossip—<u>Benny</u>? I know none his equal in that way—it is a passion with him to meddle in other folks' matters. Do you think Dr. Drake is pleased with Mr. C.? Again, my dear Edward, good-bye. God keep you and grant us a happy meeting.

Your own true Margaret

[Postscript] Good-bye till I see you and may it be in health and happiness. My love to your mother. This is a poor letter.

Adena Dec. 16th, 1838
Sunday morning.
[Postmarked Dec. 18]

How dearly I should love to write you a long letter if I only had time. I have just read your last and am partly pleased and partly <u>not,</u> my dear Edward. I believe, however, on the whole pleasure is the predominating feeling for I always love your letters. I was absent most unexpectedly last night, or I should have written to you, for I knew my <u>scolding</u> letter would bring an answer and I thought I should like to write once more before I saw you. 'Tis time now to prepare for church and I must write no more.

I stayed (and <u>quarrelled</u>) with Mrs. Coons last night. You could never talk with any patience to her— 'tis more than I, who know and appreciate her good qualities, can do. I think her head is fuller than ever of love and fictitious sentiment—such absurdities as she does utter. I shall tell you of them, and I'll just tell you that I will be tolerably glad to see you.

Don't think me silly, but indeed I could not sleep for a long while last night for thinking you would be here next Saturday night. Don't come in gloomy spirits; <u>you</u> <u>shall</u> <u>not</u> no matter how much reason you may have, and in truth, I think you have no good ones. So you see all your trouble was for nothing. I really thought you must have some mighty matter on your <u>conscience</u>, but from your letter—to me,

— 144 —

your sadness resolves itself to little more than this: your health is not good and as you are suffering from dyspepsia, I can well imagine how your spirits are in consequence depressed. You are conscious that you are wrong to give way to depression and are very glad to fancy you have <u>good</u> <u>cause</u> for the indulgence of such feelings and so, you see, you torment your memory for such causes. When I suffered as you now do, dearest Edward, every painful circumstance of my life seemed to be brought before me. My conscience accused me more than I could bear—oh, 'twas horrible. I hardly think I could endure it again.

I do think with prudence your health will be amended if not perfected, and I shall take it upon me to prescribe and forbid just as I may think proper for you. You may think me presuming, but, good sir, I have no idea of your being tormented all your life long without at least making an effort to release you. It is partly selfishness, too, because I shall not choose always to be sympathizing with you when I might rejoice in your returning health. If my strong will can be of any use to you, I shall prize it more, dearest, than I have ever done before. 'Tis time it should be of use to some one, for it has given me trouble enough. What a very modest gentleman—you would have written more frequently if you supposed I valued your letters. Why, I told you so, and I do not very often tell stories, dearie—not even about you.

I have become quite bold, indeed. I really wish to see James Campbell, and hope he will arrive before you that we may have a long talk about his affairs. Six months ago, he would not have believed me or any one if he had been told of what has just occurred. I am afraid I shall have to bear some of the blame should matters turn out differently from what we hope and expect—but Harriet evinced such plain a preference for Mr. C., and he so much needed a good wife and was determined not to be an old bachelor, that the temptation to do them each a good turn was very great. I hope they will be happy, and am glad to hear that all Harriet's family are pleased with the match. She will, I think, be well suited to the society here and will fill my place. I feel more and more convinced that I did right in making a confidant of our doings of Mr. Campbell and take some credit to myself whether you award it to me or not—for 'twas no easy matter, and recent circumstances have proved that it was <u>necessary</u>.

Why do you not write longer letters as you used to do? You may as well give me a good part of your <u>time</u> and <u>attention</u> for I assure you I shall expect it here after. Amanda G. supposes your letters must be "beautifully written." I have half a mind to show her some choice specimens of a dozen or so.

I have seen but little of Ellen Waddle for some weeks—she intended staying with me part of this week but without her knowledge, her mother promised her to Julia, and so I suppose I shall be disappointed. I believe Elizabeth Drake expects to have the command of you, as Mrs. Coons told me she would only stay a week and you were to return with her. I think she will be a little mistaken in her calculations. I am very sorry she should be here just now—it quite troubles me.

Sally S. and Mr. Thatcher are <u>progressing</u>. I am glad she fancies him, for I am very sure I could not have done so—he is scarcely agreeable to me, but there are very few gentlemen whose society is pleasing to me. I have always been sorry, too, that I could not feel more interest for the poor <u>gents</u> who were trying their best.

I have my doubts if you get this letter. I wish it could have gone by to-day's mail. This, you must know, dearest, is Monday morning in my own room by candlelight. Julia seems but little better. I fear she will scarcely be well again this winter. Mother, Willy, and <u>we</u> <u>all</u> are well. I hope the fine weather and good roads will continue till you come. Good-bye, my dear Edward. Come to me happy. Your own Margaret

[Postscript] It is light now and to my regret I discover the weather has changed during the night and it is now <u>sleeting</u>, the worst kind of weather for travelers. I hope you may not suffer—do be careful and wrap up well. I am afraid you are often very improvident, and negligent of your health. Good-bye—I shall expect you on Saturday afternoon, or at furthest [sic] at tea time. I hope you have called on Mrs. Worthington.

Adena, Jan. 3rd, 1839
Thursday evening
[Postmarked Jan. 7]

I only wish to say good-night, dear Edward, and tell you how you pleased me by promising to come soon again—it is right and best <u>I</u> think for you to do so. I do not feel nearly so sad as at our former partings—thanks to your comforting assurance. I selected several pieces of music to-night which I shall practice—since I know you wish me to attend to my music, I think I <u>can</u> find time. I do not wish you should be disappointed in any respect in me, and if you feel any <u>pride</u> in my musical talents, surely I have sufficient motive for cultivating them. I forgot to show you some of Albert's letters as I promised but I can do it again. I have just been looking over them; the omission of my design, that is, the recollection of it, brought them to my mind—some of them <u>need</u> burning.

Already I have thought of a dozen little things I wished to have mentioned to you—maybe they are as well unsaid. How brightly the moon shines. I almost wish you had kept your first intention and you would have been with me now. Good-night, I have <u>nothing</u> to keep me up to-night. You, I suppose, are talking with James just now. I miss you this evening, <u>you</u> <u>know</u>, but can't be sad for all that. It was a good thing of you to tell me with your good-bye you would come again. I shall feel more at ease about you, Edward, when your first letter tells me you are happy at home. I hope the journey will drive your enemy quite away. Oftentimes, a long ride over rough roads proves serviceable.

Friday evening. Well, the day is gone and you will not wonder that it has seemed somewhat longer than any for two weeks past. I have been very much <u>taken up</u> with housekeeping affairs and wonder that my many engagements did not shorten the time—but I believe the days <u>are</u> growing longer—I must consult my <u>almanac</u>. I have a trouble to-night and I shall tell it you—but just now at tea, Mary [Macomb?] said she had seen you in town this afternoon with Mr. Peet—could it be so? I cannot believe it—and yet Mary ought to know you, and it is also possible that circumstances may have made it necessary that you should remain in town—the unexpected delay of the stage coach or something else. But indeed, I do not like to admit the possibility of your being so near and yet not with me. I wish I could ask you—alas for me, Edward, I <u>have</u> very much of the woman about me, as you said. I feel it more now than ever in my life before—for my own peace I could wish I had much less—it will cause me much <u>suffering</u>—call it, if you will, imaginary suffering, 'tis none the less hard to bear for that. I will not write more of it to-night, by to-morrow I shall feel it less. I do not wish I was a man, thank my Creator who made me a woman—but I do wish men could enter more sympathizingly into the feelings of women. You do, dearest, more than any man I ever met, but yet even you cannot understand all my feelings—and for this reason I am often <u>ashamed</u> to express many emotions which might seem to you puerile. I know, and am sure, you are not in town to-night, yet the <u>suggestion</u> <u>of</u> <u>such</u> <u>a</u> <u>possibility</u> has made me unhappy. I have been fancying all day on just what part of the journey you might be. I do hope you are in better health than when you left me.

Saturday evening. I have it all now, dear Edward, clear enough, and imagine, for only you can, my relief—who do you think was taken for you? Why, no less important a personage than the Rev. Dr. Sparrow of Kenyon College. I went to church to-day and from there to Ellen's. She mentioned Mr. Sparrow's being in town and in an instant <u>the</u> <u>truth</u> flashed on me, and away went my sadness which in spite of everything had darkened my spirit. Am I not a silly one? Forgive me, dearest Edward, but I cannot promise entire exemption from all that is naughty. You will do me much good; you are the one of all the world to make me better—if not you—no one can.

I was in Mr. [Frank] Campbell's store[17] to-day and he asked me if <u>our</u> <u>friend</u> had left for Cincinnati—said he wished to have seen you, as James had requested him to send by you a cane for Dr. Drake. I suppose you will have Mr. [James] Campbell in your city for a week or so longer—he and Harriet will have a good opportunity of <u>settling</u> <u>their</u> <u>affairs</u> and becoming well acquainted. Some pretend to say that lovers never understand each other's character better at the end of a month's intercourse than at first—but of us that is palpably untrue, I think, I know a great deal more of you than I did when you left me in September, and if you do not know me, why 'tis your own, not <u>my</u> fault. I question, however, if such persons as Mrs. Coons would ever care about knowing aught but the brightest traits of character of their <u>idols</u>— alas, for me, if to gain your love it had been necessary to conceal my faults.

I had a letter last night from Ellen Waddle. She regrets extremely she was denied the enjoyment of your society, but hopes as I was more favored she may be permitted to share with me my pleasure—in what way, think you? Why, by narrating to her <u>all</u> <u>that</u> <u>is</u> <u>interesting</u> connected with your visit. I wonder, now, if she expects me to sit down and tell her all we talked about. When you come in <u>March</u>, I will have <u>Nelly</u> [Ellen Waddle] stay awhile at Adena. I shall not tell anyone you are coming then unless I first hear it from you.

Mother is really better to-day and for the first time in ten days, too. Poor Julia is not quite so well this evening and seems sadly disheartened. I wish I could go and nurse her. How is Mr. Drake? You are at home to-night and maybe writing to me. I almost know you are if you are in health which blessing may God grant you. Dear, dear, Edward, you are too constantly in my thoughts. Write me, as you said, often and never let my foolish jests give you a thought of anxiety. You are stronger than I— no wonder I should torment myself, but you! never—it cannot be!

I have half a dozen or more letters to write next week and cannot therefore promise to write <u>every</u> <u>day</u>. I have been counting your letters and have <u>not</u> thirty, so make up the number if you please, as speedily as may be. Only think, Amanda gets two or three letters for every one of hers. You will say Mr. Trotter has little else to do in comparison with yourself—maybe—but I wish you had as little—or at least that you had sufficient leisure to write <u>very</u> often. I do not wish to be selfish or unreasonable, but sometimes I really fear I am, but you will forgive it. Do, I pray you, be more prudent and careful of your health. I hope you found your mother and our dear little Eddy well. You are with them now. I am ashamed of myself when I think how miserable I made myself about positively nothing for I was all the while sure you would not have remained a day in town and not seen me. Good-bye, dear Edward—to God our Father I commend you.

Margaret

Adena, Jan. 8th, 1839
Tuesday evening
[Postmarked Jan. 14]

Disappointed—grievously so, yet 'tis none of your fault, I am very sure of that, my dear Edward—knowing the irregularity of the mails I could not <u>expect</u> a letter, but I could not help hoping. I need a letter to-night for I am <u>drooping</u>—and I hardly know why. Good-night—I must write to Ellen Waddle now, and what shall I say for you? I began in earnest to write letters—dispatched three this morning, all very full. I had a long letter from Sister Sarah yesterday. She complains sadly of my last letter and accuses me of having laboured under a fit of dyspepsia when I wrote it—calls you her <u>excellent</u> <u>friend</u> and says very good things of you.

Wednesday eve'g. Dear Edward, I wish I was with you that you might <u>talk away</u> some of your lesser troubles. Your letter is sad, but I understand it and only grieve to see that your health is not better than when you left me. It is very presuming for me to differ from your mother, but indeed, I do think I may judge by my own painful experience and say that at times dieting is absolutely necessary—not for any length of time, but for a day or two as your feelings may require. You ought to know better than anyone else. Your mother possibly judges not from personal experience—and all who know anything of that most terrible disease must be aware that it takes a thousand differing forms, sometimes in the same person and that each requires a different mode of treatment. You hope to be of benefit to me; now, dearest, I do think if you will submit your care to me, I will not promise a perfect cure—but I am very sure I can <u>help</u> to make you better. I shall <u>try</u> when once I have the <u>command</u> of you.

Every evening I wish for you. This day last week you were with me. I can at least write a few words every evening and that plan suits me better than writing one day in the week. I fear I said something wrong in my last letter—but oh, how miserable I did make myself and all against my reason and conviction. Now say that I am not a simpleton if you can. I have been terribly out of spirits to-day and what mode think you I took to recover me? Will you promise to try it? I assure you I found it effectual in this instance though I do not know if it would prove so a second time. Why, my dear Edward, I went to the kitchen and relieved the cook from the necessity of making biscuits for tea, by doing it myself—is not that a new idea?

I have been reading *The Chronicle* and see that Miss Beecher is <u>doing</u> <u>battle</u> for herself and Mr. McGuffy.[18] I wonder I could have forgotten the "Dirge" you spoke of. I looked over the papers and as soon as I saw it again I remembered having admired and adapted it to a plaintive air when I first read it. I am often oblivious of things I have read, and am often mortified in consequence, but a glance at the book or a single incident [?] repeated recalls the whole to me.

Thursday night—a week since you left me, Edward, and I am not sorry it is gone; the next will not be so long. I have been as industrious as the "little busy bee" this week, and have accomplished more than I anticipated—of which I am very glad for 'twas for Mother I was so busy. She prefers me as her <u>mantua</u> <u>maker,</u>[19] and I think I must promise so to continue. If I could only know you were well, how much more happy I should be—it is hard that I can do nothing for you. How much is there to remind us that earth is not our home—love and fear so closely by each other—I have a thousand anxious fears for you which it would be useless to attempt to banish. Poor Julia is worse again. I have Tom—they say he is unmanageable at home. I have many fears that Julia has still much suffering in prospect. I have been writing to Sarah [Galloway] Browne and told her it was your fault I had not written two weeks since—is that truth?—you cannot deny it. She will forgive you.

Saturday night. Edward, dearest Edward, there is no letter for me and I need one—I cannot tell you how much. I know 'tis no fault of yours but that does not comfort me. You seemed so fatigued and depressed on the evening of your arrival that I cannot but fear you are worse than you supposed at first. I was in town this evening and to my extreme regret learned that our good friend, James Campbell, was dangerously ill. You had not seen him when you wrote, and merely mentioned he was sick at Dr. Drake's, and I supposed 'twas but a trifling indisposition. If he should die! May God in mercy avert so afflictive a dispensation. I feel as though I ought to do something for him, and almost wish he was here that I might. He has been always so kind, so attentive to me—I owe him, dear Edward, a large debt of gratitude—poor fellow, and poor, dear Harriet, how much she must suffer. I hope his brother is with him to-night. I know everything will be done for him, but in sickness we pine for familiar faces. I have felt sad for some days and have with hope looked to this evening for my best earthly consolation. The knowledge of Mr. C.'s illness has excited many anxieties, my dear Edward, for you—if I could but know you were well. I fear my too great solicitude is sinful—but if so, may God forgive me, I cannot help it. Promise me to be careful in the things I have mentioned to you—do not fear to tell me anything— nothing can pain me but the knowledge that you are not happy, when by any means I could contribute to your being so. Cares will come, dearest, even I have mine, but God sends them as trials to us and as such, I endeavour to bear those that fall to me. Mother is better and sends remembrances to you. Poor Mr. C.—it makes me sad to think of him. I am not sick, but sad, and partly in consequence that the letter I expected did not come. I will hope for to-morrow, and in a few days write again. Good-bye. May our God have you ever in his holy keeping.

Your own true Margaret

[Postscripts] What news did you have that was unfavorable, and that I may not know? From whom had you letters that troubled you? Will you not tell me? But not unless you think best I should know. I am not asking, as you know, from mere curiosity but with the hope of sharing and in alleviating your trouble—do not despond, my dear Edward. We have so many blessings and mercies now, and so many more in prospect for us—I think and hope you will soon be well again and do not fear so much for your health. You do not know how much faith I have in myself and what wonders I hope to do for you. Pray have ready the thousand dollars in eagles[20] which you are to pay me for you will [need?] it. I know I shall win it fairly. I rise at half-past five every morning and have practiced a long while by candlelight every morning. Do you not feel guilty to think you are sleeping all the while—fie on you, lazy one! I shall have to get for you "Poor Richard's" wise sayings on the subject.[21] I have not read them since my childhood, but I well remember that I highly approved of them then. I cannot permit you to be sad, indeed, for I am quite determined we shall be very happy and can we be when either is sad? No, no, it must not be. If I am going to take you away from your mother, Eddy, and all your friends, you might cry just a little but you know you shall live with them and have <u>me</u> to boot and how I shall trouble you? I wish you had given me some of your hair—not because (as you kindly say of mine) 'tis the prettiest in the world, but I love to have something of yours always about me to look at—why, I might forget you.

I have kept for three months or more two very large and beautiful apples for dear little Eddy—but I forgot to send them by you—they would have pleased him as much as the very small ones. I cannot permit them to share the fate of <u>common</u> apples and so shall send them to a favorite little Sunday scholar of mine. Mother asked what Eddy thought of his <u>mittens</u>. I can fancy the little fellow saying after his <u>own</u> manner, "I think they will keep my hands very warm." Adieu.   Yours ever, M

My best love to your mother and a kiss to dear Eddy. Sunday Morning. I do thank you, dearest, for having written so soon after your arrival. You are always considerate of me. I hope I shall always be so for you. Julia said yesterday evening she was better and hoped now she should soon be well—two days before, she said she was worse than she had ever been. Her sisters wish to come and stay with her but she will not permit them—that seems strange to me for <u>we</u> do not do so. Poor James C., wish I knew he was better. All his friends here express much interest for him.

I often think I will not write such <u>brimming</u> letters, but do not like to seal them while I see a blank spot. You must be tasked sometimes.

Adena, Jan. 23rd, 1839
Wednesday eve'g
[Postmarked Chillicothe, Jan. 27]

Shall I say, my own Edward, that I am sorry to have written my last letter? I scarcely remember what expressions I used, but I clearly remember I was very miserable when I wrote it. I ought not to add to your anxieties, but ah me! I fear I very often do. I have your last letter this evening—a thousand thanks for it. I cannot but reproach myself that you have <u>my</u> <u>last</u> instead of so kind a one as yours. Dear Edward, when you know how very selfish, willful, and <u>unamiable</u> I sometimes am, you will not wonder that I have so much feared myself incapable of making you happy. You would have pitied me on the day I wrote my last letter—I do not know why, but I have not the same degree of pleasure in writing since you left me. I wish for you more and my thoughts seem <u>to</u> <u>me</u> to lose so much by being transferred to paper—nor do your letters, dear letters though they be, <u>quite</u> supply your place or fully compensate me for <u>your</u> <u>own</u> self. I think of you all the while now—more, I believe, than I have hitherto done, if that be possible—but then I will connect with thee, dearest, that painful thought of change—I love not thee the less, but my house more, as the time approaches when it will not be mine. You will say, as you have already done, "Why think of it now?" I do not know, unless I am <u>pleased</u> to make myself unhappy. I shall live through it, Edward dear—only bear with me awhile; "only three months"—as you say, and then I hope to atone for past <u>offences</u>.

Thursday. I have had a real scramble along the hillside this evening, with Miss Caldwell[22] who is visiting me this week. You and I should have had more walks together. How dearly I should love to have you here all the month of June. I have a plan in my head which I will tell thee of—not in reference to our immediate arrangements, but—some years in the future.

Tell me, dear Edward, who wrote that very good article on the proper sphere of woman—was it Mrs. Douglass? I only received *The Chronicle* this evening, and that is the only thing I have read—surely it was not written by a man—<u>no common one</u> if a man. I like it, and some of these days I will point you some sentences which in my view contain very <u>important</u> and striking truths. I don't feel disposed to write them just now, but I will remember it. Thank you for the "Monthly," too—most of the articles, however, have been in the weekly *Chronicle*.

I had a letter from Lizzy a day or so since—poor little lady is sadly troubled by your having noticed <u>seriously</u> a few silly speeches never intended for you. Now, Edward, <u>there</u> is added proof of what I told you, that Elizabeth was greatly changed—three years ago she would have made the whole a subject of merriment, and you would have had a very playful, though maybe a little sarcastic, reply. Now she takes up the affair as soberly as though great matters depended on it. She says, too, you ought to expect some exception to the general satisfaction which <u>she believes</u> attends your intended connection with the family, etc. Elizabeth said she would be in Cincinnati during the winter and when she comes, do comfort the little lady. I must say I am sorry I shall miss your first meeting, but do tell me of it. I wish she could stay with your mother whilst she is in the city. I know she would find herself more at home and happier. She says the next time she expects to find a home in <u>our</u> house.

Ask her for me, Edward, <u>what she means</u> by the "supposition" that she will not be at home in the spring—I am at a loss. If I only knew when she would be in the city I would write to her to execute some trifling commissions for me, and enclose the letter to you—but she did not tell me.

I am sincerely glad that Mr. Campbell is recovering so rapidly, but wherefore have they all changed their plans? I cannot promise to be present at Elizabeth's [Drake's] marriage for I have no such expectation. I would not now give one day at home for a thousand weddings. I hope to be present at James Campbell's—that I should not like to miss, but if they appoint it too early, I cannot go. I think they are all in a hurry, and what is the use of it?

O, that the flowers would come soon. I am weary of the winter, and of myself oftener than I should be—I can't get <u>right</u> again. I have no cold or cough, dearest, but I have been grappling with a most insidious foe, and you are witness that I have not been victorious in the contest. Benny would ascribe it all to <u>sympathy</u>, as he said on a former occasion, you remember.

By the bye, <u>what</u> <u>is</u> <u>to</u> <u>be</u> <u>done</u> with Mr. D. in the family arrangements you did not say—alas, for the Uncle Bennys and Aunt Peggys! They seldom meet with due respect and consideration. Will he live with Harriet? He much needs the kind care of his needs and the breaking up of the family must be a melancholy thing for him. It is always a sad circumstance—but change must come to us all, and as you told me, maybe mine is the easiest I could experience.

Friday. I wonder if I shall write you a pleasant letter ever again? Do not scold me for dullness, or for anything, dearest, but write as often as your many engagements will permit and I shall soon recover my equanimity. [My brother] James came in just now and said Ellen Waddle returned last night, of which I am heartily glad. She will be with me next week and you may be glad of it, for she has <u>elected</u> herself guardian of your interests and will watch me closely and for your sake do all she can to make me happy. Mother is but little better—scarcely leaves her room. Julia, I hope, is better. I cannot write more now, for you will want a letter and I must send this by to-morrow's mail. Are you well, happy and do you think very often of me? Good-bye and write oh, very often, for I need your letters.   Your own true Margaret

[Postscript] Willy told me a few days since that the ink I used destroyed the paper. What a pity if all my interesting communications epistolary should be lost to future generations—best publish them, dear—now tell me whether I am jesting or serious, is it a man, or a bear?

My regards to Dr. Drake's family and my friend, Jamie. If you would give him a message I would send one. I will just say that my pens need mending and Mr. C. usually does me the kindness, etc. I have a new knife, but I do not know how to use it skillfully. Tell Harriet she is a sad girl not to have answered my last letter long ago. I shall not write to her till she does.

Does the good fairy Order abide with thee, or is she only a transient visitor? You treat some of my queries very disrespectfully. I shall have to call out "<u>Attention</u>" unless you know your duty better. Good-bye, in haste but truth.   Margaret

Eolia, Jan'y 29th, 1839
Tuesday Morning
[Postmarked Feb. 1]

Wed. Eve'g. I dated my letter yesterday mor'g, my best Edward, and really did wish to write to you—but I could not—wherefore, I don't know, but it was that I had been much disappointed that I had not two letters last week and was afraid to trust myself to write till I had heard from you again. I have written you quite enough of dull, complaining letters for the present and hope better for the future. As I told you in my last letter, your letters do not satisfy me and no sooner have I finished reading one than I wish for and almost expect another—just as if you were by me talking, you know, and should take up one subject after another. Your last visit spoiled me, dearest—I have hardly yet recovered from grief at your departure. But you will soon be with me again and if you spoil me then why, you will be the sufferer, for but a little while afterwards and you will have to take me for good and all as children say.

I am staying with [my sister] Ellen. To-day, I went home to see Mother—she seems better than for two months, but yet unable to leave the house. Julia, too, is much better and what do you think? I have flowers in bloom—irises and jonquils—I shall have them now in the house till I find them in the woods. I had a very long and very interesting letter from Amie [Amanda] Galloway yesterday, but good-night—I have a business letter to write to-night and I have already written one—what do you think of that? And guess the nature of my business with ladies in cities.

Thursday mor'g. In my calmer moods, dear Edward, I really think myself a most unreasonable woman to expect you, with your many and multifarious pursuits, to give me so much time. It is selfish, indeed, but very natural, you must admit. I have often explained it to you, wherefore I was so selfish—why, dear Edward, my whole happiness depends on your letters now—and if I am disappointed for two or three days in succession, after the time I certainly expect a letter, I am more than good for nothing—I cannot enjoy company or music or anything. You will pardon me then, dearest Edward, and not wonder at my importunity. I did think I would be more considerate—but alas, selfishness predominated, for all men and women too, wish to be happy, you know. How often I wish you were nearer to me, that you might come at least once a week. I do not believe, however, that Mr. Thatcher and Sally [Swearingen] profit much by their opportunities, or have in fact, dearest, as frequent communications or as intimate communion as we have, a hundred miles apart—but they are not like us, you know.

I don't like you to speak too depreciatingly of yourself or to doubt, as you seem to do, that you will make me happy. Do not do it again, my own Edward, I do not like it—if you fail of making me happy, who else would have succeeded? I am much grieved at your continued indisposition. You must, unless you are soon better, give up some of your vexing cares, and, come what may, endeavour to recover your health. We must patiently submit to the great Disposer of events in all things, but ill health for either of us will be a great drawback upon our happiness—the only one, dearest Edward, I can now foresee. You often need the soothing and comforting— just as I do, dear one, and of all the earth you only can so minister to my happiness, and perhaps I to yours. If I had known how much you would have needed me in that way, it would have been the strongest temptation I could have had to consent to your first arrangement. You will think better of yourself, myself and the world in general when the cloud is removed from your spirit by returning health. Dear Edward, I know it all—how much you suffer and how little comfort, in such a state, is to be derived even from the prospect of speedy relief. I hope I shall never have to bear it again, but since it teaches me more fully to sympathize with you I cannot so much regret what I have suffered mentally and physically. It will indeed be strange if we should overlook our many mercies and blessings, and allow ourselves to dwell perversely on the comparatively few trials we have. Why, dear Edward, your love is to me the richest blessing I have on earth. We can, we must, be happy if we try to do our duty and I feel confident that will be our earnest endeavour.

Amanda has told Mr. Trotter positively she will not be married before me and many a blessing, I suppose, he has given me for delaying his happiness. I must have Amie for my bridesmaid. I like her and I must have Anne James, and I will have Ellen Waddle. Suppose we ask Mr. Frank Campbell to support Miss James? Willy, Amanda; and Mr. Drake, Ellen W.? Will it do, think you? Amanda thinks we have chosen the middle of May and says, "Oh, how delightful it will be at Adena then." We shall go to her wedding either the last week in May or the first of June— 'tis to be decided when Mr. T. comes to Ohio again, which will be next month.

I do not wish it to be known that you are coming in March—you ought to keep up your character as a gallant gentleman—in six weeks you will come again. Poor Miss Eaton—I feel very sorry for her—her mother has had much affliction. She is, I think, a most excellent woman. I cannot write as well here as in my own dear quiet little room at home. I will write soon again. Mr. Thatcher is going to Connecticut next week. Send James Campbell home; my pens need mending. I think

I can sing with more ease, and my voice is improving. Good-bye, and God bless thee, my dear one.

[Postscript] I have only been here a week and I am <u>homesick</u>—fie on me for a baby. Do you know that it is a very difficult matter for me to write to your mother? Were it not for the hope she would write to me, I should not do it—there is selfishness for you. Will you sometimes remember me to Mrs. James?[23] She ought to remember me.

Margaret

THE WIFE OF A LITERARY MAN.

A woman fit to be the wife of a literary man must indeed be a *woman;*—she must combine in her character all those pleasing attributes which we often find described, but so rarely meet with in real life. She must be neither selfish in feeling, vain, prodigal, nor passionate. She must be one who will not marry where she cannot respect, and, when she has consented to lay aside her virgin honors, one who will love her husband with a devotion that shall waive every other consideration but that of duty to her God. She must be even more than all this; she must be self-sacrificing in disposition, and be willing to endure much loneliness; and also learn, if she have not already, to have a fondness for her husband's pursuits, in which case she will receive a return that will be dearer far than all the world can offer. A man of literary pursuits sins against himself and the woman he marries, if he takes one who is but a votary of fashion, whose empire is in the drawing room, and not in the seclusion of domestic life. And if he marry a literary pedant, he will be still more unfortunate—unless the pedantry be that of a young, active, and inquiring mind, which is pleased with its first essay into the regions of learning. Sh

choosing a wife should not look so much for shining abilities as for a clear, discriminating judgment, and a warm and affectionate heart. A combination of these qualities, if *he* be not an unreasonable, cross-grained tyrant, will be sure to brin—————ic felicity.

Given to me by Edward

Dec. 1838.

From the estate of Winston Mansfield Dudley

Margaret's "Idol Home" in 2001
Courtesy of Karel Whyte

The Mansfield and King Homestead, from the Cincinnati *Times-Star*, December 8, 1932. *Courtesy of The Cincinnati Post*

Part Eight
"Time's flight will . . . take me from my idol home"
Letters to Edward Mansfield,
February 4 – April 15, 1839

Eolia, Feb. 4th, 1839
Monday evening
[Postmarked Feb. 8]

I have just received your very welcome and equally sober letter. Your last two letters are <u>very</u>, <u>very</u>, <u>very</u> <u>sober</u>—wherefore, dearest Edward? Not for that cause alone, but for others I don't care just now to mention, I do assure you if you were here to-night I should take you very seriously to task. If I had written an hour ago I should have said some things you will never hear—but I have thought better of it. You will not understand me on paper and, as we have suffered enough from misunderstandings already, I will <u>for</u> <u>the</u> <u>present</u> (mark that) deny myself the gratification of <u>ending</u> a scolding which should begin with, "How dare you, sir," etc. Now, is not that alarming? Are you not terrified at the prospect for the future? You may meekly ask, "Why, what have I done or said?" I shall not tell you. It has not <u>hurt</u> <u>me</u> but only made me a little mad and I would give a pretty thing if you could see my <u>brilliant</u> eyes just now. I have half a mind not to write to you for a week. Pray, sir, do not flatter yourself quite so highly—you are really quite presuming—oh, I wish I could just have the pleasure of . . . . Indeed I am mad, but yet I have laughed a dozen times since I began to write. You, sober, meditative, dignified, what <u>is</u> the right word? None I can think of seems to express what I wish to say. O, for the invisible coat of the redoubtable Jack the Giant killer, that I might follow you about for a little while. I have a strong inclination to ask aid of the <u>little</u> <u>people</u> who "drink the dew" and pass in and out of key-holes at pleasure. But maybe you are in your awfully sublime mood just now and so, my dear, good, but naughty Edward, for the present, good-night.

Wednesday evening. Thanks, dear Edward, for your last dear letter, which I received to-day—it has contributed more to my happiness than any one you have written since your return. I like the <u>spirit</u> of it. Do you know I thought your last letter almost, not quite to be sure, but yet very near answering the epithet of <u>saucy</u> and it put me for a little while quite in a <u>pet</u>, as maybe the last page may show you. You may think of me what you please, but mind, sir, you <u>shall</u> <u>not</u> <u>say</u> everything you think of me—to think of your telling me ever so many times, how very much <u>I</u> <u>love</u> <u>you</u>! And then, after telling me that I <u>must</u> do so and so, to say that women govern <u>always</u>—and then again to agitate a point which <u>was</u> <u>settled</u> by you months ago, and yet more recently put at rest by <u>mutual</u> <u>consent</u>, because you chose it to be so. I see how it will be bye-and-bye and I see also that I had best take advantage of my present <u>liberty</u>. You cannot possibly make me afraid of you, dearest, and I do not know that you wish it.

It is very strange to me that you should feel such a doubt as you expressed in your last letter. I do not know that it would be proper for me to make vows and protestations of ever-lasting faith—that is your part. Nor did I suppose it necessary even now, if ever so proper. In truth, dearest, I am puzzled how you can doubt me in that way—it is incomprehensible to me, for I have never had such a thought of you, though if we talk seriously of the matter I should have as good or better reason to fear I might disappoint you. I am sorry to say it of you, but as I do it often of myself, you may this time share the epithet, "simpleton," with me—what say you to that? Were you ever so called before? Do you wish me to say I am already disappointed? If it were the case, I should unhesitatingly tell you so. I have it yet in my power to save you from future disappointment with respect to myself, but unless you insist on it, my dear Edward, I shall not.

You say you know me well—am I changeable in anything—and above all in my affections? Dearest Edward, at your heart you have not a doubt, not the faint shadow of one; if I thought you had, I should not feel quite as happy in your love. Is it not strange how very strong our <u>sympathies</u> are? Now I have been better for the last ten days than I have been for six weeks. Although you did not know it, I was far from being in health when you were with me, and since then I have suffered more than from the same cause for a year or more. I am perfectly well now, and quite happy again. "The glorious sun is brighter." Mother is much better, Julia is better, Ellen Waddle has returned, and <u>everything</u> promises fair.

You are very good, indeed, to say I may stay at home till the middle of May and I rather expect to do so, for surely you will stay two or three weeks with me [after our wedding]—will you not? I had yesterday a letter from Harriet [Drake] in which she requests me to be present at her sister's marriage, but says <u>nothing</u> of her own;

but if Mr. C. ever returns he will tell me everything. Harriet speaks of you as having been an invalid and partly under her care. Ellen Waddle is not with me, for you know I am with Ellen, my sister. The two coming weeks she says she will spend with me. By the way, Ellen W. is engaged to act as bridesmaid to Miss Woodson, a friend in Lexington, Ky., who is to be married on the tenth of April. So, dear, if I wish to have her with me, we must take the very last of the month. I wish I—but no matter now —I suppose my business is of no more importance than yours, and somehow I can arrange it to suit you—but if I do cry in June, mark me—I told you so—and you must neither blame nor upbraid me. If I could but keep you here. I shall go home on Sunday and right gladly write to you from my own sanctum. Here I have no place where I can write uninterruptedly except before daylight, and then almost all my letters are written.

I send you some rose leaves. I robbed Ellen of a very sweet bud for you but did not tell her its destination. Unless Mr. Campbell comes home soon, I must employ another pen-maker. I have hardly one I can write with. I long to get home again—you don't know how much—I have only been there once in two weeks and so near. I should have gone oftener but the weather has been so seriously cold that I feared to venture out so far. Whenever you can, you will write? I need your letters more and more.

Mr. Thatcher has gone East. He and Sally [Swearingen] are much more sentimental than we—he showed me a pretty little lock of hair and bade me guess where it came from. I am going to spend the evening with Mrs. Burbridge[1] at Col. Madeira's—are you not afraid to trust me? Thursday—I am dull to-day and hope to get a letter from you—no—not till Saturday. My love to precious little Eddy—does he remember me? You will remember me sometimes to your dear mother. I hope she has good health now. Good-bye, my own dear Edward. God's blessing be ever with thee.

Your own true Margaret

Adena, Feb. 10th, 1839
Sunday evening
[Postmarked Feb. 13]

Congratulate me, dearest, on my return home—after an absence of two weeks and a day (it seems much longer). Right happy am I to find myself at home in my own darling room, a most comfortable rocking chair, by a cheerful fire writing, dearest, to you. I know you love me, and need not your last letter to confirm that fact but, indeed, it is a very dear letter and I love you for it. You are very good to me—write always twice a week, and I'll promise never to be unhappy and I think I may promise, too, that I will not be sick. It is very strange I should so much need your letters as scarcely to <u>live</u> <u>in</u> <u>peace</u> unless I have them just when I expect. I do not <u>tire</u> of them and you have given me a fair trial, too, of your most precious self.

Thank you, though, for saying I <u>may</u> tire of you sometimes and then you will send me to Adena—I shall be tempted to profess myself wearied with you sometimes. But, no—when I have once left it, home is no longer a home for me—"Whither thou goest I will go."[2] You sometimes, Edward, have expressed doubts that I should be disappointed—I don't think I clearly comprehend precisely your meaning—in yourself, dearest? Never, if you are what I now know you. I am sometimes troubled, and that not a little, lest I be discontented with a city life. I hope not. I wish to be happy wherever God shall appoint my home—but you know my manner of life from my <u>birth</u>. You do <u>not</u> know how remote from cities or towns all my visions of happiness have been. I only mention this occasionally now, to prepare you for what may happen, though I hope not. If I only thought you could be with me most of the time I should have but few fears—you cannot, you know, dear, and probably just at the time I shall most need you, you may have least time to give me.

What I said in jest once, I have half a mind to repeat in earnest and say I <u>do</u> believe it would have been wiser to have postponed our marriage till you had <u>more</u> <u>leisure</u>—I shall feel as though I am interfering with your arrangements when I make demands on your time. Do not, dearest, misunderstand me this time. I know your business is important, and surely I am interested that it should not be neglected. It would, I may not deny, have given me much pleasure to have spent the month of June at home and until your last came I hoped to do so, but, dear Edward, it is by no means necessary to my happiness as you ask. I was absent, as <u>you</u> <u>ought</u> to remember, the whole of the month last year—very much against my will I was obliged to leave home just at that time, but I went [to Cincinnati] with my sister and it best suited her plans.[3] I well remember saying and thinking, "I'll see what shall take me from Adena at this time next year." The roses all bloomed in my absence and I could not recall them, so I just set my heart on the next season. There are many little arrangements for summer which I thought I might make for Mother's comfort—but they, too, can be dispensed with, or someone else can attend to them. I don't like the uncertain season of spring much better than winter and not till June do I fairly recover the possession of my frozen faculties. I should not mention any of these matters if you had not led me by your observations to the subject—it may be better that I would not have my own way in this thing, but I must confess 'twas not [an] easy duty to yield, even, my best love, to you. I do not think you will ever ask anything I cannot more readily grant— no one but you knows this, for when I have been questioned by my family as to the <u>time</u>, I have invariably answered, "Between the month of March and the last of June." Since you left me I have had no thought but to [accede] to your wishes and am making my arrangements accordingly. One reason why I was on a certain day woefully depressed was that (added to real indisposition) Mother had said to me a few days previous, she thought I had better begin certain necessary preparations.

<u>Then</u> I felt, oh, how keenly, that I <u>must</u> leave home—it had always seemed, before, a very distant event—but I must not think of that now, for my heart is sore thus, yet. You think I do not think enough of you when I speak of these things—my heart would tell you otherwise, could it transmit its unwritten thoughts. I shall write to you twice this week, for your kind letter. You are a dear, good Edward and I promise you, you shall lose nothing by your attention to my happiness.

I am going to town this evening (for this is Monday, you must know) on a most important mission—when that is accomplished, I shall feel much more at my ease. Thanks for your very pretty songs which I shall learn forthwith—they are all pretty and I love them, for you sent them. The duet, I shall ask Amanda G. to learn with me—the air is an Italian one which I have long admired, and often tried to find words to suit—but could find none to please me—the measure is uncommon. Thank you, dearest, again, and now till to-morrow, good-bye. I did not mean to write so much—I only felt glad to be at home again and wished you to share my pleasure. My letter cannot go till Wednesday, and I will keep it and write a little to-morrow that you may have the latest intelligence.

I have been to town and seen Mr. Campbell. He looks thin and languid. I wanted to take him home, but his brother will leave home in a few days and they have some business to talk over. He says he will come and stay some day as soon as he can and then do you and Harriet fear the consequences. He looks a little as though he needed care yet. Tell Harriet I will keep him in order for her.

Tuesday morning—I <u>have done it</u>—and guess what it is that I have done? Why, dearest, what I little thought I should ever do—ordered a dress for a very special occasion and this morning the letter is on its way. I am glad it is done, for it has troubled me more than a little to have it to do myself—my sisters had me to assist them. Ellen W[addle], like a bad girl, has gone to Columbus and Ellen Carlisle,[4] too—both promised to stay with me this week.

Do you hear from Mr. Drake and will he return in the spring? Ellen W. is much pleased with Mr. Telford's [manner] and says she thinks maybe he will do.[5] I told her I should tell you how very willing she was. There is to be a wedding next week. Miss Caldwell who spent a week with me two weeks since and then told me solemnly she <u>never</u>, <u>never</u> would marry Mr. Allston—she marries him next week.[6] She had rejected him a dozen times, I do believe, and had, as she thought, given him his <u>definition</u> [?] the day before she came to stay with me. They made it up and have been engaged for a week and next Tuesday will be married.

My dearest, good-bye. Margaret

[Postscript] I should have written to you Saturday night immediately on the receipt of your letter, but was so very much engaged that I had no leisure till eleven o'clock and you know you don't allow me to keep late hours. And I should have thought I had plenty of time after midnight to write two or three letters. I shall give up some of my correspondents <u>after</u> April and you amongst the number. Since I can't write at night I find it consumes more time than I can well spare of <u>day</u>. I wish I could send you some of our very sweet irises—have your mother's yet bloomed? They need water and the next mild rain they should be set out. I have more than a dozen in bloom and more opening every day.

I am grieved to hear of your mother's illness. I do hope she is better now. My warmest love to her and to my dear little Eddy, too. What I have filled my sheet with I hardly know for I have not said much. Mother will spoil you some of these days. I see clearly you will be a great favorite, though, poor unfortunate, you are a Yankee and a friend to Dr. B[eecher?]. She is pleased with all your speeches and pronounces that on history <u>admirable</u>. Is it not a pleasant thing to see mother and daughter of the same mind? I am well, and happy if you are so—I can find no good letter paper in town —I owe you an apology for that, as I see, but can get no better.

Mrs. Worthington has sadly inconvenienced me by neglecting a very small commission I entrusted to her. I wish I had sent to Mrs. Campbell to perform it for me. I shall not send to Cincinnati for anything—I have acquaintances in Philadelphia who will attend to my wants. What if my things should not arrive in time! Why, you'd have to wait, that is all.
[In margin of p. 2] Go to Rostaing [?]—he will manage your case better than Rogers.

Adena, Feb. 12th, 1839
Tuesday evening
[Postmarked Feb. 15]

Do you know, most precious Edward, that I had just finished reading for the [nth] time your last letter when another came? Well, I was thinking of writing part of a letter to-night, but then thought I, my letter only went this morning, and so I concluded I would wait till to-morrow and send my letter by Friday's mail. Hope whispered me I should get a letter to-night but I could not expect it—you are the dearest and best Edward in all the world to write me such frequent and sweet letters.

I do believe I love you better when you write often—for the last two weeks I have been thinking pleasant thoughts of you all the while. But oh, dear Edward, for three weeks or more I was in a suffering way—in my last letter I told you one cause of my being so. It is over now and I am in perfect health and Mother is much better and all my blessings brighter than they were. When I feel as I now do, I wonder that I can ever allow myself under any circumstances to be unhappy—it seems ungrateful, wicked.

I am so glad your little Iris has bloomed—gather from it, dear, what meaning you wish. In Flora's vocabulary[7] it means "I have a message for you" and so I had— ten thousand. Let its fragrance tell you of all you would wish to know from me—bid it faithfully bear my message. I am truly grieved that your dear mother should continue ill—who has she with her? Oh, Edward, if my mother should be in as ill health next, as the present winter, can I be happy? Your mother should have some of her friends with her, though in truth little can be done. I hope I may be of use to her at some future time.

I must speak of it now lest it pass from my mind—I am so glad you spoke of Mr. Telford. I wished, but was afraid to ask, if you could bring him in case Mr. Drake could not officiate. If Mr. D. returns in health I think he will come with you; he promised it long ago. I must not take so much time to write to you, Sir, for I have more to do than can be accomplished by my ten fingers and one head. I will not turn over to-night. Good-bye.

Thursday morning. This is <u>Valentine's Day</u>—do you ever write Valentines, dearest? I wish you would think of it, to write to me to-day. I have been looking into my journal to see what I said therein this day last year.[8] It seems but yesterday—and yet it has been a most eventful year to me. But, dearest, I choose you my Valentine for the ensuing year, only the misfortune is, I <u>can't</u> choose any other, and, moreover, I must choose you this year and for aye—"Vow ye and keep your vows, else vow ye never." Several signs of spring have appeared—my expanding flowers are one promise, for their "mates of the garden" must follow them. The doves have been heard, but I did not hear them, but this morning was charmed by the sweet warblings of other birds. I wait, however, for more promise, and long to attend the first concert given by my friends, the frogs—then I shall be sure the winter is indeed past. I hope indeed, as you predicted, we may have an early spring. I long for the flowers and mild air of spring—and maybe it will bring you, too. It would have been very wrong for you not to have come once again to see me, if you could, without neglecting your duties, do so. Why, by April you would almost be a stranger to me (man or bear?)

I have already learned your songs—one, I shall sing only for you—I would rather you should first hear them. If you hear anything you like, and think would suit me, send it, my dearest, I will learn as many new songs as I can for you and I have not leisure for difficult pieces of music. Col. Taylor sent me some songs a few days before I received yours, but I have not touched them since yours came, for they are not very pretty. One is the "Bridal Wreath" which Mr. Taylor thought an appropriate subject for me.

Our cousin Jamie[9] was here all afternoon yesterday—he wished to stay in the country a week, but his brother is going East to-day, and his other brother is indisposed so that his presence is necessary at his store though he says he will not attend much to business. We had such a long talk—he says he began a letter to me the day after he and Harriet [Drake] were betrothed, acquainting me with all his proceedings. Harriet was to add a post-script, which, however, she neglected to do till he became ill and so I did not get my letter. Jamie thinks they will be married the first week of June—which, I fear, will interfere with our going to Amanda's wedding, but I will write and tell her of their plans and she can fix her time before or after, as she pleases.

I am exceedingly sorry for your mother's illness. I wish I could do something for her. The weather is so much milder for a few days, that I hope she will be better. Mother is in almost her usual health—she is going to-day to see Ellen and 'tis the first time she has been out this winter, or since you left, I mean. Poor Julia is worse again—William told me last night she was confined to bed. I have not seen her since Monday, and then she was not so well. She has had a winter of suffering. Mary Galloway is expected this week to stay with her sister [Julia], and, indeed, she needs her. Albert is coming too, and I shall be glad to see him, though he has disappointed me. I cannot forgive him that. Henry G[alloway] has been here, but I fear his case is hopeless and so I told him. Ellen Carlisle says now she never can marry him, but <u>some</u> women are so changeable that I put little faith in the generality of professions of this kind. But I think poor Henry's case is decidedly a bad one—he has already made <u>two</u> applications—he says he would make a dozen if he thought the final one would be successful.

You seem to think it wonderful that you have written two letters a week, but my dear Edward, if you wrote daily I should not complain. You are very kind, for I know you have many engagements—I think I am quite considerate and reasonable in my <u>requirements</u>—am I not? I assure you I might, with <u>reason</u>, too, exact much more and you would be <u>obliged</u> to comply. What if I were to be unreasonable and require you to be my most humble servant? Mr. Campbell says all his letters to Harriet must be punctually answered, <u>letter</u> <u>for</u> <u>letter</u>. I threatened to warn Harriet to assert her rights, but thought I would wait and see if Jamie kept his resolution. He is perfectly unreserved with me, and looks and <u>expresses</u> his gratitude—again said he owed <u>all</u> to me. I don't like him to say that. You ask what [my brother] James is doing—I don't know. There is little of anything going on that I hear of. I send you a leaf from a boquet in my room. I wish I could send you the whole. Eddy's flowers will keep me in your memory. This is Thursday, dearest, and I shall not write again for a whole week. You boasted—now this is the third letter I have written in one week—I dare you to do more and never let me be more than three or four days letterless! Good-bye, dearest.   Your own true Margaret

Adena, Feb. 15th, 1839
Friday evening
[Postmarked Feb. 18]

I said in my letter yesterday morning that I should not write to you again for a week, but, dearest Edward, I did not know then that I should have another letter to-night, or that my nonsense would have any more effect than to make you laugh. There—will that be sufficient apology for breaking my word, or shall I add yet another excuse for my writing to-night? Just by way of proving to you my perversity, ever since I said I would not write I have had a strong wish to break my resolution, and came <u>mighty</u> <u>near</u> doing it last night.

Albert G. was here yesterday afternoon and said a great many impudent things, to <u>try</u> me, he said. I'll tell you some of them when you come. Don't you think he says that I marry you for your mother's sake. He knows my deep regard for her, for I have done him the honor to take him to see her several times. Yes, he says she made the match—I told him even if she had, I would freely forgive her that which had made me happy. He said you were not handsome; I asked him if he presumed to compare himself with you. He talked about you all the while he was here—and—(don't be offended, dearest) for some of his pertness I gave him a <u>sound</u> <u>box</u> <u>on</u> <u>the</u> <u>ear</u>—no gentle one, either. Why, it is only Al—that I have known since he was a school boy.[10] He insisted on knowing our wedding day, which I could not tell him. Said he would not be wanting then, he supposed—as he would be a bird of ill omen. What did the boy mean? I like Albert—for all his misdeeds. He wants me to choose a wife for him, but says he won't promise to love her. I don't believe he thinks my heart is very deeply engaged—that is all he knows, dear Edward, and 'twas not my place to tell him better. Mary Galloway came to stay with Julia who is yet an invalid.

Why did you burn your letter? It was <u>mine</u> and now I have lost it—anything from you will please me, even a gloomy letter. You had best throw that silly letter of mine into the fire. Why, dear, it was not worth reading once, much less six times. I want to see you to-night—in a month you will be here and then how glad I shall be. Albert asked if it were possible you were not coming before <u>the</u> <u>time</u>. I evasively answered that was just as I pleased, and so it is, my own dear Edward, and I am pleased that you shall come, for I long to see you again.

I have to leave home again next week, against my inclination, too, sorely; but Arthur will be absent and Ellen needs me, but I'd much rather stay at home for a thousand reasons. At home, I can write to you when I please and without interruption. I have written every day this week, and yet I had not thought to write more than once a week—but you are my own dear Edward, and if I chose to write a <u>whole</u> letter every day—what of it? I have thought again and again, if I would write seldomer and with more care, it would be better for me, and my letters equally interesting to you—but when I sit down to write, I forget that, and scribble away for dear life.

The gentlemen have been <u>amazingly</u> <u>kind</u> in visiting me for the last week. I am impatient at their interruptions. Do you know they have almost all forsaken me since I am engaged? That is, they don't come to see me as before—for which I am their obliged servant, in true earnest. I like them all just as well as I ever did and when it does not interfere with my plans, find their society just as agreeable.

Saturday evening. Cousin H. Massie has just left here—I like him right well and so, I think, will you. I have a strong notion that he wishes again to address Ellen W[addle]. He intimated as much to me, this afternoon, without knowing that I had any knowledge of his first <u>essay</u>. He asked me how it would do—I do not think they are suited to each other and so I told him and he seemed rather disappointed. I am quite sure Ellen would not marry him. He told me to tell you, you need not be in a great hurry to come.

I had a letter from Anne James last night. She seems afraid she cannot be here by our time, and I am really apprehensive that Ellen Waddle will not have returned from Kentucky by the last of April—her friend is to be married on the tenth, and unless Ellen hurries, I shall be disappointed. To you, doubtless, these seem trifling causes, but to me they are important. Cousin Henry says "the people" will have us married on the twentieth of April. I shall not consent to name any day more than a month beforehand, for various reasons, some of which I will tell you when you come, and in sooth I wish you were here to-night for my head aches sadly, and you know you have skill in driving away that pain.

I have been entirely confined to the house this week against my intentions, and am suffering for it. Every afternoon I have ordered my horse for a ride, and been as often prevented by visitors; some of the gents have been here every afternoon from three o'clock till sunset. Has it not been delightful weather? We must have some rides when you come. I love to think of being with you, but—dearest, I have said that often enough already. I am so sorry you destroyed that full letter. I won't forgive you till I receive one written closely and with every nook filled. I have, as well as you, sad thoughts sometimes, though with much less cause, and think if I could only tell you of my troubles I should be happy again. Dear Edward, I would so much rather talk than write to you, for then you cannot misunderstand me and I fear you sometimes do—my letters.

I read with both pleasure and profit the Oration you sent—thank you, I will read what you send me and in truth I have but little time just now for much more. Company, letter writing and music must have their dues, and thus I have, with my many engagements, little leisure. I often with longing eyes look from my needle to my bookshelves. After a month I shall not be so busy. My seal will tell you, where there is love there is faith.

Mother is quite well again; Willy has been quite sick for some days. Julia is just so-so. I shall go to the wedding [of Miss Caldwell] next week, and will tell you of it. Do write very often, for I leave home reluctantly and shall need your consolations. I grieve that you were disappointed in that letter offering you comfort. Do not, my dearest, mind what I say. I would not for the world willingly cause you the slightest anxiety, much less unhappiness. Do you rise early? Then you have leisure to write daily if you please, and so you ought to do next week. You owe me a large amount of letters. Ellen W. is yet in Columbus—do you know, dear Edward, that I think she ought to have kept her word to me, rather than to have gone to Columbus? Indeed I do—but I find few persons, even the best, who seem to think small promises which involve little, at all binding. Now I do, and as an instance, once in precisely similar circumstances with the present, I kept my word though I had much stronger inducements to break it than had Ellen. She is a most excellent girl, but we are very dissimilar in many things, though we are good friends. My best and dearest Edward, good-bye, and burn no more letters.

Your own Margaret

[Postscript] Sunday Morning. It is snowing, and I fear winter will come again, but it cannot last long. Can you tell me, dearest, what day I may hope for you?—or what week, even? If the roads are very bad you should come by the river. Do guard against exposure and take care of your health. I am well except a little headache, the consequence of want of exercise. My love to your dear mother and dear little Ned—also his papa. I am sorry to see snow—the earth is quite covered and snow falling fast.

I do earnestly hope your mother is better. I feel anxious for her. Mother seems to think of her all the while. I pray your next letter may tell me she is recovering. I am pleased that Eddy's flowers are blooming. I have a large box full of the same kind and the whole house is perfumed by them. They are a sweet promise of spring and excite many pleasing emotions. You must, indeed, write—oh, how often.

Eolia, Feb. 22nd, 1839
Friday eve'g
[Postmarked Feb. 25]

A whole week, a weary week and no letters—I, too, had hoped that my shower of letters would have elicited from you a few extra ones. Last week, dearest Edward, I had three—this week—not one.

Sat. I tried my best to write last night but I was so cast down that I could not and, besides, I was very certain I should have a letter to-night and so waited. I have been at two parties this week; one was a wedding—but it did not much interest me—the people were a different set from those I am accustomed to meet, and the parties not my particular friends. Mr. Woodrow performed the ceremony, I think, in a very awkward and by no means a solemn manner—it was very tedious, and appended to it, a short lecture to all married persons present—a thing so unusual that it excited mirth in some of our giddy young people. Indeed, I scarcely blamed them, for there was little in either the good little gentleman's matter or manner to make one feel solemn. I vow he shall not marry me after that barbarous mode—shall we send for the bishop?

I have just returned from spending a sociable evening with my friend, Elizabeth [McCoy] Foulke—'tis the second anniversary of her marriage. Cousin H. Massie brought me your letter. I had asked him to go to the office for me—I knew I should have [a] letter and did not half like to go for it myself, and so asked Mr. Massie. He teased me about it, too—said our box was empty, etc. I wonder you do not write to me very, very often—if you knew all I could tell you, you would. Your letters are my rights, dearest. I have received a great number of letters within the last month—they have poured in from every direction; yours scarcely come to me alone.

Ellen says you should be postmaster to enable you to defray the expense of my extensive correspondence—but never fear—I intend deliberately to give up the business and retain very few correspondents, those only who are my best friends. I am well aware I shall not have the leisure hereafter that I have had to devote to such things, and I would much rather stop at once, than to undertake what I am sure I cannot perform. Why, even now, since you, dearest, have altered my hours, I find it a difficult matter to write many letters without neglecting something else. How do you like the weather? 'Tis the mildest February I ever remember. I shall soon go to the woods for flowers. I have been absent from Adena for a week—it seems long, and you have aided in making it weary, though you had no such intentions—'twas only neglect. Did I not tell thee, dearest, I should need thy consolations more than usual? And yet this is Saturday night, and my letter has but just come. You will not believe me, but indeed I do not jest when I say my happiness depends as much [sic] on your letters.

Ellen Waddle told me to present to you her best regards and say she would take care of me for the two next weeks. She regrets having gone to Columbus, and says she wished a thousand times she had kept her promise to me. She professes herself delighted with your account of Mr. Telford, but seems fearful she will not be the happy one. William McCoy[11] has returned to Missouri and I earnestly hope Ellen will think no more of him. She would not forgive me if she knew I had betrayed her to you; she has much pride and it was severely wounded by her admission to me, but I am sure 'twas better for her. 'Twas a relief, and the feeling now will be more easily conquered—to say nothing of the benefits arising from my advice and sympathy. Ellen has great confidence in me, nor does it seem lessened now, though I told her she must tell me nothing she did not wish you to know. I have very few, really no, opportunities of communication with you except by the mail.

I have something for Eddy which I wish to send. I hope he will always be gentle and lovely as he used to be—I rather opine, dearest, you think he is more troublesome now, because since your mother's illness he has been more under your charge and gives you more trouble. Sometimes I am alarmed at what I have taken on myself in the care of your dear little boys. If I were but fitted for it, and could have the consciousness that I had the powers of fulfilling the whole duties of a mother to them, I should not fear, for I love children and the care of them has ever been a pleasure to me. I think, dearest, I am worth taking pains with and promise to be very grateful for any you may bestow on me.

I am <u>exceedingly</u> <u>glad</u> that you at last feel the necessity of caring for your health. If I could but take you away from all your troubles for a year or so, I know I could do much for your health but as it is your duty to retain your cares, and do all possible for your health at the same time, we must be not only submissive but contented and happy, and I think in any circumstances I can be of service to you if you will only <u>let</u> <u>me</u> <u>do</u> <u>as</u> <u>I</u> <u>please</u>. I have all your promise for that, dear one. I hope your mother will soon be well—she will surely come in April—and what of Mr. Davies?[12] I think I cannot in reason ask more than three weeks of your precious time and thank you from my heart for your kindness in promising so much. I would not have asked more. Good-bye—if you love me, write often. My love to your mother.

Your own Margaret

[Postscript] Julia continues to grow better—she has had a most trying winter. Ellen is well and Mother almost in her usual health. Willy was quite sick last week; I have not seen him for some days, but he is better, I know. Sister Sarah has been in Philadelphia and flourished considerably—I hope she has enjoyed her visit—she so seldom makes one for mere pleasure that she ought to be happy when she does. When will you come? Tell me—I wish to know for good reasons. Lizzy wrote asking when she must come, but I have not yet told her—I wish she was what she once was.

I practice as much as I can—have you kept your promise in that way? I shall expect the faithful performance of every promise you have ever made to me. I have not made many to you, dearest, and in that I did wisely. O, but I shall be glad to have you with me again. <u>They</u> <u>all</u> have a suspicion that it would be proper for you to make me another visit. They don't exactly say so; and I say nothing. Good-bye again, my dear, good

Edward. Your sad letter did not trouble me as much as some of its predecessors, but indeed, dear Edward, I longed for another to tell me you were bright again.

Adena, Feb. 28th, 1839
Thursday eve'g
[Postmarked March 4]

'Tis the last day of winter and a most stormy one it has been. We thought, dearest, the spring had come—you said so <u>for sure</u>, but a glance at the driving snow will convince you of the fallacy of our hopes. Time does <u>fly</u>; you tell me so in all your letters, but indeed you need not remind me of that. I am sorry and glad, too—its flight will bring you to me, but will also take me from my idol home. I do try to convince myself that I have grieved enough about that <u>last mentioned</u>, but sometimes my heart will ache at the prospect, in spite of my best efforts to control its emotions. If I did not think you loved me very dearly I could not, oh, dear Edward, I could not go. I don't think so much on it now, for some weeks past. I hope the <u>bitterness</u> is past, and you may not hear me speak many more regrets. I did not receive your letter written last week till yesterday, and this evening, thanks to you, my own dear Edward, came another. You are very kind and I will promise to be very good, and <u>endeavour</u> <u>sometimes</u> to <u>yield</u> <u>my</u> <u>will</u> <u>to</u> <u>yours</u>. I have been wishing to see you all day, and wished to write this morning that my letter might reach you this week, but I was much engaged and could not, so by waiting I have another letter.

Dear Edward, your mother surely must come. Did I not tell thee last summer that April would be <u>too</u> <u>early</u> for our friends? Now, if it were June instead, there would be nothing in the way of your mother's coming, and I have half a mind to ask her if we shall not delay awhile for her. I had rather wait two months (understand me, now) than lose the pleasure of having her present. Mother will not take a refusal, and begs your mother not to decide so long beforehand. She could bring Eddy and [her servant] Clara with her and you could engage someone to take care of the house for a short time—even if your mother would but stay a week. I do hope she will come. Are there trees before your house? If not, 'tis a favorable time for planting them.

In two hours more I might date <u>spring</u>. March—what a matter we make of these artificial computations of time! I will not sit up late, though in truth, I'd be glad of an excuse to keep me up every night till twelve. I often wish I could do without sleep. I have not seen <u>Jamie</u> for some time; he was here last week in my absence. I shall be very much pleased if Harriet will come. If Elizabeth's wedding[13] is over, why may not Harriet and Dr. Drake leave the <u>young</u> <u>people</u> to take care of the house and come to your wedding? I feared Harriet might feel some embarrassment, but she need not—Amanda will be here and everyone knows she is soon to be married. I do hope your mother will come. Have you heard [from] Mr. Davies? I don't know whether Eddy ought to come without your mother. We'll talk of that when you come, dearest.

Ellen Waddle is here with me—she will room with me and I find her quite an <u>annoyance</u> sometimes. She goes to Kentucky in two weeks, and will barely return in time for us. Good-night. After a day of storms, the bright moon is looking out so calmly beautiful. The next moon will bring you. I must know what day to <u>look</u> for you. I have not told anyone you are coming, but think I must tell Mother next week. She is not fond of <u>sudden</u> <u>surprises</u>.

Albert shall not dare speak to me as he did when last here. The only reason I suffered it was lest he might suppose me vexed by what he said, and I would not <u>that</u> for a good deal. He <u>would</u> talk of you. Every object seemed to suggest <u>you</u> for a topic—the garden seats—the flowers, etc. I do not think he will come to our wedding.

Dear Edward, can't you come on Sat. evening, as you said, and stay till next Friday? But, just as you can; I know, my dearest, you will stay as long as 'tis right you should. I hope you will have pleasant weather. I am <u>sorry</u> the weather affects your health—'tis the same with me—we shall have trouble yet from our <u>similarities</u>.

Friday, March 1. 'Tis just dawn, and there is a sweet bird warbling most delightfully near my window—it seems a welcome to spring, but the little creature must have an instinctive knowledge that winter is past for nothing else would tell him so. The ground is covered with snow and all nature looking as dreary as at midwinter. But it <u>is</u> spring for all that, dearest, and where is my winter?

Like you, I have been very industrious, but also, like you, have but little to show. I have been incessantly employed and not always in a manner most agreeable to my wishes. Time will go—if I could, I do assure you, I would stay its speedy flight.

Sat evening. Is <u>this</u> spring? The trees, shrubs, etc., are in truth beautifully appareled, but not with the garments I love best. I wish, dearest Edward, you could witness with me some of our beautiful snow scenes in the country. You have no opportunity of seeing one in beauty in the city, for the snow is sullied almost as soon as fallen. But here we have, for days sometimes, the pure "untrodden snow." Ellen and I were engaged to take tea at Fruit Hill,[14] but the snow-storm prevented.

Yesterday, we went to Mrs. Jacob's.[15] Saw Mr. Campbell there; he says he is very sure Harriet would not come—what did she say to you about it? I love you to dream of me, dearest. I do of you, but not often. Never mind the <u>gray</u> <u>hairs</u>—that is my concern, not yours, and I don't quarrel with them. What if you come the last week in March? Or just <u>which</u> week, I do want to know. I forgive you, dearest, for having burned <u>my</u> letter; you have been very good and I hope will continue your goodness. I often wish to say something about articles in *The Chronicle* and other things I read, but I've no room. I make a free use of all the cases of the first person singular [and] of the <u>personal</u> <u>pronoun</u>, and so my pages are speedily filled. Ellen is in amazement what we write so much about. I can't tell her, indeed.

Yesterday was such a beautiful spring-like day, it made my heart glad. I fear the effects of this sudden change on your mother. My mother is in her usual health; she has a <u>little</u> cough to-day but it will leave her the first fair day. I had a very kind letter from your mother. Indeed, dear Edward, she does think much more highly of me than I deserve, for which I am sorry, for she cannot fail of disappointment. But, indeed, 'tis no fault of mine—I never wished to deceive her. I like to be appreciated but not overrated. My love to your mother. I do earnestly hope she will not yet come to a positive decision not to come.

Sunday morning. "Stern winter reigns again." The poor little birds have ceased their music and, but for my Almanac (thank <u>you</u>) I should suppose it midwinter. We have a snow of some inches, six at least, I should think, and the weather as cold or colder than at any time in the month of February. Dear Edward, I was so unreasonable as to expect a letter last night. I had no right, I admit, nor did I deserve it, so I will not grieve over my disappointment, for you are very good and will write me soon again. I hope you ride sometimes and are prudent in taking precautions against your foe. How is dear little Eddy? Don't send him to school yet— two years hence will be time enough—he will have so many rough ways with other boys. Good-bye, and fail not to be as happy as you may. Don't grieve for losses and crosses. I must say I shall need a little more than bread and cheese, which, however, is all you have ever promised; but I think we can manage to get a little more.

Adieu, dearest.
Your own true Margaret

Adena, March 6th, 1839
Wednesday night
[Postmarked March 11]

Now, Edward, I am grievously disappointed. I have had no letter for a week and was so sure I should get one to-night that I sat up an hour past my usual time awaiting Willy's return from town. I have not been well to-day—and disappointment will not relieve a nervous headache. Your last is dated twelve days ago. I should have had two since. I intended to write you by Friday's mail but I can't indeed till I feel better, much better than I am to-night. The weather confines me to the house and I have had constant headache for a week. So, dearest, you will not get this, this week. Good-night. I have not been up so late as this for a long time—since you were here. I am mad with you to-night—you so often disappoint me. But maybe I may feel more amiable in the morning.

Friday evening. I repented of my decision and was just seating myself to finish this to send yesterday, when Mr. Campbell called. He stayed to tea and of course I had no time to write. I have no words to express my disappointment— dearest, my own Edward, unless you are ill, I must think you unkind to leave me so long without a letter. It has been a gloomy world to-day with me and I did <u>certainly</u> expect to be brightened by a letter from you. Ellen [Waddle] and I talked last night of a matter which excited me very much and made me more nervous than was altogether comfortable—consequently I did not close my eyes the livelong night and you may suppose I am none the better for it to-day.

Ellen will go next week to Kentucky—the arrangements of her friends there will probably so far interfere with ours that I shall be obliged to give up the hope of having Ellen for bridesmaid. As yet we cannot tell. Ellen is anxiously awaiting letters to inform her of the definite arrangements of her friends.

My own dear Edward, I do pray you are in health—but when *The Chronicle* came this evening and <u>no</u> <u>letter</u>, I had a thousand anxieties for you. You did promise to write twice a week—have you forgotten, Edward? Believe me, I need your letters now more than ever before, for I have frequent and sore heart-aches and you who only can administer me consolation—why will you not do it? I am sad, oh, how sad—do come to me or I cannot bear it much longer. It seems hard you will not write oftener; indeed, Edward, you do not mean it, but you often pain me. Your last letter is dated <u>24th February,</u> wanting but two days of two weeks; 'tis no small trial to me that when I most need the soothing influence of your letters they are oftenest denied me. On such a day as this, I <u>need</u> to be assured of your love for me—not that I doubt it, my own, but it requires much faith in your affection to make me willing to leave all I have loved and to chase away my despondent feelings. Unless I get your letters more frequently I believe I would rather, or almost, as leave have none. <u>You</u> cannot tell how much suffering disappoint[ment] causes me. Write by Columbus, dearest, and if you love me, if you care for me, let me hear oftener. I know you have many engagements, but in a little while I shall cease to ask such favors, though in place I may ask greater, but dear Edward, I must be indulged now. Good-night—I must go to sleep, if I can, without the letter I ought to have. I know you have written once, at least, for you could not surely leave me ten days without a letter from you. I ought to have <u>two</u> instead of one.

 Saturday night. At last, and I had almost despaired of it, <u>one</u> letter has come. But indeed, I expected three, for it seems a weary time since I received your last. Am I unreasonable? Dear Edward, my dearest of the world, tell me truly—I do think you ought to write me now twice a week. If my happiness depends on your letters, ought you to make me unhappy? I have been but dull company for Ellen W. this week and often wished she was not here, or I in happier mood. And how, pray, will you bear with me? I don't like to think how much trouble I shall cause you, but, as you said, if you <u>will</u> take me, it must be for better or for worse and I trust I shall not be <u>worse</u> all the while, but I cannot promise much—I know my failings too well. Dearest Edward, you calculate too largely on my character and will assuredly be disappointed. Depend on yourself for you have but little to expect from me in the way you speak of in your last letter. I hope to be of use to you in regaining your health and I promise you, if you desire health, you shall be an early riser. If nothing else will accomplish my purpose, I shall try the cold bath, which I have found effectual in desperate cases. O, but I do want to see you badly—but I shall scold you a little, too, for breaking your promises—to think you have begun already! Alas for the future if all are as lightly broken as those I now refer to. You would write twice a week and send me <u>something</u> every mail! That was "Lightly uttered, deeply heard," my dear one, for I believed every word you said and you have failed, you know how often. I can bear a great deal when I know what to expect, but of all things, I cannot endure a state of suspense; suffering is preferable—you know this. Do not fear my heart is not warm for you. I should be much more at ease were it less so. Your next letter will tell me just what day you will come. I shall send this by Columbus and you can judge if that route be the quickest in these <u>trying</u> <u>times</u>. I don't think I shall urge your writing. You can do just as you please, but if you write to me but once in twelve days I [will] write but once a month, that is all. First, I was impatient, then anxious and lastly, really angry with you, all within the last fortnight.

I had a letter from Mrs. Worthington in Dayton. We must invite <u>them</u> and Elizabeth says she will come. There will be quite a clan-gathering if all keep their promises. Mother had a long letter from sister Sarah—she had just returned to Cambridge and seemed much gratified by her visit to Philadelphia. Tom has the offer of a very good place from a merchant there, which sister has under consideration and I think will accept though she was unwilling to take Tom from College before he finished his course.

Louis [Macomb][16] has gone to learn the <u>printing</u> <u>business</u> with Mr. Ely. He chose it, and seems, so far, pleased with his choice. Julia is recovering. Mother and all the rest, well. I have not told them you was [sic] coming, and have made no more definite arrangements than we agreed on when you were with me. I have not much leisure for music—either I am losing my fondness for it, or becoming very diffident for I don't like to play for any one.

Now, Sir, unless I get <u>letters</u> next week, I won't write to you. A pretty thing, truly!—that I must beg for what is my right, and you, too, calling yourself a conscientious man. Thee had best look to thyself or thee will get into a scrape.

Ellen W. has been with me for two weeks and a good, kind girl she is. She is going to Kentucky very soon and I fear will scarcely return in time for us. Mr. Lee,[17] the gentleman who is to marry her friend, was here this afternoon, just from Lexington and <u>Missouri</u>. He is a clever young man and his usually sunny countenance was more shining than ever. I am sorry for Miss Woodson—she must go from home and <u>all</u>, and way out to the extreme western boundary of Missouri. That is <u>almost</u> as hard as my lot—is it not? Our activities seem strangely contrary to our wishes sometimes. Now, there is Amanda envying me my city life and dreading her own in the country—and I—you know, dearest, how gladly I would exchange with her and how many fears I have for the future. I know it is wisely chosen for me but 'tis a trial too, and you must have much patience and be tender with me till I learn to bear it. Once I thought it would be impossible for me to live in a city or even a town like our own, but then, dear, I did not know how much there was in such a life to make it tolerable. You were not in my heart in those days.

I am sorry, dear, you have so much care, and sorry, too, that you so often blame yourself so much. Let by-gones be by-gones and let us endeavour to redeem the past. I have much to do to make amends for a wasted life. Paper fails, but love does not, dear.

Your own Margaret

[Postscript] My very best regards to your mother—I shall soon answer her very kind letter. A kiss to dear little Eddy. I have something for him which I shall send when I have opportunity. In looking over my childish treasures not long since, I found a whistle that I thought would please Charley and so I laid it away for him. It was given to me when I was about his age.

Adena, March 11th, 1839
Monday eve'g
[Postmarked March 13]

You do not know, dear Edward, and I am glad you do not, how sick I have been these two days. I shall be quite well before this reaches you and so you need have no anxiety on my account. I have been imprudent in confining myself too much—the weather has not been such as to tempt me out, and I have been very busily engaged within doors—and this it is which has made me sick. I have had constant head-ache for two weeks, but not severe, and every day I hoped it would go off, but yesterday it gave me a warning it would no longer be trifled with, and so I have kept to my room and am trying to be well. I have been much alone to-day and, in thinking of you, I chanced to remember that unless I wrote by Wednesday's mail you would probably get no letter from me before you left Cincinnati, for your last letter did not say explicitly what time you should be here. Indeed, Edward, your letters have been very precious of late. This is the eleventh of March and in that time, <u>eleven days</u>, I have had but one letter from you. Do read over some of my old letters and see if I have not urged sufficient reasons why you should write me very often. I have never left you a whole week without a letter. My own feelings of disappointment taught me to fear lest you might suffer as I did.

Ellen Waddle has left me, and though she is a dear, good girl, I am right glad to have my room all to myself again. I cannot be happy unless I am much alone—please remember that. Ellen Watts was here to-day—she was speaking of men and their selfish nature. I said if I thought you were like all the men I know (with but two or three exceptions) I would not marry you, even though matters had gone so far, no, nor even were it six weeks later, if I were assured you were like all the rest. Ellen said she <u>supposed</u> <u>you</u> <u>were</u>. But I cannot, I will not believe it—she does not know you. But I do know, Edward, I would not for a world be her husband's wife. I have met with but very few men whom I could even like. I see too plainly their selfishness when I contrast them with women. I could not bear what many, yes, Edward, most women bear, and this is the main reason (I have told you) that I thought myself unfitted for married life. I think so yet, Edward, and have my misgivings that you will discover that I spoke truth. I wish I was gentle, easy, <u>characterless</u> as some men would have us all to be. I think better of you than to suppose you, my dearest, would wish me so, but as men are, it would be the happiest for women to be so. I remember some years ago to have conversed with Mrs. Douglass on the subject and she, too, says marriage to a woman is but a better sort of slavery. Make me a slave! There lives not the man who could do it, and I have not the slightest fear of your playing lord and master to me.

I want to see you to-night. My head aches sadly and you could make it better. This is the first time I have sat up half an hour to-day, but I thought maybe you would wish to hear from me. I have not been happy of late, dearest Edward; my thoughts are troubled and I cannot banish them. I shall be quite well before you come and I anticipate much comfort in seeing you. I have much to make me sad, more than to gladden me. You said you would make me cry two or three times, but you have done far more than that and I fear there are yet more tears to be shed. Why, Edward I never used to cry. You have made a baby of me and now you must soothe and pet me to tranquillity again.

Tuesday. I am better to-day, dear Edward, and hope I shall be quite well by another day. I have been fasting for several days—starving myself well. I shall be quite well enough to enjoy the letter that must come this evening. You will have bad roads and an unpleasant journey, I fear—but you will be careful. Come to Adena, even if it be late. I shall be expecting you. Write two days before you start on your journey. I told Mother last night you were coming; she seemed surprised, but according to her custom, said nothing. I would rather not have told her, but as I mentioned, she does not like sudden surprises. I am very dull and tired besides, my dear Edward, and cannot write more now. How glad I shall be to have you with me. My love to your mother. I shall soon answer her very kind letter to me. Edward, she will surely come; her health will be established and what will prevent? The season is not a pleasant one, I know, but I do not think she need fear taking cold. Good-bye. May God bless you, dearest. Kiss to Eddie.

Your own Margaret

[Postscript] Do tell me, will Mr. Davies come? You have said nothing about him for some time. I hope he will; I should like well to have him here. And your mother, dearest, she must come if we wait a month for her. I have the most pleasant little room for her and Eddy you can think of. I shall be grievously disappointed unless she comes. Why, she need not stay very long unless she choose to do so. Will Harriet Drake come?

Tuesday evening. I am better, much better, almost well, my dearest, and, as proof of the same, I have just <u>finished</u> some toast and tea, the first I have eaten for three days. I hope I shall meet you in health and oh, how I long to see you—care for your health; do, dearest, remember how very much our happiness depends on it. I have some maple sugar for dear Eddy which I think he will relish greatly. Come, come soon—I want to see you. If you would but write as often as you ought to do. Matthias has come for my letter, so good-bye. I am well, dear.

Adena, April 6th, 1839
Sat. night
[Postmarked April 8]

I am tired and sleepy, both, dear Edward, 'tis late and I have already written three letters this evening—so you have but a poor chance of a pleasant letter. This is the <u>fifteenth</u> letter I have written this week and accomplished <u>wonders</u> besides in other ways—if my nights were as long as yours, I should do but little. Thank you, dear, for your letter from Portsmouth, and again, for the one Mrs. Grimble brought me. I don't care much about writing to you, and if I did not think you would feel some concern for me, should not write again. I have not much to say. I am very well and hope to be happy—too busy to allow myself to be much troubled about you or anything—don't love to think of leaving home—makes my heart ache. Oh, Edward, you must love me very much and be very, very gentle and patient with me or I can't bear it. It is hard, any way I can look at, or think of it—I know I shall try you—but you must bear it awhile, and I do hope I may in time to come repay you. I have a great deal to distress me—more than you think of, but I know it will all pass and time and God's blessings make us happy. You will be here two weeks from to-night—but not to make me a visit, but to carry me off—that is not kind, Edward, for I don't wish to go. The leaves are coming out beautifully, but no roses yet—plenty of wild flowers, but alas, my engagements just now chain me, an unwilling captive, to the house. I could find it in my heart to reproach you with that. 'Twas wrong to hurry me, and I told you so, but yet the grievance is not very great.

I had a letter from Amanda to-night; she will be here next week and stay maybe till we go to Cincinnati. You said Elizabeth Drake was to be married on the 3rd of May—surely not on Friday. Is Mr. C. in Cincinnati? <u>You</u> made <u>me</u> a visit without publishing it—I heard he had gone to Portsmouth and guessed the rest. Do bring Mr. Telford, if he will be brought. I want him to come. Mother is delighted with the idea of having your mother here. I hope the weather will be as fine as for a week past—if it should be, the journey will be of use to her—dear little Eddy will be delighted to be in the country; it will seem like a new world to him. Anne James, I think, will not come and that will be a sore disappointment to me. Her brother-in-law, Dr. Bush, is going to Europe, and Anne must stay with her sister. I have just written to her urging her to come over even if she returns immediately after our marriage and hope she will. Mr. Telford will do for her, you know.

I have written to all my distant friends and hope to see some of them. Even though Mrs. Worthington spoke so confidently of coming, I did not expect her—she has lost her character and has not energy to accomplish anything. If <u>somebody</u> would make the necessary preparations, and put her on a steamboat she would come, doubtless. I should be sorry for you, and myself, too, if I thought I should lose <u>myself</u> as Elizabeth has done since her marriage. With a husband she <u>ought</u> to have had, Elizabeth would have made an energetic and useful member of society—so much you see, we depend on you—'tis a responsibility you incur when you take me—and if I should change, I think and hope for us both it will be for the better, and not for the worse.

I am afraid we shall have trouble from our similarities. I am accustomed to have others adapt themselves to me—it has always, since my childhood, been so—and it is the same with you. Now how shall we manage this? I can't be amiable and yielding and you will not—it would be undignified in Mr. Mansfield. Well, you know it and must do as everybody else does, just as I bid you. Shame on your penetration—to love such a woman—a willful, perverse, obstinate woman. Prepare for the contest, good sir, for it is near at hand. Dear Edward, my own dear Edward, there is too much truth in my jesting, but by God's grace I have in some degree conquered my will, and by a continuance of His help I hope with your aid to do much more. Unless I am wicked, I cannot but be happy. Few have so many blessings as I, and who, dear Edward, has more? My friends are all so kind to me now that it touches my very heart—even my pets, the lilies-of-the-valley, are going to bloom for me earlier than usual. Mother said she had never seen them so forward. The garden is filled with flowers and all seems to promise us happiness. Gratitude should make me happy for my Creator has largely blessed me and his crowning blessing, my dear Edward, is yourself. If I do grieve sometimes and suffer from a change, you will, I know, sympathize with me and comfort me and I will do my very best to repress every painful feeling.

I had no letter to-night. Our post-office is under bad administration and it is a favor to get one's letters when one pleases. I will write once more, at least, to you—maybe oftener—but, in truth, I don't much care about writing. My moods are varying and I might write something that would give you pain, when 'twas not in my thought to do so. My <u>gowns</u> have not yet arrived, but are looked for daily—and I think we will say the <u>twenty-fourth</u>, decidedly.

I will not send you any more of my precious hair, but what I think nearly as sweet, some violet leaves. I hope they will retain their odor till you get them. Nothing must prevent your mother's coming. <u>You</u> must surmount every obstacle, and when you arrive, come instantly to Adena. If there are no other passengers, the stage might bring you across, or we could send the carriage—or [leave?] passengers in town, but come up immediately.

I am glad you have attended to that more important thing, the proper appareling of yourself in due season. Look and be well, now, or we shall quarrel. My love to your mother; I will write to her next week. Kiss Eddy for me, and write every mail. Adieu.

Thine own Margaret

[No heading, but postmarked April 15, 1839]

I doubt very much, dear Edward, if you get this but I just wish to write—I am sad—and faint-of-heart to-night. No matter how busy you were, you ought to have written to me—I told you so—you don't know yet, Edward, how much with me depends on what seem to you <u>trifles</u>. I know you have many very important engagements, and that just now you have little if any leisure, but I know, too, that you wish to do all you can for me. I am not happy; I cannot be—have scarcely been myself for three months. O, Edward, the heart-aches I have had in that time! I ought not to leave home, ever—I cannot be happy with strangers—what do they care for me? You—you cannot be much with me, and then my home—can I live elsewhere? My heart, as the vine, has every year been sending out and grasping with its tendrils every object about me, and now it seems transplanting would be death. I have so much to love. Will you be more than all to me? I could trust a woman but I am afraid of men—I have not known the best—that must be my excuse. I have told you that I was too selfish to be married—you think I will change—for your sake, my best loved, I hope so. I have always been [so] accustomed to the indulgence of my peculiarities that they have become my nature—they will torment you—but you must bear them. Dear Edward, I would rather die than make your life unhappy. I am oppressed with sad thoughts to-night, and though 'tis selfish in me, 'tis a relief to tell them to you. You will pardon me—when you are with me, I shall feel happy—a week more from this very night and you will be with me—but I cannot bear to think that you will take me away. I believe I had rather you would not come—it seems but yesterday you were here.

I had a letter from [my sister] Lizzy to-day which I will show you. She arrived in town to-night and will be at home to-morrow morning, but I shall not see her till my letter is closed—she bears malice against you for taking me away, and so do I, too. So pray be on your guard when you come or we shall do you some mischief—I have had a letter from my Springfield and Columbus friends—none of the Wardens will be here, which I regret. Mary [Galloway], I think, would like to come but she must be with Elizabeth Drake. I have the promise of quite a large party of pleasant acquaintances from Columbus, Miss Espy and Mrs. Wolfley[18] among the number. I wish very much Judge [James] Hall[19] would come and would send him an invitation if I thought he would accept. He was invited to Lizzy's wedding and may expect a repetition of the same civility, so I think I'll send it—and to several other of my acquaintances. Amanda will be here on Tuesday—she would have come sooner but for her father's health.

I wish it did not make me sad—this gathering of friends. You would say it should not have such an effect, but till you are a woman, and situated just as I am, you are no competent judge. All I can do, dear Edward, the future seems uncertain— I can give it no form—I cannot conceive how another home, other friends should be dear to me. I am very sorry your mother should miss the blooming of our red-bud trees—the prospect from my window is enchanting—the cherry and pear trees have been, and some of them are yet, exceedingly beautiful. You remember, they are very large. My cousins [Ellen, Sally, and Virginia Swearingen] have been very kind and stayed a great deal with me—I needed company—a rare thing for me, too, who am so fond of my own society. I wonder if I shall love yours so much, dearest?

This is Saturday. You must be here next Saturday. Will not the stage bring you over the fields to Adena? Don't go to James's; they will detain you. If your mother be not too much fatigued, come immediately up. I shall expect you surely. I am very much afraid I shall <u>cry</u>—'tis not my wont, either, but of late days there may spring up a fountain in my eyes. You opened, and must close it. Such a crowd as we shall have! But they shall not, the half of them, see me married—they have no right and 'tis not my pleasure. Invite Mr. Rankin.[20] Please, dear, call on Mrs. Worthington just before you leave town—she will have something for me. Mr. Telford will stay with us. I have no letter to-night. Good-bye. May Our Father bring you safely to me.

Your own Margaret

[Postscript] Sunday Mor'g. Lizzy is here, but Charles could not come. I am sorry for I know he much wished to be here. Good-bye—bring Lizzy a pretty thing to pacify her—I really fear she will seize you—rob you, maybe, of more hair than I did—only because you are taking me away—that is all. 'Twas pleasant for them all to have me to keep home in order for them when they come on visits.

The Rest of the Story

Margaret Worthington's marriage to Edward Mansfield took place as planned, on April 25, 1839.[1] One of the wedding gifts she received, presumably from her mother, was a tooled leather folder, inscribed inside, "For Margaret Worthington, April 24th, 1839." It held a paper packet containing a lock of Thomas Worthington's hair, a memento his daughter would have treasured.[2]

A description of Margaret's wedding dress appeared in a Lebanon, Ohio newspaper in 1948, together with the announcement that it had been given to what is now the Warren County Historical Society by Miss Helen M. Dudley of Morrow, Ohio, one of Margaret's granddaughters.[3]

> The wedding dress is of the finest quality white satin and is cut with a simple dignity, well-suited to the wearer. It is fashioned with an off-the-shoulder bodice trimmed with self folds, and real lace of exquisite beauty. The sleeves are short with pleated folds of the satin and the full skirt with unpressed pleats is ankle length. The skirt shows evidences of trim, probably festoons of lace, long since removed. The veil is a very sheer silk lace with a beautifully designed border. These were worn gathered across the head with flowers completing a wreath or halo. Margaret, who loved flowers with an artist's passion, probably wore lilies-of-the-valley, which were her favorite flower. [4]

Indications of the quality of Margaret's married life may be found in two unpublished diaries between 1847 and 1855. The earlier, from 1847 to 1852, contains expressions of grief over the death of her mother on Christmas Eve, 1848. But mourning did not keep her from caring for her family or entertaining her brothers and sisters when they came to Cincinnati. When Edward's mother died in April, 1850, Margaret reacted with mixed feelings; she had found her mother-in-law unexpectedly cold and harsh in her judgments. Only to her own mother had she confided how troubled she was over the change that had taken place in her relationship to Mrs. Mansfield.[5]

In the middle years of her married life, Margaret found family life a mixture of joys and sorrows. By then, she and Edward had four children: Elizabeth Phipps Mansfield, who was born in 1843 and named for Edward's mother; Eleanor Strode Mansfield, born in 1845 and named for Margaret's mother; Francis Worthington Mansfield, born in 1848 and named for Margaret's brother; and Margaret Edith Deering Mansfield, born in 1853 and named in part for Margaret herself.[6]

Each year on her children's birthdays she lovingly described each child's physical appearance and personality. She found great satisfaction in those rare occasions when her stepsons, Ned and Charley, were at home, so that all six of their children were under one roof. To be sure, the duties of raising small children and caring for Edward's health often taxed her patience. In addition, the servants they employed frequently failed to meet her requirements. Even so, she had a happy marriage, often expressing her abiding love for Edward. On one occasion she called him the best friend she had on earth. Although his studious habits sometimes vexed her, they agreed with each other on most issues, and shared an interest in the same friends.

Throughout her married life Margaret maintained close ties to her Worthington siblings, especially to her sisters. She seemed to grow closer to Sarah than she had been as a young woman. But she found it hard to bear the prevalence of death around her, recording the fact that between 1849 and 1853 she lost twelve close relatives and friends. She mourned the deaths of her younger brothers Frank and Willy and of her sister Lizzy, all of whom had died between 1849 and 1852. She especially bemoaned the loss of Lizzy, whom she had come to consider the best and brightest of all her siblings. She also mourned the deaths of her niece, Mary Macomb, her nephew, Tom King and Sarah's second husband, William Peter, as well as her old friends, James P. Campbell, Dr. Daniel Drake and Major James Galloway.

While in the years right after her marriage Margaret returned to Adena annually during the late summer months, after her mother's death in 1848 she seldom visited her birthplace because it no longer seemed like home and held too many sad memories.[7] Finally, in 1855, back at Adena with all four of her children, she took pleasure once again in seeing the great variety of flowers blooming in the well-ordered gardens and in revisiting the scenes of her childhood. She seemed reconciled to ever having been separated from her beloved home. That very year—1855—Edward and she had built a house near Morrow, Ohio, above the Little Miami River, in a beautiful hilly location that in many ways resembled that of the Worthington mansion near Chillicothe, above the Scioto. There, at their new home, Edward's son, Charley, helped plant trees as well as acorns Margaret had brought from Adena. At last, her children could enjoy the country delights which Margaret had long coveted for them.

Margaret Worthington Mansfield died at Morrow, Ohio on March 16, 1863 in the midst of the Civil War, from a form of typhoid fever she contracted while nursing wounded soldiers.[8] She was only fifty-one, and left children ranging in age from ten to twenty. Her sister, Ellen Watts, died the same year. Only three of the original ten Worthington siblings then survived: Sarah King Peter, who died in 1877 at the age of seventy-seven; James T. Worthington, who died in 1881 at the age of seventy-nine and Colonel Thomas Worthington, a Civil War veteran, who died in 1884 within one month of his seventy-seventh birthday.[9]

After Margaret's death, Edward Mansfield went on living at their country home near Morrow, continuing for seventeen more years the distinguished writing career that earned him the title, "The Sage of Yamoyden."[10] He died there in 1880 at the age of seventy-nine. He and Margaret are both buried in the Mansfield plot at the Spring Grove Cemetery in Cincinnati, although Margaret's remains lie in an unmarked grave.[11]

Margaret and Edward's children all lived to adulthood. Elizabeth and Eleanor both married and raised children of their own. Frank and Edith remained single but both attended college—a matter that would have greatly pleased their mother. Frank graduated from the U. S. Military Academy at West Point in 1871 and Edith, already a teacher, graduated in 1903, at age fifty, from Stanford University where she majored in education and received a Phi Beta Kappa key for academic achievement[12] (cf. 190).

The only descendants of Edward and Margaret Mansfield to survive into the twenty-first century are those of their eldest child, Elizabeth P. Mansfield Dudley (1843-1913) whose son, Adolphus Mansfield Dudley (1877-1945) had an only son, Winston Mansfield Dudley (1912-1973), for whose three children, three granddaughters and great-grandchildren, both current and future, this edition of Margaret Worthington's early diary and letters has been prepared for publication.

The guiding principle Margaret and Edward Mansfield followed wherever they lived was the motto written in her family Bible: "As for us and our house, we will serve the Lord" (Jos. 24:15). In diary entries marking her own birthdays, Margaret repeatedly vowed to become a more faithful Christian. After her death, Edward reported that because she was eager to have a church nearby where their family could worship, Margaret had contributed very generously to the erection of a Presbyterian church in Morrow. (Stained glass windows in honor of both Edward and Margaret Mansfield can still be seen in that church.) Edward summed up his estimation of Margaret's faith in the following tribute: "There is nothing marvelous in it, but when we look at it closely, we see it is something which the world has but little of. It is not merely a loud profession, nor strong doctrine, nor only prayer; but it is the practice of a Christian, who to all of these had added an unwavering fidelity–in every act, duty and business of life; and to all these added a cheerful enjoyment of every gift and grace of God."[13]

Margaret and Edward Mansfield's Children, *circa* **1861**

Standing: Charles Davies Mansfield (#295) 1834-1892; Francis Worthington Mansfield, (#298) 1848-1928. Seated from left: Margaret Edith Deering Mansfield (#299) 1853-1928, Eleanor Strode Mansfield Moulton Swiggett, (#297) 1845-1931; Elizabeth Phipps Mansfield Dudley, (#296) 1843-1913. In her hand a photo of Edward Jared Mansfield, (#294) 1831-1870. Charles and Edward were own brothers, half brothers of the other 4, both sons of Mary Peck; the others [the 3 girls and Francis] were children of Margaret Worthington. Father [of all 6 children] Edward Deering Mansfield, 1801-1880.
From the estate of Winston Mansfield Dudley; notation by Edith Dudley, 1869-1953, edited by CWW to include Mansfield Genealogy numbers and birth and death dates.

Appendix

Bold print indicates the names of persons Margaret mentioned in her writings.

A. Margaret Worthington's Closest Chillicothe Friends 1836 -1839

James P. (Jamie, JPC) **Campbell** (b. in 1790s in Pennsylvania) moved to Chillicothe to become his brother's partner in a dry goods store.[1]

Effie McArthur Coons (b. 1804) daughter of neighbors, Duncan McArthur and Nancy McDonald; was widowed and by 1836 had returned to Fruit Hill (see p. 46) and **McArthur family**, (see p. 192).

Anne James (Annie) was a daughter of Thomas James and Charlotte Massie. Mr. James, a businessman and civic leader, had come to Ohio in 1798.[2]

Elizabeth (Lizzet, Bessie) **McCoy** (b. 1809), eldest daughter of John McCoy and Jane McCracken, had attended boarding school with MW and was her closest friend in 1836-37. **William McCoy**, her brother, ran a dry goods store, McCoy and Lee.[3]

Henry Massie (b. 1811) was a son of one of Chillicothe's founders; he became an attorney. MW called him "cousin," due perhaps to a relationship to her aunt Nancy Collins.[4]

Col. John L. Taylor (b. 1805 in Virginia) studied law and was admitted to the bar in 1828. He began a law practice in Chillicothe in 1829, was a major general in the Ohio militia, and became a U.S. congressman.[5]

Eleanor (Ellen) **Waddle**, daughter of John Waddle and Nancy Mann, replaced Elizabeth McCoy as MW's closest companion after Elizabeth married **Dr. L. W. Foulke** in February, 1837.[6]

John Walke, son of Anthony Walke and Susan Carmichael; m. **Fanny Kercheval**, granddaughter of Duncan McArthur, July 20,1836 (see **McArthur family**, next page).

Margaret's **Swearingen cousins** were also important members of her social set, sometimes appearing among the guests she invited to parties at Adena. In 1798, MW's uncle, **James** Strode **Swearingen** (1782-1864) had emigrated from Virginia to Chillicothe, Ohio, with his older sister Eleanor Swearingen Worthington. The children born to James S. and his wife, **Nancy** Bedinger Swearingen (1786-1858) were:

> **Henry** Bedinger (**H. S.**) b. at Adena, 1814
> Eleanor (**Ellen**) Bedinger (**E. S.**) b. 1816
> Sarah (**Sally**) Bedinger, b. 1819, m. Nathaniel Woodbridge Thatcher, 1840
> **Virginia** (**V. S.**) b. 1821
> Nancy Calhoun, b. 1823, died in infancy
> James, b. 1826 [7]

Margaret enjoyed a neighborly relationship with the **McArthur family** who lived at Fruit Hill, on property adjoining Adena.[8] **Duncan McArthur** (1772-1839) born in Dutchess County, New York, helped in early surveys of Ohio and assisted Nathaniel Massie in laying out the town of Chillicothe. In 1796 he married **Nancy McDonald** (1777-1836). After serving in the state legislature, he was appointed colonel of the Ohio Volunteers and participated in the War of 1812. He served one term as an Ohio representative in Congress and from 1830 to 1832 was governor of Ohio; while in office he suffered a disabling accident from which he never recovered.[9] Their children were:

> Margaret C., m. Robert Kercheval (d. 1833) September 14, 1816
> > Frances (**Fanny**) **Kercheval** m. **John Walke** [10]
> Helen M., m. Alexander Bourne, October, 1816
> **Effie** (1804-1847) m. (1) Elijah **Coons**, May 1, 1830
> > m. (2) Senator **William Allen** (1803-1879) May 12, 1845
> **Allen** (1806-1858) m. Olive Whitney (1820-1885)
> James McDonald (d. 1839)
> Eliza Ann (1815-1855) m. W. Marshall Anderson, 1835
> **Mary** (1818-1842) m. Carey Allen Trimble (1813-1887) December 25, 1837
> Thomas m. **Sarah** . . . [11]

B. Margaret's Old Acquaintances in Cincinnati in 1836

Margaret had first met **Elizabeth Phipps Mansfield** (Mrs. Jared) in 1826 when Mrs. Emma Willard, at whose Female Seminary at Troy, New York, she was then a pupil, took her to visit the Mansfields at West Point (See diary excerpt and transcription on p. 114).

In 1836, when Margaret first visited Cincinnati, Mrs. Mansfield was widowed and living in the city with her son Edward, his wife Mary, and their two sons. In June, 1838, more than a year after Mary's death, Margaret made a second visit to Cincinnati, this time as a guest of Edward Mansfield's mother, and while still there became engaged to Edward in July.[12]

Margaret's relationship to **Elizabeth Phillips Worthington**, at whose Cincinnati home she stayed in 1836, was not, as one would suppose, based on a family tie, but rather on her having known Elizabeth before her marriage, probably in Chillicothe.[13] MW described her friend as one who "used to be energetic, gay . . . but now seems listless. . ."[14] Margaret's interest in Elizabeth lasted throughout her writings of this period, from the time she was the Worthingtons' house guest in the spring of 1836 until she was considering her wedding guest list in the spring of 1839. Elizabeth's husband, **John G. Worthington**, was an attorney-at-law in Cincinnati between 1825 and 1850.[15] He was the son of Dr. Charles Worthington (1759-1836) of Georgetown, D.C., who was the son of Colonel Nicholas Worthington and Catherine Griffith of Anne Arundel County, Maryland.[16] Margaret, on the other hand, was descended from Robert Worthington, "The Quaker," (1667-1735) a lineage already described in the Chronology of Margaret's Parents (p.13). This line of Worthingtons came into this country by way of Pennsylvania and Virginia, and therefore had no direct link to that of John G. Worthington. Another clue to their lines being separate is that Margaret never referred to John as "cousin," a term she used rather freely in other situations where a relationship might be claimed.

During her three-week visit in Cincinnati, Margaret met the following people, whom she already knew:

Dr. Daniel Drake (1785-1852) and his brother, **Benjamin Drake** (1795-1841) were both important to Cincinnati's cultural development.[17]

James Graham was a paper manufacturer whose daughter married **Dr. William Ridgely**, a physician.[18]

Judge James Hall (1793-1868) enjoyed a fine reputation as a writer, citizen and man of business. He edited *The Western Monthly Magazine.*[19]

Rufus Hodges and **William Rankin, Jr.** were both attorneys.[20]

William Oliver was president of the Cincinnati Insurance Company; and **Benjamin Whiteman** was secretary of the same firm.[21]

MW also mentioned Messrs. **Edward Cranch** and **Samuel Eells**. Cranch was an attorney and also a member of Dr. Daniel Drake's Semicolon Club, a Cincinnati literary group.[22] Samuel Eells (1810-1842) was a law partner of Salmon P. Chase, future chief justice of the U. S. Supreme Court (1864-1873).[23]

Miss Wallace was a former classmate of MW's at Miss Baskerville's school in Chillicothe.[24]

C. Margaret's New Acquaintances in Cincinnati in 1836

Margaret's diary entries during her Cincinnati visit recorded the names of many women who called upon her or at whose homes she made calls. Among them was her sister Lizzy's mother-in-law, **Mrs.** Samuel W. **Pomeroy.**[25] In addition, the following young women were contemporaries she presumably met for the first time:

Miss **Booth**, possibly a daughter of William Booth, a clerk at the Commercial Bank.[26]
The Misses **Carneal**, the daughters of Thomas D. Carneal and Sarah Howell Stanley.[27]
Harriet and **Elizabeth Drake,** the daughters of Dr. Daniel Drake.[28]
Olivia Groesbeck, a daughter of John G. Groesbeck, a Cincinnati merchant; she was a reputed "town toast."[29]
Miss **Shoenberger**, the daughter of an iron merchant.[30]

D. Margaret's Lancaster and Columbus Acquaintances in 1836

Margaret already knew **George Myers**, husband of Rebecca Galloway, as well as his brother, **Henry Myers**, who in 1835 had joined the firm of Myers, Fall and Dresback; the **Mrs. Fall** she met was presumably the wife of Henry's partner John C. Fall.[31] MW met for the first time:

Mr. Belding who was himself visiting Lancaster. Nothing more has been learned about him, nor about Messrs. **Graham, Heart** and **Tennant**.
Miss **Clarke**, who was possibly related to Arthur Clarke of Lancaster.[32]
Thomas Ewing (1789-1871), an attorney and United States senator from 1831 to 1837, who later became Secretary of the Treasury under President Harrison, and from 1841 to 1845, Interior Secretary under President Tyler.[33]
General William Henry Harrison, who became the ninth President of the United States in 1841, but died shortly after taking office.
Eleanor Ann (Ellen) and **Louisa Irwin,** whom MW already knew, were daughters

of Judge **William W. Irwin**. Ellen married **Lewis Wolfley** in 1837.[34]

Elizabeth McCoy's aunt, **Sarah Craft McCracken**, was the wife of Samuel McCracken (1785-1857).[35]

Mrs. William J. Reese (1812-1900), whom MW seemed already to know, was a sister of William T. Sherman of future Civil War fame. **Mr. Reese** (1804-1883) was a Lancaster attorney and merchant.[36]

John G. Willock (1820-1881) who was born in Glasgow, Scotland; married Julia Sherman and became a prominent citizen of Lancaster.[37]

Miss **Lavinia Espy** who was a reigning belle of Columbus.[38]

Dr. Lincoln Goodale (1792-1868) who had called on MW at Adena on October 29, 1836, also met her in Columbus.[39]

Miss **Kell(e)y** who was a daughter of Alfred Kelley and Mary Seymour Welles. Mr. Kelley, a member of the Ohio General Assembly, owned an especially fine home in Columbus.[40]

E. Edward D. Mansfield's Parents and Early Years

Edward D. Mansfield's parents were Col. Jared Mansfield (1759-1830) and Elizabeth Phipps Mansfield (1776-1850). In 1803, after President Jefferson appointed him Surveyor General of the Northwestern States and Territories, Col. Mansfield, his wife and two-year-old Edward moved from West Point, New York, to Marietta, Ohio. From this headquarters and successive locations near Cincinnati, Mansfield supervised land surveys in the new state until 1812 when his family, now including a daughter, Mary Ann, returned to New England. In 1814, Col. Mansfield resumed his teaching post at the U.S. Military Academy at West Point.[41]

Edward graduated from West Point in 1819, but gave up a military commission to pursue further education at the College of New Jersey (later Princeton University) from which he graduated with first honors in 1822. After studying law under Judge Gould at Litchfield, Connecticut and being admitted to the bar, in 1825 he moved to Cincinnati, Ohio to practice law, but left that profession in 1836 to become a newspaper editor and writer.[42]

F. Edward's Own Family

Edward Deering Mansfield b. August 17, 1801, New Haven, CT
    m. (1) April 25, 1827, Litchfield, CT
        Mary Wallace Peck (d. March 10, 1837, Cincinnati, OH)
        Children:
        Edward Jared Mansfield (Eddy or Ned)
            b. February 2, 1831, Phillipstown, NY
        Charles Davies Mansfield (Charley)
            b. August 26, 1834, Cincinnati, OH
        William Virgil Mansfield
            b. February 26, 1837, Cincinnati, OH
            d. a day or two later
    m. (2) April 25, 1839, at Adena, Chillicothe, OH
        Margaret Worthington
            b. July 25, 1811, at Adena, Chillicothe, OH [43]
            Children: see p. 190.

Mary Ann Mansfield (EDM's sister)
    b. January 23, 1807, Ludlow Station, near Cincinnati, OH
    m. October 11, 1825, at West Point, NY, to **Charles Davies**,
        Professor of Mathematics at the U.S. Military Academy.
            Two of their five children were named for Jared and Elizabeth
            Mansfield. Edward and his first wife reciprocated by naming
            one of their sons Charles Davies Mansfield.[44]

G. Edward's Cincinnati Friends in 1838 and 1839

Edward Mansfield developed many friendships during his long career in Cincinnati and its environs. The three listed below, one a minister, one a physician and one an educator, are representative of the social group into which Margaret Worthington moved when she married Edward.

When he was a law student in Litchfield, Connecticut in the 1820s, Edward Mansfield boarded in a house across the street from the home of the **Reverend Lyman Beecher** (1775-1863), pastor of the local Congregational Church, which Edward regularly attended. In 1832, Rev. Beecher accepted the presidency of Lane Theological Seminary in Cincinnati and to supplement his limited salary was pastor for ten years at the Second Presbyterian Church. Edward, who had also moved to Cincinnati, again joined the Rev. Beecher's church. He also knew his pastor's daughters: Harriet, who married Calvin Stowe, a professor at Lane Theological Seminary in 1836, and Catharine, who was a strong advocate of education for women. In the early 1830s Edward and the Beecher sisters attended literary reunions at Dr. Daniel Drake's Vine Street home, where Harriet, the future author of *Uncle Tom's Cabin*, read aloud some of her earliest stories.[45]

Dr. Daniel Drake (1785-1852) figures prominently in the history of the Mansfield family in Cincinnati, as his wife Harriet Sisson, was Edward Mansfield's first cousin. Drake was born in New Jersey, but soon moved with his parents to Mayslick, Kentucky. In 1800, he became the first student of medicine under Dr. William Goforth of Cincinnati. In 1814, his brother, **Benjamin Drake**, came from Mayslick to become Daniel's partner in opening a Cincinnati drugstore. A year later, after receiving further medical training under the famed Dr. Benjamin Rush, Daniel received the degree of Doctor of Medicine from the University of Pennsylvania at Philadelphia. In the next decade, he served as professor at both the Medical College and Transylvania University in Lexington, Kentucky. After his wife's death Dr. Drake never remarried, but established himself again in Cincinnati, where he continued a distinguished career as one of the city's cultural leaders.

Edward Mansfield's relation to Dr. Daniel Drake's wife, Harriet Sisson, is as follows: Richard Mansfield (d. 1655) the first of his family to settle in America, came to Boston in 1634 from Exeter, Devonshire, England, and moved to New Haven, Connecticut in 1639. Stephen Mansfield (b. 1716), a great-grandson of Richard, married in 1745, Hannah Beach (d. 1795). Among their eight children were **Jared** Mansfield (1759-1830) and **Sarah** Mansfield (b. 1765).

Jared Mansfield married Elizabeth Phipps in 1800. Their surviving children were **Edward Deering Mansfield** (b. 1801) and Mary Ann Mansfield (b. 1807). (See Appendix F).

Jared's sister, Sarah Mansfield (b. 1765) married James Sisson in 1784. Among their nine children was **Harriet Sisson**, b. in New Haven in 1787. Thus it was that Edward Mansfield's first cousin, Harriet Sisson, married **Dr. Daniel Drake**, December 20, 1807 at Col. Mansfield's home, Ludlow's Station, Ohio, near Cincinnati. Harriet died in October, 1825 of autumnal fever.

Children of Daniel and Harriet Sisson Drake:
    Harriet Drake (b. 1809, d. in infancy)
    Charles Daniel Drake (1811-1892)
    John Mansfield Drake (1813-1816)
    Elizabeth Mansfield Drake (1817-1864);
        m. Alexander H. McGuffey, May 9, 1839
    Harriet "Echo" Drake (1819-1864);
        m. James P. Campbell, late 1839[46]

Also closely affiliated with Edward Mansfield was **William H. McGuffey** (1800-1873) In 1837 he began compiling a collection of textbooks including the popular *McGuffey's Eclectic Reader*. When he became president of Cincinnati College in 1836, Edward Mansfield became professor of Constitutional Law and History at the same institution, bringing the two men into close professional association. William named his third son Edward Mansfield McGuffey, and during his tenure as president of Ohio University between 1839 and 1843, invited Edward Mansfield to visit him at Athens. Alexander H. McGuffey, who married Edward's cousin, Elizabeth Drake, collaborated with his brother, William, in producing the *Readers*.[47]

Abbreviations

Abbreviations used in sections of Introduction, Appendix and Notes

Adena = Adena from 1807 to 1839
EDM's Fam/Fr = Edward D. Mansfield's Family and Friends
ESWL = Eleanor Swearingen Worthington's Life from 1827 to 1839
M's PC = Chronology of Margaret's Parents from 1773 to 1827
M's Pers = What Was Margaret Worthington Really Like?
M's Sibs = Margaret's Siblings between 1836 and 1839
MW to 1839 = Margaret Worthington's Formative Years from 1811 to 1839
WFT = Worthington Family Table

Abbreviations used in Text, Notes and Bibliography:

CHS = Cincinnati Historical Society
CWW = Charlotte W. Wells
EDM = Edward D. Mansfield
ESW = Eleanor Swearingen Worthington
LRP = Laura R. Prieto
MW = Margaret Worthington
OHS = Ohio Historical Society
RCHS = Ross County Historical Society
TW = Thomas Worthington (father)
WCHS = Warren County Historical Society
WRHS = Western Reserve Historical Society

Notes

Preface

1. A.M. Dudley to Charlotte W. Dudley, August, 1938, owned by CWW.
2. Mansfield 1885, 43-45, 77-87.
3. Dudley 1976, 231-246.
4. Mansfield, Margaret W. Diary, November 1847 to April 1852, CHS; Diary July 13, 1852 to August 17, 1855, privately owned by CWW.
5. Sears 1958.
6. Peter 1882; King 1889; McAllister 1939.
7. Bennett 1901; Brown 1976, 29; Brown 1987; Cole 1903. Mansfield 1860; Mansfield 1879; Mansfield 1880; Renick, Fullerton and Nipgen 1896; Southward 1950; Utter 1942; Weisenburger 1941.
8. Bleser 1981; Hedrick 1994; Sklar 1976; Taylor 1991.
9. Buber [1923], 1958.
10. Buber 1964.
11. Mallon 1986, xvii.
12 Butterfield, Friedlaender and Klein 1975, 10.
13. Conway 1992, vii-xiii.
14. Beauchamp 1967, xxxii.

Introduction

A. Margaret Worthington's Formative Years, 1811 to 1839

1. Cf. 13-17, 21.
2. Cf. 7-12.
3. Cf. 17-20.
4. "Chronology of Chillicothe, Ohio," 1947.
5. Weisenburger 1941, *97*.
6. Sears 1958, Chapters iii, iv.
7. Drake and Mansfield 1827, 19.
8. Weisenburger 1941, *52-55*.
9. Sears 1958, 162.
10. Worthington, Margaret 1852-55 Diary, 170; Laura R. Prieto (LRP) interview with Mary Anne Brown, May, 1996.
11. *The Supporter and Scioto Gazette* December, 1822; Renick, Fullerton and Nipgen 1896, 107; Ellen Worthington to Albert Worthington, February 8, 1822, Thomas Worthington Family Papers, OHS; cf. 4, 5.
12. Kelhofer 1975; Elizabeth Worthington to MW, June 29, 1826, Pomeroy Family Papers, RCHS; Renick, Fullerton and Nipgen 1896, 155-63.

13. Sage 1898, 125.
14. Wilson 1983, 104.
15. Sage 1898, 125; Sears 1958, 233-34; Spiler et al. 1963, 240.
16. Obituary, "Mrs. Mansfield," Unknown newspaper, April 3, 1863.
17. Brown 1976, 29; December 12, 1836 entry, MW's 1836-37 diary, OHS; cf. M's Sibs, pp. 20-24.
18. Worthington, Margaret, Music book; cf. 4.

B. Adena from 1807 to 1839 (Adena)

1. Cuming 1810, 218-19, cited by Thwaites 1904.
2. Worthington 1811, cited by Sears 1958, 33.
3. "Adena" 1966, 1; cf. 15, 1802 entry.
4. Mansfield 1880, 7.
5. Sears 1958, 30; Reps 1991, *52.*
6. Hamlin 1955, 199-201.
7. Sears 1958, 31, 33.
8. Ibid., 31.
9. "Adena, Location of House and Dependencies,1800-1827," 1971.
10. Rodabaugh and Caren 1947, 4.
11. Sears 1958, 30-33.
12. *Scioto Gazette* July 9, 1904, 105: No.11.
13. Hitch, Neal V. and Cheryl Lugg. "Wallpaper Documentation and Reproduction at Adena: The Estate of Thomas Worthington." *APT Bulletin: The Journal of Preservation Technology* V. 33, 2002, 57-64.
14. *Columbus Sunday Dispatch Magazine* February 8, 1953, 7, 8; February 15, 1953, 19.
15. Williams and Williams 1969, 94-103.
16. Sears 1958, 179, 205.
17. Ibid., 204-05.
18. Ortman 1946, n.p.; Sears 1958, 31.
19. Sears 1958, 224, 229.
20. *Cincinnati Enquirer,* April 10, 1946.
21. Mansfield 1880, n.p.
22. Brown 1976, 29.
23. MW to EDM, September 20, 1838, Edward Deering Mansfield Papers, OHS; McAllister 1939, 43, 131.
24. Weisenburger 1941, 207-08; cf. 116.
25. "Adena Restoration Multi-Faceted," *Echoes,* October/November, 2000.

C. Chronology of Margaret's Parents
from 1773 to 1827 (M's PC)

1. Sears 1958, 4-10; Worthington genealogy, Worthington-L-request@rootsweb.com.
2. Sears 1958, 10.
3. Whyte 1999, 1-3, 10, 12, 22, 60-61, 104-05.
4. Sears 1958, 10.
5. Ibid., 10-11.
6. Whyte 1999, 60-61.
7. Sears 1958, 11.
8. Ibid., 12.
9. Peter 1882, 44-45.
10. *Family Register* 1894, 7; Cole 1903, 5; Whyte 1999, 60-61.
11. Sears 1958, 15.
12. Cole 1903, 5.
13. Sears 1958, 23; February 20, 1855, entry, MW's 1852-55 diary, privately owned by CWW.
14. Hood, ed. 1970, 9; Bennett and Bennett 1901, 12.
15. Cole 1903, 29, 30.
16. Peter 1882, 30-31; *Scioto Gazette* May 23, 1903, 18; Finley and Putnam 1871, 140.
17. Cole 1903, 30; Sears 1958, 26.
18. Utter 1942, 4; Peter 1882, 56.
19. Sears 1958, 85, 107; Cole 1903, 30.
20. Utter 1942, 30, 31.
21. Cole 1903, 31.
22. Sears 1958, 30.
23. Ibid., 142.
24. Cole 1903, 31.
25. Sears 1958, 149.
26. Ibid., 153.
27. Ibid., 162-3.
28. Ibid., 153.
29. Renick, Fullerton and Nipgen 1896, 78; Sears 1958, 173.
30. Cole 1903, 31; Sears 1958, 45, 213.
31. Cole 1903, 29, 30, 32; Sears 1958, 200-02.
32. Cole 1903, 32.
33. McAllister 1939, 57; Peter 1882, 98-9.
34. Randall and Ryan 1912, 431.
35. Sears 1958, 216-17.
36. Ibid., 233-34.
37. Ibid., 232-33.
38. Ibid., 231-35.

D. Eleanor Worthington's Life from 1827-1839 (ESWL)

1. McAllister 1939, 64.
2. Sears 1958, 230; Cullum 1868, 313.
3. MW to William Worthington, August 29, 1834, Thomas Worthington Family Papers, OHS.
4. Sears 1958, 16.
5. Newspaper files at American Antiquarian Society, Worcester, MA.
6. Jones 1983, 82-85.
7. February 7, 1853 entry about "a beautiful inheritance — that 1,800 acres of land," Worthington, Margaret, Diary 1852-55; Sears 1958, 236.
8. Sears 1958, 113.
9. Edith Mansfield to Winston Dudley, June 9, 1928, privately owned by CWW; Elizabeth Pomeroy to ESW, June 13, 1836, Pomeroy Family Papers, RCHS.
10. Finley and Putnam 1871, 140.

E. Margaret's Siblings from 1836 to 1839 (M's Sibs)

1. Brown 1976, 29; Cole 1903, 29-32; *Family Register 1894*, 14-16; Sears 1958, passim; MW's Diaries, 1836-37, 1847-52, 1852-55.
2. Cullum 1868, 1:313.
3. Sears 1958, 200.
4. ESW to Elizabeth Pomeroy, December 21, 1836, Pomeroy Family Papers, RCHS; obituary, Mary T. Macomb, *The Scioto Gazette*, December 7, 1836; cf. 97.
5. Venable 1891, 431.
6. McAllister 1939, 80.
7. King 1889, 1:13-14.
8. Sklar 1976, 120.
9. King 1889, 1:51.
10. DeVerter 1959, 299-304.
11. Howe [1847], 1889, 1:113.
12. McAllister 1939, 97.
13. Elizabeth Pomeroy to Elizabeth McCoy, February 2, 1837, Swearingen-Franklin-Foulke Papers, RCHS.
14. Cf. ESWL, Note 3.
15. After leaving Harvard and graduating from medical school in Philadelphia, Frank set up a medical practice in Cincinnati. (John Marye, Gambier, Ohio to Henry Swearingen, Chillicothe, Ohio, Tues. 4th, 1834 [sic], RCHS; ESW to MW, August 30, 1840, Thomas Worthington Family Papers, OHS; Mansfield 1879, 260).

F. What was Margaret Worthington Really Like? (M's Pers)

1. Howe [1847], 1886-90, reprint 1908, 2:766.
2. Worthington, Margaret, Diary 1847-52, April 24, 1852 entry.
3. MW misquoted the last two lines of "Evening Prayer at a Girls' School," by Felicia Hemans (1793-1835). In the original it read: "Earth will forsake. O! happy to have given The unbroken heart's first fragrance unto Heaven" (Hemans 1826, 156-58).

Part One

1. **Lizzy and James** are the first of nine siblings appearing throughout MW's diary and letters (cf. 20-24); . . **the circle of industry** probably meant the members of St. Paul's Circle, affiliated with the Episcopal Church in Chillicothe, which met and sewed weekly at private homes, following which men would join the circle for a social gathering (Renick, Fullerton and Nipgen 1896, 178).
2. **Mr. Taylor** was Col. John L. Taylor (presumably "the honorable judge"), the first of eight special friends MW mentioned (cf. 191).
3. **Uncle James** is MW's first mention of the Swearingen family. He was her mother's brother (ibid.).
4. **Rebecca Myers** was a sister of Julia Galloway Worthington, wife of MW's brother, James T. Worthington (cf. 23).
5. **Frank** was MW's youngest brother, Francis Asbury Worthington. He was named for the Methodist circuit rider and was attending Kenyon College in Gambier, Ohio (cf. 21, 24; Howe [1847], 1891, 1:146).
6. **Charles Pomeroy** was Lizzy's husband (cf. 23); **Sister S** was Sarah Worthington King, one of MW's older sisters (cf. 21, 22-23); **Miss Delano** was Susan, the daughter of a Chillicothe druggist (Southward [1811] 1950).
7. This **Miss Irvin** may or may not have been one of the daughters of Judge William W. Irwin of Lancaster. MW always spelled this name Irvin (cf. 194-95, 207n1).
8. MW's misspelling of **Tuesday** as Teusday is corrected throughout.
9. Cousin **Henry Massie** was an especially congenial friend (cf. 191).
10. **Mr. [Edwin P.] Cranch** was a Cincinnati attorney (cf. 193).
11. **Mr. Randolph.** One may infer from the first sentence of the next entry (April 5, 1836) that "Mr. R," lived in Xenia, as MW gave him letters to take to Sarah and Mary Galloway there. Otherwise, he has not been identified.
12. **Sally S.** was one of MW's local cousins (cf. 192, 221n7); by "**the boys**" MW meant her younger brothers, Willy and Frank (cf. 23, 24). **Fruit Hill** was the McArthur estate next to Adena on the plateau just west of Chillicothe (*Weekly Scioto Gazette*, Saturday, May 23, 1903, cf. 46).
13. **Anne James** was another of MW's close friends (cf. 191).
14. **Xenia** was a pioneer town in Greene County, Ohio. **Sarah** and **Mary** Galloway were sisters of Julia Galloway Worthington (cf. 23); **Sally** was Sarah Galloway's nickname.
15. **Steubenville** was a town on the eastern border of Ohio where a Female Seminary was founded

in 1829 (Sherzer 1913, 13-17). Mary Galloway did not attend this school for long, if at all.

16. **Tom** was one of MW's older brothers and **Sister Mary** was her eldest sister, Mary Worthington Macomb (cf. 14, 16, 21,22); **Mr. K** was Sarah's husband, Edward King, who had died in February, 1836 (cf. 15, 16, 17, 21-23).

17. **Ellen** and **Arthur**, the only family members not previously identified, were MW's sister, Eleanor Worthington Watts and her husband Dr. Arthur Watts (cf. 15, 17, 21, 23).

18. **Arthur's mother** was Elizabeth May Roberts Watts, born in Maryland (Cole 1903, 31).

19. **My enemy of lang syne** was possibly a headache, which may have been brought on by tight-laced corsets, stress at entertaining suitors, or other "provocations" (Farnham 1994, 171).

20. **Miss Luckett's.** MW probably meant Jane Luckett (1809-1900), who was very active in the Episcopal church (Renick, Fullerton and Nipgen 1896, 170).

21. **such exigencies** as a breach in the canal were often due to the wood and dirt construction of early canals. Spring floods caused this particular breach. (*Scioto Gazette,* April 13, 1836; Sears 1958, 229).

22. **Mrs. [Effie McArthur] Coons** lived at Fruit Hill (cf. 191, 192).

23. **Eolia** was the home of MW's sister Ellen and her husband, Dr. Arthur Watts (cf 205n17).

24. **Mr. Walke** (cf. 191).

25. Regarding the persons in MW's traveling party, only her sister **Lizzy**, **Susan Delano**, and **Mr. Buchanan** appear in later entries. Although she does not mention her sister Sarah in this April 19 entry, she does mention her having left the boat in Cincinnati on April 21. Henry Buchanan was cashier of the Commercial Bank of Scioto in Portsmouth. MW recorded his visit to her at Adena on June 3 and 6, and in her October 27, 1836 entry wrote that he was "wife-hunting" again (*Scioto Gazette,* April 6, 1837; cf. 42, 60).

26. **Piketon** is a town on the Ohio Canal, midway between Chillicothe and Portsmouth.

27. **Portsmouth** is a town at the confluence of the Scioto and Ohio Rivers, with a population in 1830 of about one thousand people (Weisenburger 1941, 17).

28. The first **steamboat** on the Ohio arrived at Cincinnati in 1811; between that date and 1827 over two hundred fifty steamboats were built along the river, providing meals and beds for passengers who could afford the extra fare (Ambler 1932, 121; Meyer 1917, 108).

29. **Mr. W[orthington]** and, in the next sentence, **E[lizabeth] W[orthington]**, referred to John G. Worthington, a Cincinnati attorney and his wife, Elizabeth Phillips Worthington, MW's hosts during part of her stay in Cincinnati (cf. 193).

30. **Mrs. [James] Lodge**, a widow, kept rooms on 4th Street between Walnut and Vine *(Cincinnati City Directory 1836/37, 106).*

31. Cincinnati's commercial importance in the early decades of the 19th century led to her being called the "**Queen City of the West**" (Miller 1938, 34).

32. MW would have had her choice among two or three **dentists**. Charles Wilson Peale had been the first American to use the French process of molding porcelain into artificial teeth. (*Cincinnati Mirror Advertiser* May 28, 1836; *New Columbia Encyclopedia* 1975, s.v. Dentistry; Lindsay 1933). From 1827 to 1830 Dr. John Harris conducted a dental school 20 miles southwest of Chillicothe in Bainbridge, Ohio, where the Dr. John Harris Dental Museum is now located. (Information courtesy of Mary Anne Browne).

33. This passage shows MW's aversion to the **Yankee** traits of the **Pomeroy** family, into which

NOTES TO PAGES 33-36

her sister Lizzy had married; they had emigrated to Ohio from the Boston area."Yankee" connoted a preoccupation with business at the expense of sociability. Condemnation of Yankees was widespread in the West in the 1830s (*Dictionary of American Biography*, s.v. Pomeroy, Samuel W.; Miller 1938, 38-39).

34. **Mr. and Mrs. Pendleton** were Nathaniel Pendleton (1795-1861), prominent attorney and politician, and his wife, Jane Frances Hunt Pendleton (d. 1839). Col. Pendleton was a leading member of the bar in Cincinnati, a member of the Ohio State Senate, and in 1840 was elected to the U.S. Congress (Mansfield 1879, 145).

35. **Sally, Mary and Albert G.** This is the first time MW mentioned Albert Galloway; he played an important part in her writings from 1836 to 1839 (cf. 23).

36. **Edw**[ard] **Mansfield**, son of Col. Jared and Elizabeth P. Mansfield, was the editor of the *Cincinnati Chronicle* (cf. 195, 223n41).

37. **Dr.** [Daniel] **Drake** and his brother **Ben**[jamin] were, in the 1830s, leading lights in Cincinnati's intellectual community (cf. 197, 198); **Judge** [James] **Hall** was a prolific writer and editor of the *Western Monthly* magazine (Mansfield 1860, 304).

38. **Universal** [Yankee] **Nation** was a pejorative term based on the character trait alleged to be peculiar to New Englanders: "It is an ardent, unquenchable love of money: money the Yankee will and must have" (*Cincinnati Mirror and Western Gazette of Literature, Science and the Arts*, February 20, 1836; Thornton [1912] 1962, 2: 919, 962; Miller 1938, 38-39).

39. Sally **Carneal** was said to be one of the two most beautiful girls in Cincinnati (Harlow 1950, 381-2; de Chambrun 1939, 204).

40. **Old Acquaintances** (cf. 192-94).

41. The Western Female Institute in Cincinnati was founded in 1832 by educator and writer Catharine **Beecher** (1800-1878). Although she intended the Institute to become a model for Western education, the school collapsed completely in 1837 (Sklar 1976, 112-21).

42. **Miss Groesbeck** and **Miss Shoenberger** (cf. 194).

43. **Mrs. Mansfield** was Edward D. Mansfield's mother (cf.192-93, 195).

44. **Mr. Graham** and **Mr. Eells** (ibid., cf. 193-94).

45. The **Hygean Well** was located two blocks from the Ohio River near Covington, Kentucky, and named "Hygeia" by William Bullock of London's Piccadilly Museum. Bullock had purchased the country estate in 1827 from Thomas D. Carneal, Cincinnati merchant-capitalist (Yoseloff, 1958 1891-95, Plate CLI (151), 19; *American Guide: Cincinnati* 1943, 527-528).

46. Here MW drew a small cup.

47. Frances Trollope and her son Anthony initiated the construction in 1828 of **the Bazaar**, located a block west of Fort Washington. The Bazaar included an exhibition hall (after 1831), coffee house, bar room, saloon, and ballroom as well as retail stores. It was a favorite spot among Cincinnati's ultrafashionables (Lancaster 1950, 97; Clubbe 1992, 131).

48. In the Chinese custom of **footbinding**, perhaps originally in imitation of the club feet of a popular empress, the arches of girls' feet were broken and tightly bound, so that they remained small as in childhood. (Mason 1937, 163).

49. Though MW used the present tense in this entry, it appears to have been written retrospectively after her return home from Cincinnati.

50. MW's view of city life was shared by Frances Trollope, who considered Cincinnati blatantly

commercial (Trollope [1832] 1949).

51. This was a line from the familiar song, "Home! Sweet Home!" part of the 1823 opera "Clari, or Maid of Milan" (Dichter and Shapiro 1941, 40).

52. **Eliza Longworth** was the daughter of Nicholas Longworth, a well-known attorney, who had come to Cincinnati from New Jersey in 1803 and built a fortune through real estate. He owned a magnificent residence, specialized in raising strawberries and grapes for commercial purposes, and was also a major patron of the arts in the city (Howe [1847], 1889: 1:817-18; Weisenburger 1941, 66-67).

53. **Miss Booth** (cf. 194).

54. **Miss Wallace** (cf. 194); the **Misses Drake** (cf. 198).

55. Page torn, fragments follow.

56. **Mr. [John] Carlisle** was a prominent Chillicothe businessman (Southward [1811], 1980, 1, 3).

57. James Hall celebrated **the Ohio** River's beauty in the poem, "La Belle Rivière" (Hall 1829, 155).

58. The relationship of **Mary** to the Irvin family is unclear; (cf. 207n1).

59. **Mrs. James** was Jane Claypoole James, second wife of Thomas James; **Anne James** and the newly married **Charlotte James Bush** were her step-daughters (Bennett 1901, 13).

60. Mary **Baskerville** (1787-1856) was a revered Chillicothe teacher (Renick, Fullerton and Nipgen 1896, 155-163).

Part Two

1. **Judge and Mary Irvin.** William W. Irwin of Lancaster had been an Ohio Supreme Court Judge and active in state and national politics (Weisenburger 1941, 217, 224, 269; Utter [1942] 1968, 54; cf. 204n7, 207n58).

2. **Mrs. [Richard] Douglass** was Mary Douglass (d. 1858), a writer who was considered an unusually intelligent woman (Herbert 1993, 122; [Douglass was MW's spelling of Douglas]. (Bennett 1902, 4-5).

3. **Mr. [John] Shillito** (1808-1879) was a Cincinnati dry goods merchant (*History of Cincinnati and Hamilton County* 1894, 476-77).

4. The **belle** was the Southern model of the ideal young woman between childhood and marriage, at which point she would become a Southern "lady" (Wilson and Ferris 1989; Farnham 1994, 170-175).

5. MW may have bought her **dress** from one of the local dressmakers. Most clothing was still produced in the home, so purchasing a dress was a special event, often involving multiple fittings.

6. **The Angel's Whisper** was a song for piano and voice written by Samuel Lover (1797-1868), first published in London as number 4 of *The Songs of Superstition of Ireland* (*Complete Catalog of Sheet Music* 1870).

7. **James P. Campbell** (cf. 191).

8. **Henry Buchanan** (cf. 205n25).

9. Proverbs 14:10.

10. **Ice cream** remained a luxury until the turn of the 19th century. Firms like D. M. McKee and Co. were the first to sell it. By the 1830s, ice cream parlors and street vendors started to appear in major American cities (Dickson 1978).

11. **Mr. [John] Madeira** (b. 1763) was a successful Chillicothe hotelier; **Miss Madeira** was

probably his daughter, Harriet (Sears 1958, 229; Finley and Putnam 1871, 131).

12. **Miss Clarke** (cf. 194).

13. **Amanda** [Galloway] (cf. 23).

14. Like MW, **Sunday School teachers** in the 1830s tended to be young, female volunteers (Utter [1942], 1968, 384).

15. **Mr. Lee** was William McCoy's business partner per multiple ads in the *Scioto Gazette* in 1836 (cf. 191, 221n3).

16. **Gen.** [William Henry] **Harrison** (1773-1841) ran unsuccessfully as a Whig candidate for President of the U.S. in 1836.

17. **John** [Walke] and **Fanny K**[ercheval] (cf. 191).

18. Since the War for Independence, American women frequently participated in public ceremonies of this type (Ryan 1990, 173).

19. **Mr.** [William S.] **Murphy** was an active Whig politician and popular orator (McCabe 1884, 122).

20. **Terpsichore** was, in classical mythology, the muse of lyric poetry, choral song and dancing (Bell 1991, 413).

21. The **Misses Belt** were probably nieces of Levin Belt, former mayor of Chillicothe (Brown 1987, 151-52); **Mrs. Carson** may have been Elizabeth Carlisle Carson (1816-1895), according to records in Chillicothe's Grandview Cemetery.

22. **Mantua** is a corruption of the French word "manteau" referring to a loose gown worn by women in the 17th and 18th centuries (*Oxford English Dictionary*).

23. **Miss Wallace** (cf. 194, 222n24); **Mr.** [Nathaniel Woodbridge] **Thatcher** (1807-1874) would marry MW's cousin, Sarah Bedinger Swearingen, in 1840 (cf. 192, 221n7); **Mr. F**[rancis] **Campbell** (b.1792) was James Campbell's eldest brother and his mercantile partner (*Biographical Cyclopedeia . . . of the State of Ohio* 1884, 407-08).

24. Fruit Hill picture (*Weekly Scioto Gazette*, May 23, 1903, 19).

25. **Gen. McArthur** (cf. 192, 210n23).

26. **The** [Yellow] **Springs** [Ohio] was a popular destination for those members of Cincinnati high society who sought "pleasure, health and rural scenery" (Harlow 1950, 169-170).

27. Ps. 90:12, recast in the first person.

28. Daniel Webster, the noted politician, had visited Ohio in 1833, but he did not visit the state in 1836. (Curtis 1870, 462, 538). I assume that the **Daniel Webster** of this diary was James P. Campbell's horse.

29. **The pale monotrope** may have been MW's name for the Indian Pipe (*Monotropia uniflora*) a white waxy plant of woodlands (Newcomb 1977, 172).

30. **Mary** [Worthington] was the four-year-old daughter of Julia Galloway and James Worthington (cf. 23).

31. **Araminta Rice** [Walton] (d. 1893) was MW's schoolmate at Troy Female Seminary; she studied there from 1824 to 1826 and after graduation taught at Troy, and later in New Orleans (Sage 1898, 94).

32. The **unexpected guest** was Lizzy's baby, named Eleanor W. Pomeroy (Cole 1903, 31).

33. **Aunt Collins** was Nancy Calhoun (d. 1847), second wife of Eleanor Worthington's brother, Samuel Swearingen (d. 1832). Apparently she later married David Collins of Chillicothe. (Whyte 1999, 61; Mills 1902, 52).

34. **Sister S**[arah] and **Tom** [King] (cf. 22-23). According to MW's brief diary notations, her

sister Sarah left Cincinnati for New York on April 28, and returned to Adena about June 26. She left Chillicothe for Cincinnati on July 18, where I presume she finalized plans for leaving her home there for an extended period. On July 30, Sarah returned to Adena and on August 9, she and her son Tom left for Cambridge, Massachusetts.

35. A.R. VanDeren came to Chillicothe circa 1835, claiming his companion to be his sister, but they left town when the scandal broke that she was not his sister after all. (Pat Medert, to CWW, July 9, 2004; reminiscences by "Sixty," *Chillicothe Leader*, Jan. 15, 1887).

Part Three

1. **Miss Kelly** [sic] was a daughter of Mary Seymour Wells (b. 1799) and Alfred Kelley (1789-1859), canal commissioner and state senator (Cummings 1952, n.p.). She may or may not be the same Miss Kelly as in MW's December 1, 1836 entry.
2. **I've been preserving.** (cf. 51).
3. **John Marye** had attended Kenyon College with MW's cousin, Henry Swearingen, and met MW in 1834 (Swearingen-Franklin-Foulke Papers, RCHS).
4. **J.B. Hearne** may have been a Xenia relative of Daniel W. Hearn, superintendent of the Chillicothe Academy for Boys, or of Josiah L. Hearne, member of the First Presbyterian Church of Chillicothe (Renick, Fullerton and Nipgen 1896, 144-47).
5. **Young Men's Whig . . . Convention.** The "Young Men of Ross County" was a Chillicothe political club which sent over 200 to attend the state Convention of Young Whigs. James P. Campbell and Nathaniel W. Thatcher were among the leaders of the group, which had rallied to defeat Jacksonianism and the Democratic party (*Scioto Gazette*, August 31, September 14 and 21, 1836; Weisenburger 1941, 320-21).
6. **Mrs. Luckett** was Elizabeth G. Luckett (1785-1869) per gravestone at Chillicothe Cemetery, probably the mother of Jane (cf. 29, 205n20).
7. Although Julia's father was James E. Galloway, Jr., MW called him "Mr. G., Sr." to distinguish him from his sons (cf. 23).
8. **Miss {Ellen} Bond** was a daughter of Col. William Key Bond (1792-1864), Chillicothe attorney and Ohio congressman, 1835-39 (Williams Bros. 1880, 76).
9. **"The Messenger Bird"** was a duet for two voices and piano accompaniment (Owen [1828], 1834).
10. **Mr. [James Liggett] Grover** (b. 1806), was a son of Martha McClure and Josiah Grover (Kilner 1988, 75).
11. **Sarah** was the wife of Thomas **McArthur** (cf. 192, 221n11).
12. **Mr. and Mrs. Gooding** were Matthew and Cynthia Swearingen Gooding (1808-1856), daughter of MW's uncle, Thomas Van Swearingen [1779-1863] (Whyte 1999, 105).
13. Two yellow flowers were pressed here in the diary. **Consumption** was the source of one-quarter of all deaths in the U.S. during the 1830s, afflicting wealthy and poor alike. A community of women usually came to the aid of female invalids, helping them with child care and other domestic responsibilities (Teller 1988, 12).
14. The **little boy** was James Henry Myers (b. January 1, 1836) son of Rebecca Galloway and George Myers (DeVerter 1959, 302).

15. **E. Carlisle** was Eleanor (Ellen) Carlisle (1814-1854), daughter of John Carlisle (1771-1847) and Elizabeth Mann (1786-1849). John was a prominent Chillicothe businessman and a son of Andrew Carlisle (d. 1821) who came to Chillicothe in 1798 (*Ross County, Ohio Families* 1976, 2:118; Index of Grandview Cemetery Records).

16. Elizabeth (**Lizzet) McCoy** was MW's close friend (cf. 191, 221, Appendix A, n9).

17. The **synod** was the Ohio Conference of the Methodist Church which met in Chillicothe in 1836 (Versteeg 1962, *55).*

18. As part of biannual housecleaning, the **carpet** would typically be unfastened and removed in the summer, then put down again in the autumn to help provide warmth throughout the winter. Though they were formerly luxuries, carpets came into general use in American homes by the 1830s (Garrett 1990, 39, 192).

19. **Mrs. McA** was Nancy McDonald McArthur (cf. 192, 221, Appendix A, n11).

20. **Miss Deane** operated the Ladies Select School on Paint Street (*Scioto Gazette,* Aug. 3, 1836).

21. **Uncle George Townsley** was probably the brother of Martha Townsley Galloway, mother of Julia Galloway Worthington (DeVerter, 1959, 299).

22. **Who by searching can find out God?** MW's question is based on Job 11:7.

23. **Gen. McA** suffered a crippling accident while governor of Ohio (Finley and Putnam 1871,134-39).

24. **Miss Cook**'s family was active in the Methodist Church of Chillicothe. **Miss Welsh** was Jane Welsh, the "& Co." of Welsh & Co., which manufactured iron (Renick, Fullerton and Nipgen 1896, 138; per LRP interview with Pat Medert, RCHS 1996).

25. **Friend after friend departs** is a line from the poem "Friends" by James Montgomery [1771-1854] (Stevenson 1937, 2:3888).

26. **Lucy** [Sperry] had been MW's roommate at the Troy Female Seminary; she taught in Georgia and South Carolina before marrying Isaac Kirtland (Sage 1898, 107).

27. **Lancaster** is the county seat of Fairfield County, east of Columbus and northeast of Chillicothe. The town was laid out in 1800 on one of the tracts of land awarded to Ebenezer Zane by Congress for his work in opening Zane's Trace (Miller 1938, 29).

28. **Dr.** [Lincoln] **Goodale** (cf. 195, 222n39).

29. **Mr.**[George] **Myers** (cf. 194, 222n31).

30. A copy of the sheet music for **The Raindrop** [and] **Minstrel** survives in MW's songbook at OHS. Reverend J.C. Richmond wrote the lyrics and O. Shaw composed the music to this undated sentimental piece.

31. **Henry** [Myers] (cf. 194, 222n31).

32. **Mr. Ewing** and **Mrs. Reese** (cf. 194, 195, 222n33, 222n36).

33. **Mrs. Fall** and **Mr. Belding** (cf. 194).

34. **Hockhocking** (now Hocking) was the name of the river bordering Lancaster. In the language of the Delaware tribe, Hockhocking means "a bottle" (Howe1889, 1:927).

35. **Mt. Pleasant** was "a unique pile of rocks on the northern boundary of Lancaster." A local legend says that Mary Sherman jumped from a 200-foot bluff on Mt. Pleasant to test William Reese's love (*Biographical Record of Fairfield County* 1902, 235-36).

36. Both of the books mentioned are examples of "sentimental flower books." They incorporated aspects of gift books, annuals and almanacs in their literary allusions and lavish illustrations (Seaton 1995, 112-14).

37. **There's nothing true but Heaven** is the last line of the first verse of "This World is All a Fleeting Show," a poem by Thomas Moore [1779-1852] (Stevenson 1937, 2:3699).

38. **Mr. Willock** and **Mr. Heart** (cf. 194, 195, 222n37).

39. **My friend Harry** has not been identified; MW mentioned him again in her December 14, 1836 entry as "hopeful Harry" (cf. 73).

40. **Pilgrim Fathers** was a duet with piano accompaniment (Owen 1830).

41. **Columbus Route.** MW's party planned to go from Lancaster to Chillicothe by a stagecoach route through Columbus (Utter 1942, 201; Weisenburger 1941, 99).

42. **Dr. [Lewis A.] Wolfley** (1807-1844) was a naval surgeon and graduate of Ohio Medical College (Kramer 1951, 167-68).

43. **Miss Espy** was Lavinia Espy Morehead (1818-1900), one of the "reigning belles" of Columbus, who became a poet (Coyle 1962, 456; McCabe 1884, 170).

44. **Dr. [L. W.] Foulke** (1809-1887) was a graduate of the Medical University of Maryland, who established his medical practice with offices on Second Street in Chillicothe in 1836 (Evans 1987, 138, 376; Chillicothe Cemetery gravestones).

45. **"Zanies"** denoted buffoons, mimics or clowns; by allusion, the term refers to parasites or toadies. MW may also have been making a pun, referring to the people of Zanesville, Ohio, who had held a Van Buren celebration that summer (*Oxford English Dictionary; Scioto Gazette* July 27, 1836).

Part Four

1. **Mr. M.** was David Betton Macomb (1793-1837), husband of MW's sister Mary (cf. 20).

2. Deuteronomy 6:5.

3. Exodus 20:3.

4. **Hair** was often given, preserved, and even made into jewelry as a token of love and friendship or remembrance of the dead.

5. Possibly **Maria** Webb, one of the McArthur family's servants (Elizabeth Pomeroy to Eleanor S Worthington, June 13, 1836; RCHS 1952.210.39; *Chillicothe, Ross County Census 1840*).

6. The prairie land between the Scioto and Little Miami Rivers in Clark and Madison Counties is known as **the Barrens** (Jones 1983, 6, 83).

7. **Aunt** [Nancy Bedinger] **Swearingen** (cf. 192).

8. Liquor may have been the substance from which MW's brother Tom was **being weaned**.

9. By **Lizzy's loss**, MW meant her sense of loss following her sister Lizzy's marriage to Charles Pomeroy in November, 1835.

10. **Oscar** was possibly Oscar Craig, a schoolmate of MW's brother Willy. The former died of yellow fever in 1838 (MW to Elizabeth Pomeroy, January 4, 1838, OHS).

11. Had **Christmas** not fallen on Sunday, MW might have mentioned traditions such as decorative greenery, caroling, a Yule log, as well as special foods such as fried oysters and eggnog (Renick, Fullerton and Nipgen 1896, 182).

12. **The key** that MW's mother mistakenly carried away was to the storeroom. She was normally

in charge of running the Worthington household, but MW bore the responsibility in her mother's absence. Without the key, pies kept in the storeroom were inaccessible, so MW had to "knock up a pie" to feed her guests (Garrett 1990, 100, 185).

13. **New Year's** was a gift-giving holiday long before Christmas presents became a custom. Other traditions included making prophecies, as described in MW's January 2, 1837 entry in Part Five (Myers 1972, 5,7).

14. **. . .dear friend Elizabeth.** Intimate friendships between 19th century women were common, often beginning at school and continuing throughout the women's lives. However, marriage often diminished the intensity of such relationships (Smith-Rosenberg 1975).

Part Five

1. **"glorify God and enjoy Him forever"** was the answer to a Westminster catechism question about the chief end of man.

2. 1 John 3:19.

3. Habakkuk 2:14.

4. **Allen McA**[rthur] (cf. 192).

5. Francis Scott Key (1779-1843) wrote the poem *The Star Spangled Banner* on September 14, 1814 after witnessing the British bombardment of Fort McHenry. It grew popular across the nation as a tune sung to the music of a British drinking song. Congress adopted it as the national anthem in 1931. Numerous versions were published in the United States during the early 19th century. *Auld Lang Syne* is a Scottish song based on the expression first used in 1692 meaning "the good old times."

6. **Hope's gayest wreaths are made of earthly flowers** is a line from "Love Not," a poem by Caroline Elizabeth Sarah Norton [1808-1877] (Stevenson 1937, 1:871).

7. The Mexican President, Antonio López de **Santa Anna** (1794-1876) and the Mexican diplomat Juan Nepomuceno **Almonte** (1803-1869) passed through Chillicothe on their way to Washington D.C. after their capture in the Battle of San Jacinto in Texas on April 21, 1836. They stayed overnight at Chillicothe's famous Madeira Hotel, arriving in the capital on January 18, upon which President Andrew Jackson returned them to Mexico (*Diccionario Porrúa* 1976; Mansfield 1850, 324-27).

8. Here MW wrote in tiny letters **rpb** for Robert Patterson Browne (cf. 23).

9. **Little Bo-Peep** was from a so-called "Mother Goose rhyme" (actually a body of similar types of nursery rhymes, rather than the work of a single author named Mother Goose) and had already been widely published by the 18th century (Delamar 1987).

10. **Mrs. Eckert** [sic] was possibly Ellen Carlisle's future mother-in-law, because Ellen would marry William R. Eckart on August 27, 1840 (ESW to MW, August 30, 1840, Thomas Worthington Family Papers, OHS).

11. *Three Eras of Woman's Life* may have been written by Elizabeth Elton Smith.

12. MW had already received a gift of "a beautiful paragraph Bible" from James P. Campbell, but John L. Taylor presented her with the more commercial choice of an **annual**. The first Western annual, compiled by James Hall in 1829, was titled *The Western Souvenir, a*

Christmas and New Year's Gift (Seaton 1995, 66-67).

13. **This is na my ain, ain lad,** etc. is MW's paraphrase of the first line of Robert Burns's "O this is no my ain lassie."

14. **Nemo,** Latin for "no one," is used by MW here and on February 13 to refer to Albert Galloway. She wrote his name as "Albert G.," "Albert," or simply "A" eleven times in her diary entries during the spring of 1836, but in this entry confessed that she feared to see her own thoughts in writing.

15. **Wm.** [William] **Allen,** a "Van Buren man," had defeated the Whig incumbent, Thomas Ewing, by three votes on the thirteenth round of balloting in a joint session of the state Senate and House. On May 12, 1845, Allen would marry MW's Fruit Hill neighbor, Effie McArthur Coons (*Scioto Gazette* May 23, 1903, 20).

16. **St. Helena's prison rock** referred to the exile of Napoleon I on the island of St. Helena after his defeat at the Battle of Waterloo (June 18, 1815); he remained there from October, 1815 until his death in May, 1821.

17. **Elizabeth Waddle,** a sister of Ellen Waddle, had been a schoolmate of MW's at Steinhauer's boarding school (cf. 191).

18. **my new bonnet and cloak.** MW's sister, Elizabeth Pomeroy, arranged for the shipment of MW's clothing by riverboat from Cincinnati to Portsmouth and overland to Chillicothe (Elizabeth Pomeroy to Eleanor S. Worthington, December 27, 1836, Pomeroy Family Papers, RCHS 1952.210.34).

19. **Messrs. Tennant and Beecher of L.** Mr. John H. Tennant is listed among the famous and well-known men of Lancaster (Wiseman 1901, 86); considered an eminent lawyer, Mr. Philemon Beecher came from Lancaster to Chillicothe when court was in session (Southward 1950, 7).

20. **sent for an emetic.** In early 19th century medical thought, disease signified an imbalance in the body; therefore, the presence of illness required some type of catharsis, such as bleeding or vomiting, in order to redress that imbalance (Leavitt and Numbers 1985; Vogel and Rosenberg 1979; Warner 1986).

21. Roswell Hill had begun a **singing school,** specializing in sacred music, for both ladies and gentlemen, on September first of the previous year (*Scioto Gazette* August 31, 1836).

22. *The Scioto Gazette* published a short essay on February 15, 1837 about the death on February 8 of **Martha Fullerton** (b. 1813 or 1814) from consumption.

23. **My total education has been a most faulty one.** MW had a good share of formal education, attending boarding schools in Chillicothe before spending the 1825-26 academic year at Emma Willard's prestigious Female Seminary in Troy, N. Y. Throughout her life, however, she regretted not having been "trained to think"—and write—better. By the 1830s, public schools were spreading across Ohio. Girls at academies studied composition, logic, rhetoric, natural philosophy, sciences and advanced mathematics. MW thus witnessed many advances in education which had been unavailable to her just a few years before hand (cf. 3).

24. **The Broken Heart** appeared in Washington Irving's *Sketch Book,* number 1 (1819), the first work by an American author to garner international acclaim.

Interlude Between February, 1837 & July, 1838

1. Eleanor Worthington, Adena, to Elizabeth Pomeroy, December 21, 1836 (Pomeroy Family Papers, RCHS 1952.210.38).
2. Elizabeth Pomeroy to Eleanor Worthington, December 27, 1836 (Pomeroy Family Papers, RCHS 1952.210.39).
3. Date of **David Macomb's** suicide, per interview of Mary Anne Brown, Adena Site Manager, by Laura Prieto in May, 1996.
4. **Ellen** and **Thomas Macomb** (cf. 22).
5. **Sally's wedding. Sarah** Galloway married Robert Patterson Browne (cf. 23).
6. H[arriet] **Madeira** was a daughter of John Madeira (*Ross County, Ohio, Marriage Records* 1989, 114; cf. 207n11).
7. MW implies that rumors in Chillicothe still had it that she would marry James P. Campbell.
8. **Mary McArthur** married Carey Allen Trimble (cf. 192).
9. William M. **Anderson** married Eliza McArthur (ibid.).
10. **Aunt Collins** (cf. 208n33).
11. **Mrs. Foulke** was formerly Elizabeth McCoy (cf. 191).
12. **Ellen** or **Elly** was Eleanor, first child of Lizzy and Charles Pomeroy (cf. 49, August 4, 1836).
13. Eleanor **Waddle** (cf. 191); Miss **Woodrow** may have been the daughter of Eleanor Worthington's minister (cf. MW's diary entry, January 20, 1849; Ross County 1840 Census, Chillicothe Township, p.328); Susan **Creighton** was the daughter of William Creighton, president of a Chillicothe bank (Brown 1987, 154); she married Jesse L. Williams (cf. 125).
14. **Mrs. Luckett and Jane** (cf. 205n20, 209n6).
15. **Mrs. Pomeroy** was Lizzy's mother-in-law (cf. 194).
16. **John Marye** (cf. 209n3); **Oscar Craig** (cf. 211n10).
17. **Sarah** Worthington King and sons (cf. 22-23).
18. MW at Adena to Mrs. C. R. Pomeroy, Salisbury, Meigs County, Ohio, January 4, 1838, postmarked Chillicothe January 11, 1838 (Edward Deering Mansfield Papers, OHS).
19. William Worthington to Elizabeth Pomeroy, March 22, 1837 (Pomeroy Family Papers, RCHS 1952.210.40).
20. Editor's inference from MW's statement in June 2,1838 letter: "Ellen and Arthur left on Thursday for home on the river boat" (cf. 101).
21. **Mary Peck Mansfield** and her children (cf. 196).
22. **Dr. and Mrs. Catlin** (EDM to MW, October 14 and 23, 1842, Edward Deering Mansfield Papers, OHS).
23. **Mr. B[enjamin] Drake** (cf. 197).
24. **Amanda** Galloway was Sarah Galloway Browne's sister (cf. 23).
25. EDM gave an **address**, "The Worth Of The Mechanic Arts," on June 1, 1838, at the conclusion of a three-day fair. It was published in Cincinnati as part of the *Report of the First Annual Fair of the Ohio Mechanics Institute* (copy owned by editor). MW's letters to EDM, beginning in Part Six, reveal that at some time during her stay at the Mansfield home in June, she and EDM became engaged.

26. William H. **McGuffey** was at that time president of Cincinnati College and a professor of moral and intellectual philosophy. EDM wrote of him, "[H]is Sunday morning discourses in the college chapel were always numerously attended, and his manner of treating metaphysics was universally popular" (Mansfield 1879, 289; cf. 198).

27. **Dined at Mr. Worthington's** (cf. 193).

28. MW, Cincinnati, to Mrs. R. P. Browne, Dayton, Ohio, June 2, 1838 (Edward Deering Mansfield Papers, OHS).

29. 1838-39 correspondence between Margaret Worthington and Edward Mansfield (ibid.).

Part Six

Chronology

1. While the date of their **engagement** is uncertain, the reality of it is confirmed by the tone and subject matter of their letters dating from July 1838; for example, MW's October 2 letter to EDM informed him that Elizabeth Worthington "knows of our engagement" (cf. 118).

2. The purpose of **EDM's trip East** in 1838 has not been researched. At earlier times, he had traveled to the Southeastern states in regard to developing a railroad connecting Cincinnati to Knoxville, Tennessee and Mobile, Alabama; at other times, he went to New York City to visit his publisher, A.S. Barnes.

3. *Scioto Gazette* April 25, 1839 Notice: "Married last evening, at Adena, near Chillicothe, by the Rev. E.W. Peet, Edward D. Mansfield, Esq. of Cincinnati and Miss Margaret Worthington, daughter of the late Governor Worthington."

July 27, 1838

4. **Mrs. Coons** (cf. 191).

5. **Mr. [Ben] Drake and Harriet.** Dr. Daniel Drake's brother and daughter (cf. 197-98). Ben Drake and EDM were well acquainted, having co-authored a small book, *Cincinnati in 1826* (Drake and Mansfield, 1826).

6. **Col. Madeira** (cf. 207n11).

7. **Miss C[atharine] B[eecher]** (cf. 206n41). She had visited Adena in the summer of 1835, so MW had met her personally (Sklar 1976, 118; cf. 22, 23, 197).

8. The gentleman EDM knew was apparently an educator (cf. 132, Nov. 14, 1838).

9. *Chronicle.* The Cincinnati Chronicle went through several owners and name changes during its publication; EDM was its editor from 1836 until around 1851 (cf. 223n42).

September 9, 1838

10. **My only sister.** EDM's sister was Mary Ann Mansfield Davies (cf. 196).

11. **pecuniary affairs.** EDM's worries about money matters may have been due in part to the Panic of 1837 (Weisenburger 1941, 339).

12. **Poor Mary** was EDM's deceased wife, Mary Peck Mansfield (cf. 196).

13. **Gen'l Hodges** may or may not have been the Rufus Hodges MW met in Cincinnati (cf. 193).
14. The **Misses Galloway** were Amanda and Mary; the wedding EDM did not attend was Sally's on October 31, 1837 (cf. 23).
15. **Albert Galloway** (cf. 23, 213n14).
16. Charles **Davies** was EDM's brother-in-law (cf. 196).
17. **Mrs. King**. MW's sister Sarah (cf. 22) was well acquainted with EDM because from about 1833 to 1835 both attended literary meetings hosted by Dr. Drake, to which "she contributed several interesting articles for the circle" (Mansfield 1860, 225).
18. **Elizabeth D[rake]** was another daughter of Dr. Drake (cf. 198).

September 14, 1838

19. **Lucy** Sperry (cf. 210n26).
20. **Elizabeth Worthington** (cf. 193).
21. **"The earth Languisheth."** (Isaiah, 24:4).
22. **The Madison place** was part of TW's estate (cf. 19).
23. **Ellen Waddle** (cf. 191).
24. **Cousin Henry Massie** (ibid.).

September 20, 1838

25. MW's mother may or may not have known that in 1812, her husband, Thomas Worthington corresponded with EDM's father, Jared Mansfield, about the possibility of war with Britain. (TW, Washington, to JM, Feb. 21, 1812, Thomas Worthington Family Papers, OHS).
26. **Mrs. Jesse Williams** was formerly Susan Creighton (cf. 125, 214n13).

October 12, 1838

27. **Mr. Trotter** (cf. 23).
28. **Mrs. Galloway** and **Mr. G.** were visiting their daughter, Julia (ibid.).
29. **Constitutional law, political economy, etc.** were subjects that EDM taught at Cincinnati College ca. 1835-36 (Mansfield 1879, 288).
30. **Mrs. [Abel] Catlin** was EDM's first wife's mother (cf. 100, 214n22).
31. **Mrs. [Richard] Douglas[s]** (cf. 207n2; *Chillicothe, Ross County Census 1840*, OHS, 318c).
32. **Sarah and Patterson Browne** (cf. 23, 214n5).
33. **Anne James** (cf. 191).
34. **Mr. Chase**, probably Salmon P. Chase (1808-73), Cincinnati attorney (Weisenburger 1941, 190).

October 19, 1838

35. By **Athens College** MW probably meant Ohio University, founded in 1804 at Athens, Ohio (Miller 1938, 71, 101).
36. It was assumed [William H.] **McGuffey** would be reluctant to leave Cincinnati College where he had been president only since 1836 (Mansfield 1860, 287-88; cf. 198).

October 31, 1838

37. **Caleb Atwater** was an author and politician, who lived in Circleville and was active in the establishment of Ohio's public school system (Weisenburger 1941, 166, 204).

Part Seven

November 10, 1838

1. **Brainard.** The poet, John Gardiner Calkins Brainard (1796-1828), was born in New London, Ct. (Stevenson 1937, 3855).

2. MW's mention of Effie McArthur Coons might remind Edward that he had first met Effie when he was ten and she about eight (Mansfield 1880,10).

3. **Mr. and Mrs. Peet.** Edward W. Peet had been an Episcopalian minister in Chillicothe since 1833. MW may have been implying EDM should speak with him about conducting their wedding ceremony (Finley and Putnam 1871, 130; cf. 80).

4. **Mary Macomb.** MW's mention of her niece is evidence that Mary and her brothers, Louis and David Macomb, were still at Adena eleven months after MW wrote Lizzy that she was teaching them (cf. 99).

5. **Mr.** Nathaniel Woodbridge **Thatcher** (1807-1874) was a well-educated man, a druggist and a great churchman (Bennett, 1901, 9; cf. 208n23).

November l4, 1838

6. **How blessings brighten.** The line MW quotes is from *Night Thoughts* by the English poet, Edward Young [1683-1765] (Stevenson 1934,168).

7. **Ellen Pomeroy** (cf. 214n12).

8. *She Stoops to Conquer,* a comedy from 1773, is the best known play of English author Oliver Goldsmith (1728-1774).

9. EDM's lecture on *The Qualifications of Teacher*s, delivered before the College of Professional Teachers at Cincinnati, was printed by D. S. Johnson in 1836. A copy of this lecture appears in a bound volume, *Lectures,* by E. D. Mansfield, owned by CWW.

10. **Col. Taylor** (cf. 191).

November 21, 1838

11. **Merry laughs** (Howe reprint 1908, 2:767).

November 28, 1838

12. The classic study of American culture, *Democracy in America,* by Alexis **de Tocqueville**, based on his travels throughout the U.S. in 1831, was first published in French in 1832; its English version is still widely read.

13. One definition of **wafer** is "an adhesive disc of dried paste used as a seal."

November 30, 1838

14. **Mrs. Wyllys Pomeroy** was Charles Pomeroy's mother, Mrs. Samuel W. Pomeroy (cf. 24).
15. **"Mother quite sick."** In the latter part of her life, ESW was periodically indisposed by a chronic cough, so that in winter she seldom left the house (MW to EDM, Jan. 23, 1839; Edward Deering Mansfield Papers, OHS; ESW to MW, Dec., 1846, Thomas Worthington Family Papers, OHS).

December 13, 1838

16. MW considered **Mr.** Thomas **Woodrow**, a Scottish-Presbyterian minister (and maternal grandfather of the future president, [Thomas] Woodrow Wilson), as a possible clergyman to officiate at her wedding to EDM, but later chose instead Rev. Edward Peet of St. Paul's Episcopal Church (cf. 171-72).

January 3, 1839

17. [Frank] **Campbell** (cf. 208n23).

January 8, 1839

18. **Miss Beecher.** Catharine Beecher wished to promote the education of women as moral educators, presuming New England methods were superior to those in the West. Although she and William H. McGuffey became friends (cf. 198, 215n26) her ideas may not have meshed with the standards he applied in selecting for his *Eclectic Readers* those stories and articles that would teach ethical principles to young readers. (For a full discussion of C.B.'s failure to win over the intellectual leaders of Cincinnati, see Sklar 1976, 107-21).
19. **Mantua-maker** means dress-maker (cf. 208n22).
20. **Eagles** were ten-dollar gold coins with an eagle on the reverse.
21. *Poor Richard's Almanack* by Benjamin Franklin (1706-1790) was published between 1733 and 1758.

January 23, 1839

22. **Miss Caldwell** (not identified) is mentioned again in Part Eight when MW reports to EDM her attendance at Miss Caldwell's wedding and her displeasure over Mr. Thomas Woodrow's manner of conducting the ceremony (cf. 165).

January 29, 1839

23. **Jane Claypoole James** was Anne James's stepmother (cf. 191, 207n59).

Part Eight

February 4, 1839

1. **Mrs.** Roland W. **Burbridge**, the former Harriet Madeira, at whose wedding in 1837 MW was a bridesmaid (cf. 98; *Chillicothe Ross County Census, 1840*, 330c).

February 10, 1839

2. Ruth 1:16.
3. **best suited her plans** (cf. 214n20).
4. **Ellen Carlisle** (cf. 209-10n15).
5. **Mr.** [Charles] **Telford** was a professor at Cincinnati College in the 1830s and a law partner of William S. Groesbeck (Mansfield 1860, 291-92; Mansfield 1879, 290).
6. **Caldwell/Allston** wedding (cf. 165, 171-72).

February 12, 1839

7. *Flora's Vocabulary* refers to one of the books on flowers MW had access to (cf. 64, 210n36).
8. **looking into my journal** indicates that MW kept a diary in 1838, which has so far not come to light.
9. **cousin Jamie** was a relationship MW claimed because of the anticipated marriage of James P. Campbell to Harriet Drake, EDM's first cousin, once removed (cf. 197-98).

February 15, 1839

10. **It is only Al—that I have known since he was a schoolboy**, a somewhat dismissive statement considering that Albert Galloway and MW were both born in 1811 (cf. 23).

February 22, 1839

11. **William McCoy** was the brother of MW's friend Elizabeth McCoy Foulke (cf. 208n15).
12. **Mr.** [Charles] **Davies** was EDM's brother-in-law (cf. 196).

February 28, 1839

13. **Elizabeth's wedding** refers to the marriage of Alexander McGuffey to Dr. Drake's elder daughter, Elizabeth, to take place on May 9, 1839. "On that occasion Uncle Ben Drake spent twenty-two dollars for a very handsome breast-pin for the bride." (Ruggles 1940, 87).
14. **Fruit Hill**, home of the McArthur family, is mentioned frequently in Parts One through Five (cf. 46, 204n12).
15. **Mrs. Jacob's** may have meant the home of Thomas Jacob, a businessman with an establishment on Paint Street in Chillicothe (Finley and Putnam 1871, 144).

March 6, 1839

16. **Louis** [Macomb] was about 18 years old. ESW's supervision and MW's teaching seem to have led to a good outcome (cf. 22, 98).

17. **Mr. Lee** may or may not have been William McCoy's partner in the McCoy and Lee store (cf. 66-68).

April 15, 1839

18. **Miss Espy and Mrs. Wolfley** [the former Ellen Irvin] (cf. 195, 211n42, 211n43).

19. **Judge Hall** (cf. 193).

20. **Mr. Rankin** (ibid.).

The Rest of the Story

1. On April 25, 1839, the *Scioto Gazette* in Chillicothe, Ohio, published the announcement: "Married—last evening, at Adena, near Chillicothe, by the Rev. E. W. Peet, Edward D. Mansfield, Esq. of Cincinnati, and Miss Margaret, daughter of the late Governor Worthington" (A duplicate of 215n3).

2. The packet containing a lock of Thomas Worthington's hair (Item #7 in a list of articles donated to Adena, per letter from Charlotte W. Dudley, Flossmoor, Illinois, to Dard Hunter, Jr., at the Adena State Memorial, August 7, 1960; cf. 211n4).

3. Excerpted from "Our Museum," a column by Hazel Spencer Phillips in the *Western Star,* Lebanon, Ohio, September 23, 1948.

4. Margaret's wedding dress is in the keeping of the Warren County Historical Society Museum in Lebanon, Ohio.

5. No page numbers are given for materials based on Margaret's 1847-52 and 1852-55 diaries because they are derived from transcription drafts which, when completed, may have different pagination. The original 1847-52 diary is at the Cincinnati Historical Society, Cincinnati, Ohio; Margaret's original 1852-55 diary is currently (2004) in the possession of Charlotte W. Wells, who intends to donate it to the OHS.

6. Names and birth dates of the children of Edward and Margaret Mansfield (Mansfield 1885, 133-34).

7. Margaret's late summers at Adena between 1840 and 1847 (per letters between E. D. Mansfield, Cincinnati and Margaret W. Mansfield, Chillicothe at OHS).

8. The illness from which Margaret Mansfield died was described as "Typhoid neuralgia" (Cemetery records, Spring Grove Cemetery, 4521 Spring Grove Avenue, Cincinnati, OH 45232).

9. Death dates of Sarah Worthington King Peter, James T. Worthington and Thomas Worthington (Brown 1976, 29).

10. "Sage of Yamoyden" the title given to Edward D. Mansfield by his Ohio friends and neighbors "because [he was] so philosophical in his thoughts and utterances, and so filled with many knowledges," [sic] ("Traveling Notes: Recollections of Yamoyden" (Howe reprint, 1908, 2:766).

11. One explanation for Margaret being buried in an unmarked grave is that she died from a highly contagious disease (cf. Note 8 above).
12. Facts about Francis W. Mansfield's graduation from West Point and his subsequent career in the U.S. Army may be found at the USMA Library at West Point, New York; Margaret Edith Deering Mansfield's diploma from Stanford University in 1903 together with a letter about her election to Phi Beta Kappa are owned by Edith Dudley Sylla of Raleigh, N.C.
13. Excerpts taken from the typed transcript of an article, "Mrs. Mansfield," dated April 3, 1863 and signed simply "M," appear from the context to have been written by Edward Mansfield, her husband. It was printed in the same Cincinnati newspaper that published her obituary a few days earlier. (Scrapbook of E.D. Mansfield's newspaper columns at OHS).

Appendix

A. Margaret's Chillicothe Friends between 1836 and 1839

1. *Biographical Cyclopedia of Ohio* 1880, 407-08; many ads in *Scioto Gazette* 1836.
2. Renick, Fullerton and Nipgen 1896, 227-28; Southward 1950, 2-3.
3. Evans 1987, 491; Renick, Fullerton and Nipgen 1896, 107; multiple ads for McCoy and Lee in *Scioto Gazette* 1836-37.
4. *Ross County, Ohio Families* 1976, 1:39; *Ross County, Ohio Marriage Records 1789-1849,* 1989, 119; Sears 1958, 14.
5. *Biographical Dictionary of U S. Congress* 1989, 1916-17.
6. Evans 1987, 490-91.
7. Whyte 1999, 106.
8. Mansfield 1879, 8-10; *Weekly Scioto Gazette* May 23, 1903, 21, 24.
9. Brown 1987, 152-54; *Harper's New Monthly Magazine* 1903, 866; MW to Elizabeth Pomeroy, January 4, 1838, Edward Deering Mansfield Papers, OHS; cf. 210n23.
10. Walke-Kercheval wedding *(Scioto Gazette,* July 27, 1836; cf. 47).
11. *Ross County, Ohio Families* 1976, 1:80; *Scioto Gazette*, October 26, 1836.

B. Margaret's Old Acquaintances in Cincinnati in 1836

12. Mansfield 1885, 43, 44, 77.
13. ESW to Nancy Swearingen, June 30, 1830, Swearingen-Franklin-Foulke Papers, RCHS 1987.
14. MW's diary entry May 19, 1836.
15. *Cincinnati City Directories* 1825-1850, CHS.
16. Newman 1933, Book #229.
17. Mansfield 1879, 188-89; *Cincinnati City Directory 1825-1850,* 145; cf.197.
18. Mansfield 1879, 263-65.
19. *National Cyclopedia of American Biography* 7:198.

20. *Cincinnati City Directory 1825-1850*, 83, 140.
21. Ibid., 129, 186-87.
22. Cist 1851, 86; McAllister 1939, 94.
23. *Biographical Cyclopedia . . . of Ohio* 1884,187-88.
24. Renick, Fullerton and Nipgen 1896, 101.

C. Margaret's New Acquaintances in Cincinnati in 1836

25. Cf. 23-24.
26. *Cincinnati City Directory 1825-50.*
27. de Chambrun 1939, 204.
28. Cf. 198.
29. Harlow 1950, 381-82.
30. *Cincinnati City Directory 1825-1850*, 156.

D. Margaret's Lancaster and Columbus Acquaintances in 1836

31. Wiseman 1898, 57-60.
32. Ibid., 123; Finley and Putnam 1871, 146.
33. Wiseman 1898, 75-78.
34. Cf. 204n7, 207n1, 207n58.
35. Wiseman 1898, 57-60; *Ross County, Ohio, Marriage Records 1789-1849*, 1989, 112.
36. *Biographical Record of Fairfield County, Ohio* 1902, 62, 63, 234-36.
37. Wiseman 1898, 102.
38. McCabe 1884, 170.
39. Dr. Lincoln Goodale was the brother of Theodocia Goodale, who married MW's uncle, Thomas Van Swearingen (1779-1863) in 1806 (Tyler 1939, 234, Whyte 1999, 105).
40. Ryan 1912, 347-58; cf. 209n1.

E. Edward D. Mansfield's Parents and Formative Years

41. Edward D. Mansfield's **Parents'** Data (Mansfield 1879, 12; Mansfield 1885, 43-45; Dudley 1976, 231- 46; Pattison 1970, 227).
42. Edward Mansfield wrote accounts of his education and of his years as editor of *The Cincinnati Chronicle* in his *Personal Memories* (Mansfield 1879, 48-140, 292-95).

F. Edward's Own Family

43. **His own family** (Mansfield 1885, 77; Brown 1976, 29).
44. **Mary Anne Mansfield** and **Charles Davies** (Mansfield 1885, 87-89; Alice Allan, Montclair, N. J. to Charlotte [Dudley] Wells, Flossmoor, Illinois, April 26, 1961).

G. Edward's Cincinnati Friends

45. **Reverend Lyman Beecher and Family** (Mansfield 1879, 123, 261-66, 278-79; records in a family Bible show that Eleanor Strode Mansfield, second child of Edward and Margaret Mansfield, was "Baptized by the Rev. Lyman Beecher, 31st of May, 1846").
46. **Dr. Daniel Drake** and family (Mansfield 1885, 46; Mansfield 1860, 399-400; Mansfield 1879, 167-173).
47. **William H. McGuffey** (Ruggles 1940, 72-73, 80; Mansfield 1879, 288; Wm. H. McGuffey, Athens, Ohio to EDM, Cincinnati, June 23, 1840; cf. 215n26).

BIBLIOGRAPHY

Unpublished Sources

Bennett, Martha T. "Early Years." 1901. Ross County Historical Society, Chillicothe, Ohio.

Cook, Matthew Scott. Papers. Western Reserve Historical Society, Cleveland, Ohio.

Goodale, Lincoln. Papers. Ohio Historical Society, Columbus, Ohio.

Kelley, Alfred. Papers. Ohio Historical Society, Columbus, Ohio.

Mansfield, Edward Deering. Papers. MSS 69. Ohio Historical Society, Columbus, Ohio.
    Mansfield, Edward D. "More Personal Memories." 1880.
    Worthington, Margaret. Diary, 1836-37; Music book.

Mansfield, Jared. MSS 68. Ohio Historical Society, Columbus, Ohio.

Mansfield, Margaret W. Diary, 1847-52. Cincinnati Historical Society, Cincinnati, Ohio.

———. Diary, 1852-55. Privately owned by Charlotte W. Wells.

Peter, Sarah Worthington. Memoirs, "Hon. Thomas Worthington, Fourth Governor of Ohio 1814 to 1818." Western Reserve Historical Society, Cleveland, Ohio.

Pomeroy Family Papers. Ross County Historical Society, Chillicothe, Ohio.

Ross County Bible Society. Records. Manuscripts, Western Reserve Historical Society, Cleveland, Ohio.

Swearingen-Franklin-Foulke Papers. Ross County Historical Society, Chillicothe, Ohio.

Trimble, Allen. Papers. Western Reserve Historical Society, Cleveland, Ohio.

Worthington, Thomas. Family Papers. MSS 54. Ohio Historical Society, Columbus, Ohio.
    Worthington, Eleanor. Letters to Margaret Worthington Mansfield.

———. Collection. Western Reserve Historical Society, Cleveland, Ohio.

Published Primary and Secondary Sources

Aaron, Daniel. *Cincinnati: Queen City of the West, 1819-1838*. Columbus, Ohio: Ohio State University Press, 1992.

"Adena: A Restoration by the Ohio Historical Society." Columbus, Ohio: Ohio Historical Society, 1959.

"Adena." Columbus, Ohio: Ohio Historical Society, 1966.

"Adena: The Early Nineteenth Century Estate of Thomas Worthington." Columbus, Ohio: Ohio Historical Society, 1971.

"Adena Plantation Complex." *Echoes* 11: 5. (May 1972).

"Adena Restoration Multi-Faceted." *Echoes* 39:5 (October/November 2000).

Ambler, Charles H. *A History of Transportation in the Ohio Valley.* Glendale, Calif.: Arthur H. Clark Company, 1932.

Ambler, Charles H. and Festus P. Summer. *West Virginia, The Mountain State.* New York: Prentice-Hall, 1958.

American Guide. Cincinnati, Ohio, 1943.

Asbury, Bishop Francis. *The Journal of the Rev. Francis Asbury (1771-1815).* New York: N. Bangs and T. Mason, 1821.

Barnhart, Terry A. "Chillicothe: Ohio's First Capital." *Preview* 3:2 (Spring 1994).

Bates, James L. *Alfred Kelley: His Life and Work.* Cincinnati and Columbus, Ohio: Robert Clarke & Co., 1888.

Beauchamp, Virginia Walcott, ed. *A Private War: Letters and Diaries of Madge Preston 1862-1867.* Piscataway, N. J.: Rutgers University Press, 1987.

Beecher, Catharine. Letter in the *Cincinnati Gazette,* February 21, 1837.

BIBLIOGRAPHY

Bell, Robert E. *Women of Classical Mythology: A Biographical Dictionary.* Santa Barbara, Calif.: ABC-CLIO, 1991.

Bennett, Henry Holcomb, ed. *The County of Ross.* Madison, Wi.: Selwyn A. Brant, 1902.

Biggs, Rev. H.W. *A History of the First Presbyterian Church of Chillicothe, Ohio.* Cincinnati, Ohio: A. H. Pounsford & Co., 1877.

The Biographical Cyclopaedia and Portrait Gallery with an Historical Sketch of the State of Ohio. Vols. 1-6. Cincinnati, Ohio: Western Biographical Publishing Company, 1884.

Biographical Dictionary of the United States Congress, 1774-1989. Washington, D. C.: United States Government Printing Office, 1989.

A Biographical Record of Fairfield County, Ohio. New York and Chicago: S. J. Clarke Publishing Co., 1902.

Blesser, Carol. *The Hammonds of Redcliffe.* New York: Oxford University Press, 1981.

Board of Music Trade of the United States of America. *Complete Catalogue of Sheet Music and Musical Work, 1870.* New York: Da Capo Press, 1973.

Boles, John B. *The Great Revival: 1787-1805.* Lexington, Ky.: University Press of Kentucky, 1972.

Bond, Beverley W., Jr. *The Foundations of Ohio: A History of the State of Ohio.* Vol. 1. Carl Wittke, ed. Columbus, Ohio: Ohio Historical Society, 1941, reprint 1968.

Boydston, Jeanne. *Home and Work: Housework, Wages and the Ideology of Labor in the Early Republic.* New York: Oxford University Press, 1990.

Brown, Irene Quenzler. "Death, Friendship, and Female Identity during New England's Second Great Awakening." *Journal of Family History* 12 (1987).

Brown, Jeffrey P. "Chillicothe's Elite: Leadership in a Frontier Community." *Ohio History* 96 (1987).

Brown, Mary Anne, compiler. "Worthington-Swearingen." *Ross County, Ohio Families: Bicentennial Edition.* Chillicothe, Ohio: Ross County Genealogical Society, 1976.

Buber, Martin. *I and Thou.* New York: Charles Scribner's Sons, 1958.

———. *Daniel: Dialogues on Realization: Translated with an Introductory Essay by Maurice Friedman.* New York: Holt, Rinehart and Winston, 1964.

Bunkers, Suzanne L. and Cynthia A. Huff. *Inscribing the Daily: Critical Essays on Women's Diaries.* Amherst, Mass.: University of Massachusetts Press, 1996.

Bushman, Richard. *The Refinement of America: Persons, Houses, Cities.* New York: Vintage Books, 1992.

Butterfield, L. H., Marc Friedlaender and Mary-Jo Klein. *The Book of Abigail and John: Selected Letters of the Adams Family, 1762-1784.* Cambridge, Mass. and London: Harvard University Press, 1975.

Callcott, Wilfrid Hardy. *Santa Anna: The Story of an Enigma Who Once Was Mexico.* Norman, Okla.: University of Oklahoma Press, 1936.

Catalogue of the Officers and Students of Chillicothe Academy. Chillicothe, Ohio: Samuel W. Halsey, 1849.

Chillicothe Business Directory for 1855-56. Chillicothe, Ohio: John B. Doyle and Company, 1855.

Chillicothean. Chillicothe, Ohio, 1826-28.

Chillicothe, Ross County Census 1840. Ohio Historical Society.

"Chronology of Chillicothe, Ohio 1796-1947." *Chillicothe Gazette & Chillicothe News-Advertiser.* Chillicothe, Ohio: October 1947.

Cincinnati Chronicle. Cincinnati, Ohio: April 3, 1863.

Cincinnati City Directory. Cincinnati, Ohio: 1825-1850.

Cincinnati Enquirer. Cincinnati, Ohio: March 10, 1946.

Cincinnati Mirror Advertiser. Cincinnati, Ohio: May 28, 1836.

BIBLIOGRAPHY

Cincinnati Mirror and Western Gazette of Literature, Science and the Arts. Cincinnati, Ohio: February 20, 1836.

Cist, Charles. *Cincinnati in 1851.* Cincinnati, Ohio: Wm. H. Moore & Co., 1851.

Clark, Marie Taylor, compiler. *Tombstone Inscriptions of Grandview Cemetery, Chillicothe, Ohio, Ross County.* Unigraphic, January 1972.

Clubbe, John. *Cincinnati Observed: Architecture and History.* Columbus, Ohio: Ohio State University Press, 1992.

Cole, Frank Theodore. *Thomas Worthington of Ohio: Founder, Senator, Governor and First Citizen.* Columbus, Ohio: 1903.

Conway, Jill Ker. *Written by Herself: Women's Memoirs from Britain, Africa, Asia and the United States.* New York: Vintage Books, 1996.

Cowan, Ruth Schwartz. *More Work for Mother: The Ironies of Household Technology from the Open Hearth to the Microwave.* New York: Basic Books, 1983.

Coyle, William. *Ohio Authors and Their Books.* Cleveland and New York: World Publishing Company, 1962.

Cullum, George W. *Biographical Register of the Officers and Graduates of the U. S. Military Academy at West Point, N. Y. from its Establishment, March 6, 1802 to the Army Reorganization of 1866-67.* Vol.1, 1802-1840. New York: D. Van Nostrand, 1868.

Cummings, Abbott Lowell. *The Alfred Kelley House of Columbus, Ohio; with Mrs. Kelley's Recollections and Some Family Letters.* Columbus, Ohio: Franklin County Historical Society, 1952.

Curtis, George Ticknor. *Life of Daniel Webster.* New York: D. Appleton & Co., 1870.

Daily Gazette. 1827-1881. Cincinnati, Ohio: Hamilton County Chapter, Ohio Genealogical Society, 1993.

de Chambrun, Clara Longworth. *Cincinnati: Story of the Queen City.* New York: Charles Scribner's Sons, 1939.

Delmar, Gloria T. *Mother Goose from Nursery to Literature.* Jefferson, N. C. and London: McFarland & Co., Inc., 1987.

DeVerter, Ruth Hendricks. *Our Pioneer Ancestors: The Genealogy of the Scott and Galloway Families.* Baytown, Tex.: 1959.

Devine, George John. *American Songsters 1806-1815.* MA Thesis in English. Providence, R. I.: Brown University, 1940.

Dichter, Harvey and Elliot Shapiro. *Early American Sheet Music, Its Lure and Its Lore: 1768-1869.* New York: R. R. Bowker Co., 1941.

Dickson, Paul. *The Great American Ice Cream Book.* New York: Atheneum, 1978.

Dohn, Norman H. "The Restoration of Adena." *Columbus Sunday Dispatch Magazine.* (February 8, 1953).

Drake, B. and E. D. Mansfield. *Cincinnati in 1826.* Cincinnati, Ohio: Morgan, Lodge and Fisher, 1827.

Drummond, James E. "James T. Worthington." MA thesis, Ohio State University, 1971.

Dudley, Charlotte W. "Jared Mansfield: United States Surveyor General." *Ohio History* 85:3 (Summer 1976).

Early Marriage Records of Fairfield County, Ohio, 1803-65. Compiled by Elizabeth Sherman Reese Chapter, Daughters of the American Revolution, Lancaster, Ohio: n.d.

Edgar, John F. *Pioneer Life in Dayton and Vicinity: 1796-1840.* Dayton, Ohio: U. B. Publishing House, 1896.

Evans, Lyle S. *A Standard History of Ross County, Ohio.* 2 vols. Baltimore, Md. and Chillicothe, Ohio: Gateway Press, [1917] 1987.

Evans, Nelson W. and Emmons B. Stivers. *A History of Adams County, Ohio.* West Union, Ohio: E. B. Stivers, 1900.

Family Register of Gerret Van Sweringen and Descendants. 2d ed. Washington, D.C.: 1894.

Farnham, Christie Anne. *The Education of the Southern Belle: Higher Education and Student Socialization in the Antebellum South.* New York: New York University Press, 1994.

BIBLIOGRAPHY

Federal Writers Project of Ohio. *Chillicothe and Ross County.* Chillicothe, Ohio: Ross County Northwest Territory Committee, 1938.

Finley, Isaac J. and Rufus Putnam. *Pioneer Record of Ross County, Ohio.* Cincinnati, Ohio: 1871.

Finley, James B. *Sketches of Western Methodism, Biographical, Historical and Miscellaneous.* Cincinnati, Ohio: 1854.

Fischer, Roger A. *Tippecanoe and Trinkets Too: The Material Culture of American Presidential Campaigns, 1828-1984.* Urbana, Ill.: University of Illinois Press, 1988.

Galbraith, R. C. *History of the Chillicothe Presbytery.* 1889.

Galloway, William A. *Old Chillicothe: Shawnee and Pioneer History; Conflicts and Romances in the Northwest Territory.* Xenia, Ohio: The Buckeye Press, 1934.

Gannett, Cinthia. *Gender and the Journal: Diaries and Academic Discourse.* Albany, N. Y.: SUNY Press, 1992.

Garrett, Elisabeth Donaghy. *At Home: The American Family, 1750-1870.* New York: Harry N. Abrams Inc., 1990.

Goss, Rev. Charles Frederic. *Cincinnati, The Queen City: 1788-1912.* Chicago and Cincinnati, Ohio: S. J. Clarke Pub. Co., 1912.

Graham, A. *A History of Fairfield and Perry Counties, Ohio.* Chicago: W. H. Beers & Co., 1883.

Greve, Charles Theodore. *Centennial History of Cincinnati and its Representative Citizens.* Chicago: Biographical Publications Co., 1904.

Gunderson, Robert Gray. *The Log Cabin Campaign.* Lexington, Ky.: University of Kentucky Press, 1957.

Guthrie, Jane. "The Story of an Old Garden." *Harper's Monthly Magazine* 104 (1903).

Hall, James. *The Western Souvenir, a Christmas and New Year's Gift for 1829.* Cincinnati, Ohio: N. and G. Guilford, 1829.

Hamlin, Talbot. *Benjamin Henry Latrobe.* New York: Oxford University Press, 1955.

Harlow, Alvin F. *The Serene Cincinnatians.* E. P. Dutton & Co., Inc., 1950.

Hatch, Jane M., ed. *The American Book of Days.* 3d ed. New York: H. W. Wilson Co., 1978.

Hedrick, Joan D. *Harriet Beecher Stowe: A Life.* New York: Oxford University Press, 1994.

Hemans, Felicia D. *The Poetical Works of Felicia D. Hemans.* London: Oxford University Press, 1914.

Herbert, Jeffrey G. *Index of Death Notices and Marriage Notices Appearing in the Cincinnati Daily Gazette, 1827-1881.* Cincinnati, Ohio: Hamilton County Chapter, Ohio Genealogical Society, 1993.

Hinding, Andrea. *Women's History Sources: Guide to Archives and Manuscript Collections in the United States.* New York: R. R. Bowker, 1979.

"Historic Adena Undergoing Restoration." *Echoes 39:5.* (October/November 2000).

History of Cincinnati and Hamilton County, Ohio: Their Past and Present. Cincinnati, Ohio: S. B. Nelson & Co., 1894.

Hitch, Neal V. and Cheryl Lugg. "Wallpaper Documentation and Reproduction at Adena: The Estate of Thomas Worthington." *APT Bulletin: The Journal of Preservation Technology* 33 (2002).

Hollinger, David A. and Charles Capper, eds. *The American Intellectual Tradition.* New York: Oxford University Press, 1993.

Hood, Marilyn G. "Eleanor Swearingen Worthington: First Lady 1814-1818." *The First Ladies of Ohio and the Executive Mansions.* Columbus, Ohio: Ohio Historical Society, 1970.

Howe, Henry. *Historical Collections of Ohio.* Cincinnati, Ohio: Henry Howe, 1847, 1889, 1891.

Hurt, R. Douglas. *The Ohio Frontier: Crucible of the Old Northwest, 1720-1830.* Bloomington and Indianapolis, Ind.: Indiana University Press, 1996.

Isaac, Rhys. *The Transformation of Virginia: 1740-1790.* New York: W. W. Norton, 1982.

BIBLIOGRAPHY

Jones, Robert Leslie. *History of Agriculture in Ohio to 1880.* Kent, Ohio: Kent State University Press, 1983.

Kagle, Steven E. *Early Nineteenth-Century American Diary Literature.* Boston: Twayne Publishers, 1986.

Kelhofer, Elizabeth. *The Memory of Years Sped in their Flight: A History of the Public Schools of Chillicothe, Ohio, Factual and Nostalgic.* Chillicothe, Ohio: 1975.

Kercheval, Samuel. *A History of the Valley of Virginia.* 2d ed. Woodstock, Va.: J. Gatewood, Printer, 1850.

Kilner, Arthur R. *Greene County, Ohio Births Prior to 1869.* Bowie, Md.: Heritage Books, Inc., 1988.

King, Margaret R[ives]. *Memoirs of the Life of Mrs. Sarah Peter.* 2 vols. Cincinnati, Ohio: Robert Clarke & Co.1889.

Klamkin, Marian. *Old Sheet Music: A Pictorial History.* New York: Hawthorn Books, 1975.

Knopf, Richard C., transcriber. *Thomas Worthington and the War of 1812.* Vol. 3 of Document Transcription of the War of 1812 in the Northwest. Columbus, Ohio: Ohio Historical Society, 1957.

Kramer, Howard D. "An Ohio Doctor in the Early Navy." *Ohio State Archaelogical and Historical Quarterly* 60 (1951).

Lancaster, Clay. "The Egyptian Hall and Mrs. Trollope's Bazaar." *Magazine of Art* 43:3 (March 1950).

Leavitt, Judith Walzer and Ronald L. Numbers, eds. *Sickness and Health in America: Readings in the History of Medicine and Public Health:* 2d ed. Madison, Wis.: University of Wisconsin Press, 1985.

Lee, Henry. *History of the Campbell Family.* New York: R. L. Polk & Co., Inc., 1920.

Lewis, Virgil Anson. *The Soldiery of West Virginia.* Baltimore: Genealogical Publishing Co., 1967.

Lindsay, Lilian. *A Short History of Dentistry.* London: John Bale & Sons & Danielsson, Ltd., 1933.

Lodge, Henry Cabot. *American Statesman: Daniel Webster.* Boston: Houghton, Mifflin and Co.,1889.

McAllister, Anna Shannon. *In Winter We Flourish: Life and Letters of Sarah Worthington King Peter.* New York and Toronto: Longmans, Green & Co., 1939.

McCabe, Lida Rose. *Don't You Remember?* Columbus, Ohio: A. H. Smythe, 1884.

McCormick, Robert W. "Challenge of Command: Worthington vs. Sherman." *Timeline* 8 #3 (June/July 1991).

MacKenzie, Donald R. "Early Ohio Painters: Cincinnati, 1830-1850." *Ohio History* 73:2 (1964).

Mallon, Thomas. *A Book of One's Own: People and their Diaries.* New York: Penguin Books, 1986.

Mansfield, Edward D. *Memoirs of the Life and Service of Daniel Drake, M. D. ...* Cincinnati, Ohio: Applegate & Co., 1860.

_____. *The Mexican War.* New York: A. S. Barnes & Co., 1850.

_____. *Personal Memories.* Cincinnati, Ohio: Robert Clarke & Co., 1879.

Mansfield, H., compiler. *The Descendants of Richard and Gillian Mansfield Who Settled in New Haven, 1639.* New Haven, Conn.: H. Mansfield, 1885.

Marshall, Carrington T. *A History of the Courts and Lawyers of Ohio.* New York: American Historical Society Inc., 1934.

Martin, Michael and Leonard Gelber. *The New Dictionary of American History.* New York: Philosophical Library, 1968.

Martzolff, C. L. "Zane's Trace." *Ohio State Archaeologial and Historical Quarterly* 13 (1904).

Mason, Mary Gertrude. *Western Concepts of China and the Chinese.* Westport, Conn.: Hyperion Press, 1937.

Massie, David Meade. "General Nathaniel Massie." *The Old Northwest Genealogical Quarterly* (April 1900).

———. *Nathaniel Massie, A Pioneer of Ohio: A Sketch of his Life and Selections from his Correspondence.* Cincinnati, Ohio: Robert Clarke & Co., 1896.

Matthews, Glenna. *Just a Housewife: The Rise and Fall of Domesticity in America.* New York: Oxford University Press, 1987.

BIBLIOGRAPHY

Meese, Elizabeth. "Archival Materials: The Problem of Literary Reputation." In *Women in Print I: Opportunities for Women's Studies Research in Language and Literature,* Joan E. Hartman and Ellen Messer-Davidow, eds. New York: Modern Language Association, 1982.

"Meigs County, Ohio." *Historical and Geographical Encyclopedia.* Chicago and Toledo, Ohio: H. H. Hardesty & Co., 1883.

Meyer, Balthasar H., ed. *History of Transportation in the United States Before 1860.* Washington: Carnegie Institution of Washington, 1917.

Miller, James M. *The Genesis of Western Culture: The Upper Ohio Valley, 1800-1825.* Columbus, Ohio: The Ohio State Archeological and Historical Society, 1938.

Miller, Tamara G. " 'Those with Whom I Feel Most Nearly Connected': Kinship and Gender in Early Ohio." In *Midwestern Women: Work, Community, and Leadership at the Crossroads,* Lucy Eldersveld Murphy and Wendy Hamand Venet, eds. Bloomington and Indianapolis, Ind.: Indiana University Press, 1997.

Mills, Edward C. "Monumental Inscriptions within the Old Methodist Cemetery and City Burial Plot in Lancaster, Ohio." *The Old Northwest Genealogical Quarterly* (January 1900).

Mills, William B. "Burials in the Western Methodist Graveyard, Chillicothe, Ohio." *The Old Northwest Genealogical Quarterly* (April 1902).

Morehead, Mrs. L. M. *A Few Incidents in the Life of Professor James P. Espy, by his niece.* Cincinnati, Ohio: Robert Clarke & Co., 1888.

"Mrs. Mansfield," newspaper obituary. Cincinnati, Ohio newspaper, April 3, 1863.

Myers, Robert J. *Celebrations: The Complete Book of American Holidays.* Garden City, N. Y.: Doubleday & Co., Inc., 1972.

Nelson, Larry L. "Here's Howe: Ohio's Wandering Historian." *Timeline* 3:6 (December 1986-January 1987).

Nerone, John C. *Press and Popular Culture in the Early Republic - Cincinnati, 1793-1848.* New York: Garland Press, 1989.

Newcomb, Lawrence. *Newcomb's Wildflower Guide.* Boston/Toronto: Little Brown and Company, 1977.

Newman, Harry Wright. *Anne Arundel Gentry: A Genealogical History of Twenty-Two Pioneers of Anne Arundel County, Md., and Their Descendants.* Book #229. Maryland Pioneer Series, 1933.

Niven, John. *Martin Van Buren: The Romantic Age of American Politics.* New York: Oxford University Press, 1983.

Notable American Women. Cambridge, Mass.: Harvard University Press, 1971.

Ogden, Annegret S. *The Great American Housewife: From Helpmate to Wage Earner, 1776-1986.* Westport, Conn.: Greenwood Press, 1986.

Ortman, E. A. "Showplace of the West in the 1800's Available to Ohioans in Ross Mansion 'Adena.' " *Cincinnati Enquirer* (April 10, 1946).

Owen, Harriet Mary Browne. "The Messenger Bird: A Duet." New York: Dubois and Stodart, 1828 and 1834.

———. "The Pilgrim Fathers." Boston: C. Bradlee, 1830.

Pattison, William D. *Beginnings of the American Rectangular Land Survey System 1784-1800.* Columbus, Ohio: Ohio Historical Society, 1970.

Peter, Sarah W. *Private Memoir of Thomas Worthington.* 1882.

Randall, Emilius 0. and Daniel J. Ryan. *History of Ohio.* New York: Century History Co., 1912.

Randall, Randolph C. *James Hall, Spokesman of the New West.* Columbus, Ohio: Ohio State University Press, 1964.

The Reader's Companion to American History. Boston: Houghton Mifflin Company, 1991.

Renick, L. W., M. D. Fullerton and M. P. Nipgen. *Che-Le-Co-The: Glimpses of Yesterday.* Chillicothe, Ohio: 1896.

Reps, John W. *Washington on View: The Nation's Capital Since 1790*. Chapel Hill, N. C. and London: The University of North Carolina Press, 1991.

Rice, Otis K. and Stephen W. Brown. *West Virginia: A History*. 2nd ed. Lexington, Ky.: University Press of Kentucky, 1993.

Risse, Gunter B., Ronald L. Numbers and Judith Walzer Leavitt, eds. *Medicine Without Doctors: Home Health Care in American History*. New York: Science Historical Publications/U. S. A., 1977.

Rodabaugh, James H. and Henry J. Caren. "ADENA: The Home of Thomas Worthington." *American Antiques Journal*, (May 1947).

Room, Adrian. *Room's Classical Dictionary: The Origins of the Names of Characters in Classical Mythology*. London: Routledge & Kegan Paul, 1983.

Roseboom, Eugene H. and Francis P. Weisenburger. *A History of Ohio*. Columbus, Ohio: Ohio State Archaeological and Historical Society, 1961.

Ross County, Ohio, Marriage Records, 1789-1849. Nathaniel Massie Chapter, D. A. R., Kokomo, Ind.: Selby Publishing, 1989.

Rothman, Ellen. *Hands and Hearts: A History of Courtship in America*. New York: Basic Books, 1994.

Rothman, Sheila M. *Living in the Shadow of Death: Tuberculosis and the Social Experience of Illness in American History*. New York: Basic Books, 1994.

Ruggles, Alice McGuffey. "Unpublished Letters of Dr. Daniel Drake." *The Ohio State Archaeological and Historical Quarterly* 49 (1940).

Ryan, Daniel J. *History of Ohio: The Rise and Progress of an American State*. New York: Century History Co., 1912.

Ryan, Mary P. *Women in Public: Between Banners and Ballots, 1825-1880*. Baltimore, Md.: Johns Hopkins University Press, 1990.

Sage, Mrs. Russell. *Emma Willard and Her Pupils, or Fifty Years of Troy Female Seminary 1822-1872*. New York: Mrs. Russell Sage, 1898.

Santmyer, Helen Hooven. *Ohio Town*. New York: Harper & Row, 1984.

Scioto Gazette. Chillicothe, Ohio: Various Dates, 1830s.

Scott, Hervey. *A Complete History of Fairfield County, Ohio: 1795-1876*. Columbus, Ohio: Siebert & Lilley, 1877.

Sears, Alfred B. *Thomas Worthington: Father of Ohio Statehood*. Columbus, Ohio: Ohio State University Press, 1958.

Seaton, Beverly. *The Language of Flowers: A History*. Charlottesville, Va.: University Press of Virginia, 1995.

Seidel, Kathryn Lee. *The Southern Belle in the American Novel*. Tampa, Fla.: University of Southern Florida Press, 1985.

Sherzer, Jane. "The Higher Education of Women in the Ohio Valley Previous to 1840." *Ohio Archaeological and Historical Quarterly* 25 (1913).

Sklar, Kathryn Kish. *Catharine Beecher: A Study in American Domesticity*. New York and London: W. W. Norton & Co., 1976.

Smith-Rosenberg, Carroll. "The Female World of Love and Ritual: Relations between Women in Nineteenth-Century America." *Signs, Journal of Women in Culture and Society* 1:1, (1975).

Sonneck, Oscar George Theodore. *A Bibliography of Early Secular American Music*. New York: Da Capo Press, 1964.

Southward, W. R. *Chillicothe Reminiscences: 1811*. Chillicothe, Ohio: privately printed by David K. Webb, 1950.

Spiller, Robert E., et. al. *Literary History of the United States*. New York: Macmillan Publishing Co., [1940] 1963.

Springer, Haskell, ed. *Washington Irving: The Sketch Book of Geoffrey Crayon, Gent*. Boston: Twayne Publishers, 1978.

Stevenson, Burton Egbert, ed. *The Home Book of Verse: American and English, 1580-1920*. Vol. I and II. New

BIBLIOGRAPHY

York: Henry Holt and Company, [1912, 1918], 1937.

———. *The Home Book of Quotations: Classical and Modern.* New York: Dodd, Mead and Company, 1934.

Supporter & Scioto Gazette. Chillicothe, Ohio, Dec. 18, 1822.

Taylor, P.A.M., ed. *More than Common Powers of Perception. The Diary of Elizabeth Rogers Mason Cabot.* Boston Beacon Press, 1991.

Teller, Michael E. *The Tuberculosis Movement: A Public Health Campaign in the Progressive Era.* New York: Greenwood Press, 1988.

Temple, Judy Nolte and Suzanne L. Bunkers. "Mothers, Daughters, Diaries: Literacy, Relationship, and Cultural Context." *Nineteenth-Century Women Learn to Write,* Catherine Hobbs, ed. Charlottesville: University Press of Virginia, 1995.

Thornton, Richard H. *An American Glossary: Being an Attempt to Illustrate Certain Americanisms Upon Historical Principles.* New York: Frederick Ungar Publishing Co., 1962.

Thwaites, Reuben G., ed. *Early Western Travels, 1748-1846.* Cleveland, Ohio: A. H. Clark Co., 1904.

Trollope, Frances. *Domestic Manners of the Americans.* London: [1832], 1949.

Tucker, Louis Leonard. "Cincinnati: Athens of the West." *Ohio History* 75 (1966).

———. "The Semi-Colon Club of Cincinnati." *Ohio History* 13:1 (Winter 1964).

Tyler, James J. "The Part that the Pioneer Physicians of Ohio Played in the Church and Lodge." *The Ohio State Archaeological and Historical Quarterly* 48 (1939).

———. *Chillicothe and the Beginning of the Grand Lodge of Ohio.* Reprinted from the Proceedings of the Grand Lodge of Ohio, 1938.

Utter, William T. *The Frontier State: 1803-1825. A History of the State of Ohio.* Vol. 2. Columbus, Ohio: Ohio State Archaeological and Historical Society, 1942, 1968 reprint.

Venable, William H. "Personal Recollections and Anecdotes of Thomas Buchanan Read." *Cincinnati Historical Society Bulletin* 23 (1965).

———. *Beginnings of Literary Culture in the Ohio Valley.* Cincinnati, Ohio: R. Clarke & Co., 1891.

Versteeg, John M., ed. *Methodism: Ohio Area (1812-1962).* Ohio Area Sesquicentennial Committee, 1962.

Vitz, Robert C. *The Queen and the Arts: Cultural Life in Nineteenth-Century Cincinnati.* Kent, Ohio: Kent State University Press, 1989.

Vogel, Morris J. and Charles E. Rosenberg. *The Therapeutic Revolution: Essays in the Social History of American Medicine.* Philadelphia: University of Pennsylvania Press, 1979.

Walnut Street Methodist Episcopal Church, Chillicothe, Ohio. Souvenir Programme. Chillicothe, Ohio: Scholl Press,1905.

Warner, John Harley. *The Therapeutic Perspective: Medical Practice, Knowledge, and Identity in America, 1820-1885.* Cambridge, Mass.: Harvard University Press, 1986.

Webb, Rebecca. *Some Source Notes on... St. Paul's Episcopal Church.* Chillicothe, Ohio: 1952.

Weekly Scioto Gazette, May 23, 1903.

Weisenburger, Francis P. *The Passing of the Frontier: A History of the State of Ohio,* Vol. 3. Columbus, Ohio: Ohio State Archaeological and Historical Society, 1941.

Western Star. Lebanon, Ohio. September 23, 1948.

Whitton, Mary Ormsbee. *These Were the Women: U. S.A., 1776-1860.* New York: Hastings House, 1954.

Whyte, Karel L. *Swearingen, Vansweringen and Related Families.* Aiken, S. C.: Karel L Whyte, 1992. Revised 1997, 1999.

Williams Brothers. *History of Ross and Highland Counties, Ohio.* Cleveland, Ohio: Williams Brothers, 1880.

BIBLIOGRAPHY

Williams, Henry L. and Ottalie K. Williams. *Great Homes of America*. New York: G. P. Putnam's Sons, 1969.

Wilson, Charles Reagan and William Ferris, eds. *Encyclopedia of Southern Culture*. University of North Carolina Press, 1989.

Wilson, Jr., Vincent. *The Book of Distinguished American Women*. Brookville, Md.: American History Research Associates, 1983.

Wiltse, Charles M. and Harold D. Moser, eds. *The Papers of Daniel Webster*. Hanover, N. H. and London: University Press of New England, 1980.

Winship, Marion. "Enterprise in Motion in the Early American Republic: The Federal Government and the Making of Thomas Worthington." *Business and Economic History* 23:1 (Fall 1994).

Wiseman, C. M. L. *Centennial History of Lancaster and Its People*. Lancaster, Ohio: C. M. L. Wiseman, 1898.

———. *Pioneer Period and Pioneer People of Fairfield County, Ohio*. Columbus, Ohio: F. J. Heer Printing Co., 1901.

Xenia City and Greene County Directory. 1850.

Yoseloff, Thomas. *Official Atlas of the Civil War*. New York: T. Yoseloff, 1958.

INDEX

61308377R00148

Made in the USA
Middletown, DE
19 August 2019